DIRTY WARS

DIRTY WARS

ELITE FORCES VS THE GUERRILLAS

LEROY THOMPSON

BCA

LONDON · NEW YORK · SYDNEY · TORONTO

For T. J. Mullin and David Scott-Donelan, two good soldiers and good friends, both of whom know the jungle really is neutral

(pp 6–7) A rather motley group of Navy SEALs prepared to depart on a recon/raiding invasion mission into Communist-controlled territory in South Vietnam *(US Navy)*

This edition published 1991 by
BCA by arrangement with
David & Charles plc
Brunel House Newton Abbot Devon

CN 8092

Typeset by Ace Filmsetting Ltd, Frome, Somerset
and printed in Great Britain by Butler & Tanner Ltd
for David & Charles plc
Brunel House Newton Abbot Devon

CONTENTS

SELECTIVE CHRONOLOGY OF GUERRILLA AND INSURGENT WARS

c350 BC — Sun Tzu's *Art of War* set forth the strategy of indirect approach

329–8 BC — Alexander the Great fought a counter-guerrilla campaign against the Scythians and other irregulars

218 BC — Hannibal faced guerrillas as he crossed the Alps

206–179 BC — Roman counter-insurgency campaign in Spain

73–1 BC — Romans quelled Spartacan revolt

AD 66–70 — Romans fought against Jewish insurgents

582–602 — Under the Emperor Maurice, the Byzantines fought various counter-guerrilla campaigns

c775–900 — The Vikings carried out guerrilla raids from the sea throughout much of Europe

c965 — The Byzantine Emperor Nikepharos Phokus ordered the preparation of *On Shadowing Warfare*, perhaps the first counter-guerrilla manual

c1175–1300 — Mongol irregulars expanded into Europe and China

1277 — Edward I invaded Wales and faced irregulars, including those armed with the longbow

1729–69 — Corsican guerrillas fought successfully against the Genoese and French

1741 — Frederick the Great encountered irregulars during his First Silesian Campaign, causing him to organize special counter-guerrilla light cavalry

1754–63 — Rogers Rangers and other irregulars proved effective during the French and Indian Wars in North America

1775–83 — Francis Marion and other irregulars effectively used guerrilla tactics against the British during the American Revolution

1760s–70s — British forces fought various irregulars in India

1793–1812 — French encountered various guerrillas, including Spanish irregulars (who first used the term 'guerrilla') fighting with Wellington, and also including the Russians

1834–1939 — The French began more than a century of warfare against North African irregulars, much of the campaigning carried out by the French Foreign Legion

1835–90s — Seminole uprising began the US Army's half-century of counter-guerrilla wars against the American Indians

1861–5 — Partisan Rangers of Mosby and other irregulars operated during the American Civil War

1885–95 — French faced insurgents in Indochina where Hubert Lyautey first put his 'oil slick' theory into practice

1896 — Charles Callwell's book *Small Wars – Their Principles and Practice* was published, setting forth techniques for guerrilla and counter-guerrilla warfare

1896–8 — The Spanish faced a guerrilla campaign in the Philippines

▲ MACV/SOG Reconnaissance Team operating out of Phu Bai during 1970

1899–1903 US troops fought against Moro and other guerrillas during the Philippine insurrection

1899–1902 In South Africa, Boer Commandos fought a highly successful guerrilla war against the British

1910–20 During the Mexican Revolution various irregular bands fought as guerrillas against the government and against the US Army

1914–18 During the First World War, Von Lettow-Vorbeck and T. E. Lawrence fought highly creative and successful guerrilla campaigns

1917 During the Russian Revolution, the Reds made use of guerrillas, as did the Whites later

1919–24 The US Marines intervened in a counter-guerrilla campaign in the Dominican Republic

1921–7 The Spanish and the French fought against the Rif Rebellion in Morocco. During this campaign the Spanish Foreign Legion got its baptism of fire

1927–49 The Chinese Communist Revolution took place, during which Mao formulated his theory of People's War, which has influenced virtually all guerrilla campaigns since

1927–34 The US Marines became involved in counter-guerrilla operations in Nicaragua against Sandino

▲ In an attempt to win hearts and minds, US Army Special Forces medics in Vietnam distributed sweets to children, as well as giving medical assistance *(US Army)*

1920–30s	The British were engaged in various colonial counter-guerrilla campaigns (as they had been throughout virtually the entire nineteenth century), innovatively using the RAF in some of them
1936–9	The Spanish Civil War was fought, though guerrilla operations played only a relatively small part. However, due to Hemingway's *For Whom the Bell Tolls*, many believe there was extensive use of guerrillas, particularly on the Republican side
1939–45	The Second World War was fought, with officially sanctioned guerrillas such as the OSS, SOE, and SAS working with resistance movements such as the Maquis in France and the Partisans in Yugoslavia. NOTE: The basis for many post-war guerrilla campaigns was laid during the Second World War among resistance groups, particularly

	Communist ones, who fought against the Germans and Japanese
1946–9	Counter-guerrilla campaign was fought with British assistance against KKE during the Greek Civil War
1946–9	The British faced an insurgency in Palestine among Jews seeking independence
1946–54	Philippine forces faced the Huk insurgency in the Philippines
1946–54	Ho Chi Minh's Viet Minh defeated the French in their guerrilla war for independence
1948–60	The British fought a successful counter-insurgency against Communist guerrillas in Malaya
1952–6	The British fought against Mau Mau terrorists in Kenya
1953–8	Fidel Castro came to power through a guerrilla campaign in Cuba
1954–63	The French fought a bitter counter-guerrilla war in Algeria, a war which came close to toppling the French Republic
1955–9	British forces fought against EOKA guerrillas seeking to merge Cyprus with Greece
1957–75	The United States and the Republic of Vietnam fought a counter-insurgency war against the Viet Cong and a semi-counter-guerrilla war against North Vietnamese regulars
1957–80	Rhodesian security forces fought against Black nationalist groups seeking independence, which was achieved in 1980
1960–75	The Angolan War of Independence was fought using guerrilla tactics against the Portuguese
1963–6	Malaysian and British forces fought against Indonesian-supported guerrillas and regulars during the Borneo confrontation
1963–7	British forces fought against guerrillas, before pulling out of Aden
1964–75	The Mozambique War of Independence was fought by guerrillas against the Portuguese
1965–75	The British and the Sultan's forces fought a successful counter-guerrilla campaign in Oman

▶ Contra guerrillas in training for their war against the Sandinista regime in Nicaragua

▲ Contras, most armed with the Second World War M1 Carbine, but one armed with a crossbow, still an excellent silent killer

◀ Afghan freedom fighters with a stockpile of ammunition, a luxury they weren't always afforded *(Soldier of Fortune)*

1972–9	Philippine forces fought against a Muslim revolt
1976–	The South Africans have been fighting against SWAPO guerrillas in Namibia
1976–	UNITA has been carrying on an anti-Marxist guerrilla war against the MPLA in Angola
1977–	RENAMO has been carrying on an anti-Marxist guerrilla war against FRELIMO in Mozambique
1979	The Sandinistas carried out a successful guerrilla war against the Somoza regime in Nicaragua
1979–89	The Soviet Union fought an unsuccessful counter-guerrilla campaign against the Mujahideen in Afghanistan
1982–	Contras have been waging a guerrilla war against the Marxist Sandinista regime in Nicaragua

1 INTRODUCTION: GUERRILLA WARFARE BEFORE 1900

If Milton's *Paradise Lost* is to be believed, after his conventional assault in heaven was defeated, Satan waged a form of guerrilla warfare against God. The first instance of guerrilla warfare occurring between men was probably when a couple of cavemen ambushed another group of cavemen to make off with the day's mastodon kill; or perhaps they just 'interdicted supply lines' by stealing parts of the carcass before the hunters could return for more meat. Or maybe they waged an early form of psychological warfare, visiting the hunters' caves and suborning their womenfolk. In any event, guerrilla warfare is certainly more than 2,500 years old, though it was not known by that term until the nineteenth century.

One early example of a pre-eminent military power running foul of guerrilla warriors – a situation which will sound familiar to many today – took place in 512 BC when Darius of Persia tried to march across Scythian territory, but faced a scorched-earth strategy which denied his troops food. And it will be of particular interest to students of Britain's colonial conflicts, and of the Soviet Union's recent adventure in Afghanistan, that Alexander the Great faced his toughest guerrilla opposition while passing through what is now Afghanistan, on his way to India. Ancestors of today's Mujahideen harried his rear from horseback, while others attacked him from the heights. Alexander, one of the most astute and flexible generals in history, countered by using light infantry and mounted javelin-men, recognizing that mobility was required to counter irregulars.

The same Scythians who had harried Darius also faced Alexander, their mounted archers using hit-and-run tactics against his advancing columns. As did many later commanders, Alexander resorted to a counter-guerrilla food-denial campaign, destroying the villages that supplied the Scythian bowmen.

Some Bactrians who opposed Alexander took refuge in the mountains, a traditional redoubt for guerrillas throughout history. Alexander recruited a special group of troops with mountain-climbing experience, who scaled the peaks at night to surprise and conquer the Bactrians. This operation by Alexander's 'special forces' must represent one of the earliest uses of élite volunteers as counter-guerrillas. Always appreciative of a brave enemy, Alexander often recruited defeated irregulars and added them to his army, frequently to be used against the next irregulars encountered.

Hannibal, another great commander of the ancient world, faced guerrillas in many Alpine passes, particularly in what is now Switzerland, where guerrilla warfare is viewed as a sound tactic in the nation's defence. Since all Hannibal needed was enough time to get his army and supply train through the passes, he merely fought delaying actions against the guerrillas on the heights, while the bulk of his army cleared the passes.

At various times the Romans faced insurrections, including the famous slaves' revolt – a rebellion of gladiators led by Spartacus in 73 BC – which eventually involved 90,000 former slaves, but lack of cohesiveness with no common ethnic background eventually proved its undoing. Constant incursions by Barbarian guerrillas against Roman outposts, and raids by pirates, forced the Romans to develop at least a minimal counter-insurgency capability. Julius Caesar encountered guerrilla warfare in Gaul and Britain, where he made good use of the rivalry among the native tribes to divide and conquer. His use of a combination of good intelligence-gathering and a primitive type of psychological warfare was the foundation of many future counter-guerrilla campaigns.

In Spain, Rome faced two centuries of guerrilla warfare. In 212 BC two Roman armies were destroyed in Spain, but then Scipio Africanus waged a brilliant counter-guerrilla campaign. Later generals proved far less competent. As a result, large parts of the country were lost to insurgents. Another problem the Romans encountered in Spain, which would haunt American armies in Indochina thousands of years later, was the citizen soldier system, roughly equivalent to twentieth-century conscription. Long-term service abroad was not popular with

◀ When operating in the jungle, members of the Special Air Service were trained never to relax; hence, while one man cleans his mess tin, the other remains alert to possible ambush

these citizen soldiers, a situation which would recur throughout history whenever conscript armies were sent against guerrillas.

Another lesson learnt in Spain was that those generals who led large, heavy formations into the Spanish interior usually suffered heavy losses to ambushes, while those who used lighter counter-guerrilla formations normally proved successful. The same was to prove true for the SAS in Malaya and Borneo, the French and the US airborne troops in Indochina, and the Soviet paratroopers in Afghanistan.

In 81 BC, Quintus Sertorius, a brilliant Roman general, was banished to Spain for taking part in a democratic revolution. He led a guerrilla force against the Romans, waging a classic hit-and-run war against the legions' lines of communications for almost a decade. With a force of 5,000 or less, he managed to tie down as many as 130,000 Roman troops, graphically illustrating the value to a guerrilla leader of detailed knowledge of the enemy's army. When the Roman legions kept their good leaders, rather than driving them into the enemy camp as with Sertorius, and when they gained the support of the local population, they were normally successful; when not, they normally fared poorly. These two obvious necessities – able leadership and the support of the local populace – remain critical in counter-guerrilla operations today.

The heavy Roman legions had great difficulty pursuing lightly equipped guerrillas, and as a result Roman light troops – auxiliaries – had to be developed. A good example of this difficulty can be seen in their defeat at Carrhae by Parthian mounted archers. Rather than closing with the heavy Roman infantry, the Parthians used the tactic of firing their bows to the rear, as they wheeled their horses away; this was the famous 'Parthian shot' which has entered our vocabulary. Such tactics came naturally to warriors from the East, perhaps through secondary contact with China, where Sun Tzu's theory of *chi* dictated the indirect use of unorthodox attacks, what Liddell Hart would later call the strategy of indirect approach.

Just as other conventional forces would find throughout history, the best counter-guerrilla is often a former guerrilla, and the Romans often made use of barbarians, who were accustomed to the hit-and-run tactics of the enemy.

Belisarius, the great Byzantine general, realized that guerrillas could sap an army's strength and, therefore, during the reconquest of North Africa, stressed the importance of winning over the local population. In fact, the Byzantines probably coped with irregulars better than any other military system of the Middle Ages. Using a small professional army, the Byzantines made warfare an art and a science, creating an excellent intelligence system and making use of deception. Their possession of Greek Fire, the 'nuclear deterrent' of the time, also enhanced their ability to establish and defend citadels at critical locations.

Although it never came to pass, it was astutely suggested that the best deterrent to barbarian incursions would be the arming of every free male in the Empire, to form local militias, a system the Swiss, Israelis and Swedes use to this day.

Later Byzantine armies, by the tenth century facing numerically superior enemies, often used hit-and-run guerrilla tactics themselves. Such tactics were formalized in the Emperor Nikephoros Phokas's *On Shadowing Warfare*, one of several pragmatic Byzantine military manuals. To form the bodyguard for the Byzantine emperors – the Varangian Guard – the foremost guerrilla warriors of Europe at the time, the Vikings, were chosen. Using a form of guerrilla warfare which to some extent foreshadows Mao's precepts, the Vikings would begin their campaigns with strikes against coastal towns. As resistance weakened, they would often 'liberate' entire provinces, such as Normandy, to establish their own mini-states.

Of course, as the Norman Vikings later became a conventional army, and conquered England, they themselves would face guerrilla warfare. During the Norman conquest of Ireland, for example, the Irish fought a fierce guerrilla campaign from the bogs. Later, in Wales and Scotland, the English fought what were basically guerrilla wars. Robert the Bruce waged a classic guerrilla war against English castles during the early fourteenth century.

In the thirteenth century, the most formidable warriors of the time, the Mongols, found themselves facing a guerrilla war – including boobytraps – when they attempted to invade Vietnam. Under Marshal Tran Hung Dao, the Vietnamese successfully drove the Mongols from their country, establishing a tradition which Ho Chi Minh would emulate six centuries later.

During the late Middle Ages, occasional peasant revolts turned into guerrilla campaigns, but normally the peasants were brutally crushed. In the early fifteenth century, however, the Hussites, held together by their religious beliefs, developed tactics around 'wagon castles' which allowed them to move across country as they wished. To counter armoured knights, the Hussites used poles with hooks to yank the heavily armoured cavalryman from his charger and thus successfully defeated virtually all sent against them. It was only when schisms and internal dissent developed within their ranks that the Hussites were finally defeated.

During the Hundred Years War, although the English longbow had hitherto ensured consistent defeat of the French, the French eventually retook Brittany under Bertrand du Guesclin, who proved a master of guerrilla warfare.

Elizabeth I's soldiers crushed an Irish rebellion by combining the twin concepts of mobility and food denial. Farms of rebel supporters were burned, while mobile cavalry patrols were sent to hunt the rebels down, thus dealing with the revolt swiftly and successfully. That 'hearts and minds' were never won is still obvious in Northern Ireland today.

Throughout history, even the greatest generals have often found themselves initially frustrated by irregulars, and Frederick the Great was no exception. During the Silesian and Seven Years Wars, the Austrians very successfully used Moravian and other irregulars as a screen against Frederick's advances. Because of the authoritarian nature of Frederick's reign, indigenous light infantrymen capable of independent counter-guerrilla action were never available. He was obliged to recruit mercenary 'Free Battalions' as light infantry; however, most did not prove particularly effective. Later, though, German *Jäger* units, recruited from foresters and hunters, would prove particularly good in this function.

In contrast to Frederick's Prussians, American settlers in North America were mostly of an independent nature, well suited to irregular warfare. The earliest settlers found the American Indians formidable guerrilla foes, but they adapted and learned from the Indians, soon becoming expert themselves at working in small units, moving swiftly, maintaining highly accurate and disciplined rifle fire, and using ambush and surprise. As a result, during the French and Indian Wars, Rogers Rangers and other Ranger detachments were formed as guerrilla and counter-guerrilla forces. American élite forces, charged with guerrilla or counter-guerrilla activities today still draw inspiration from these original Rangers.

Based on the experience of the Prussians, and of the British and French in North America, by the late eighteenth century most European armies possessed light infantrymen capable of some of the flexibility of guerrillas, often armed with rifles, and frequently wearing green uniforms. Some of these European light infantrymen saw action against American irregulars and regulars during the American Revolution.

Although there were certain aspects of guerrilla warfare in American campaigns in the North, it was in the South that guerrillas played the most critical part during the 'American War of National Liberation', as at least one prominent military historian has termed it. In 1775, a group of 'Liberty Boys' acted as guerrillas in the South, intimidating loyalists, among other classic guerrilla acts. British atrocities hardened resistance in the South and created an atmosphere conducive to guerrilla warfare. The British suffered particularly from lack of intelligence, since most of the locals gave them incorrect information.

The greatest American guerilla warrior of the Revolution was Francis Marion, 'The Swamp Fox'. When Cornwallis invaded North Carolina, Marion and his irregulars harried British columns and used terror tactics against Tory sympathizers, thus denying Cornwallis virtually all local support. General Nathanael Greene, commanding the American regulars, encouraged Marion and other irregulars to harry Cornwallis's already tenuous supply and communication lines, thus eroding his capability to engage in a major battle.

While losing the American colonies, Great Britain continued to colonize other areas, often encountering guerrilla warfare while doing so. In India, for example, the Marathas proved formidable opponents. Colonel Arthur Wellesley, later the Duke of Wellington, who was to make proficient use of irregulars during the Peninsular Campaign against Napoleon, proved more successful against Indian irregulars than most British officers. Fighting only when advantageous, moving fast, attacking during the monsoon, and clearing possible ambush sites along his route of advance, Wellesley established many precepts which are still valid in guerrilla warfare.

The French Revolutionary armies, former guerrillas themselves against the monarchy, were soon engaged in battles throughout Europe, and faced irregulars of various nationalities, even in France itself. Among the most successful of these were the *Lazzaroni* in Italy, who tied down as many as 40,000 French troops between 1806 and 1808. Nevertheless, in 1807, the French Army entered Spain on its way to Portugal, and was soon engaged in fighting the war which is now generally accepted to have given rise to the term *guerrilla*. In 1808, Wellesley and a small British expeditionary force arrived to support the Portuguese guerrillas. As in many future guerrilla wars (e.g. the recent one in Afghanistan), most of the guerrilla bands were regional and independent, but were loosely allied against the common enemy. The French Republican Army was never known for its restraint, and its atrocities against the populations of Spain and Portugal generated great support for the guerrillas.

Wellesley returned to England, but by 1809 was back in the Peninsula, determined to make utmost use of the guerrilla forces. (He was created Duke of Wellington after his victory at Talevera de la Reina.) Taking advantage of guerrilla control of most of the countryside, Wellington spent a year training the Portuguese Army, preparing to go on the offensive and building fortifications. When the French general Masséna finally attacked Wellington, the French suffered heavy casualties, before the Iron Duke retreated into his waiting redoubts. When Masséna laid siege, the guerrillas harassed his forces, necessitating their withdrawal in March 1810. So successful were the guerrillas against French lines of communication that a single courier often needed a three-hundred-man escort, and so efficient was the guerrilla intelligence network, that any time the French pulled troops from a garrison to use elsewhere, the garrison came under immediate attack. Proving inflexible, the French continued to use torture and destruction as their primary counter-guerrilla tactics, thus alienating an ever increasing portion of the population. The French did try to raise local counter-guerrilla bands, but after receiving weapons and equipment they deserted to join the guerrillas!

Though Napoleon is considered one of the greatest military thinkers of all time, he proved incapable of either dealing with the threat of irregulars or taking it seriously. Perhaps as an artilleryman he could not grasp that this was a foe firepower could not defeat.

Having learned little apparently from their previous counter-guerrilla failures, the French invaded Russia in 1812, making no attempt to gain the support of the local population. On the contrary, they were so cruel to the peasants along the route of march that guerrilla bands quickly began to spring up, killing French soldiers and taking their arms. The Russians, realizing that the great size of their country left an invader particularly exposed to irregular warfare, allowed Lt-Colonel Dennis Davydov to form a force of hussars and Cossacks to work with the guerrillas. This force would eventually evolve into several mixed bands of partisans and Cossacks. It should be noted that during the Second World War the Soviets used virtually the same strategy, mixing paratroopers or other regulars with partisans.

French counter-guerrilla units slaughtered local peasants indiscriminately, thus stimulating even more guerrilla action, which often consisted of lying in wait for starving French soldiers foraging for food, then picking them off. When the French began their long retreat, the partisans and Cossacks continued to wage a bitter war of attrition, often attacking stragglers within sight of the retreating columns, much as packs of wolves stalk their prey. By the time the retreat was completed, the French had lost 500,000 men in Russia – many to cold and starvation, but countless others to the partisans.

The two great military theorists of the nineteenth century – Clausewitz, in his *On War*, and Jomini, in his *Art of War* – both discussed guerrilla warfare, but neither really offered tactics to counter guerrillas. This omission may possibly be attributed to the fact that both men were professional soldiers, albeit intellectuals, who could not bring themselves to view irregulars, often drawn from a rabble, as serious enough a threat to justify a tactical discussion. Another likely possibility is that both viewed irregulars as an interesting phenomenon, but not as a force warranting a tactical discussion. Ironically, Jomini spent the latter 1820s in Russia, where he should certainly have learned of the partisan and Cossack successes against Napoleon.

After consistently proving incapable of dealing with irregulars during the Napoleonic Wars, the French once again found themselves engaged in a counter-guerrilla campaign against the Berbers, following their 1830 invasion of Algeria. Initially, they met with little better success than previously, but in 1836 General Bugeaud, who had fought against the guerrillas in Spain, formed highly mobile 'flying columns' mounted on camels and mules to pursue and defeat the irregulars. These predecessors of the later French *corps d'élites* of the desert – the *Méharistes* – used ruses, raids and ambushes, the guerrillas' own tactics, to defeat them.

France was not the only European power which found itself involved in guerrilla warfare during the nineteenth century. On the contrary, the colonial powers, particularly Great Britain, fought irregulars almost continuously somewhere across the globe. Among the most formidable guerrillas the British faced were the Afghans, who (rather ironically, in light of recent events) received assistance from the Russians in their protracted guerrilla war against the British. France, Belgium and Great Britain also faced irregulars in Africa, though the Zulus, Britain's most ferocious antagonists, had a highly organized military system, more regular than irregular. Spain also faced guerrilla warfare as its former colonies in Latin America fought for independence.

From the earliest days colonists in North America had faced guerrilla warfare from the American Indians; however, it was against the plains Indians that the classic counter-guerrilla campaigns of the American Indian Wars were fought. An earlier and successful counter-guerrilla campaign had been waged against the Seminoles in Florida, first by Colonel Zachary Scott, then by Colonel William Worth. The Seminoles were 'pacified' by a combination of dividing operational areas into twenty-square-mile grids, with a stockade in each, to exert continuous surveillance and control, then vigorously patrolling each area, while crops which supplied the Seminoles were burned. Once again, a classic combination of mobility, food denial and area control was used to counter guerrillas.

The American Civil War interrupted the Indian campaigns and denuded the frontier of troops. At one point, in fact, captured Confederate cavalrymen were asked to give their parole and were sent west to fight against the Indians.

Although the Civil War is best remembered for decisive battles and major campaigns, there were classic guerrilla actions as well. John Brown and other militant abolitionists had even attempted to foment a major slave rebellion prior to the beginning of hostilities. Border warfare in Missouri and Kansas also saw the rise of guerrilla raiders such as Quantrill. The most famous guerrilla of the Civil War, however, was John Mosby, who along with other Confederate cavalry officers such as Nathan Bedford Forrest and John Morgan, became master of the hit-and-run cavalry raid on the flanks and rear of the Union Army. 'Ranger' Mosby and his Partisan Rangers even captured a Union general in his own HQ. The increasing use of technology in the Civil War gave guerrillas more scope to disrupt the enemy's rear, by tearing up railway lines and cutting telegraph wires. The Union did not resort to guerrilla warfare very frequently or very successfully, though Colonel Grierson did launch a cavalry raid deep into the Confederacy. Mosby's successes are particularly noteworthy since they showed the value for harassment and intelligence-gathering of a guerrilla force as an adjunct to regular forces.

During the post-Civil War Indian campaigns, the cavalry became an excellent counter-guerrilla force, able to move fast and keep constant pressure on the enemy. In a tradition harking back at least to Alexander the Great, the US Cavalry used irregulars against irregulars, employing Indian scouts to provide intelligence. By campaigning throughout the winter, the Cavalry allowed the numerically inferior Indians little time to recuperate, thus undermining their will to fight. Although many guerrillas (e.g. the Viet Minh and Viet Cong) have been willing to suffer casualties out of all proportion to their numbers, the American Indians found themselves unable to fight the white man successfully, and were eventually defeated.

No doubt to native Americans the Indian Wars were a colonial campaign, but it was Cuba which led the United States into a series of colonial wars, which were to include a classic counter-guerrilla campaign in the Philippines. In 1895 the Cubans launched an insurrection against the Spanish, under the leadership of effective guerrilla leaders such as Maximo Gomez and Jose Maceo. So widespread was their support that by 1896 Maceo was approaching Havana, while other guerrilla leaders controlled various provinces. Spain was fortunate, however, in having in General Weyler, a military commander who understood how to conduct a counter-guerrilla campaign. He divided the island into operational sectors, developing town militias, creating mobile formations to respond rapidly to guerrilla incursions, and forming local counter-guerrilla forces from men who knew the country and knew the guerrillas. Though all of these moves were sound, Weyler still lacked timely intelligence from the local population.

The sinking of the USS *Maine* has been widely debated, but whatever the circumstances, it did bring the United States into the war against Spain, resulting in the eventual acquisition of both Cuba and the Philippines. The US declaration of war was in 1898, and an insurgency had been raging in the Philippines since 1896. To be precise, in fact, a Moro insurgency had been going on intermittently for over one hundred years. Following the American victory over Spain in 1898, the Filipino guerrillas became confident that independence was near, particularly since they had aided the Americans against the Spanish. The treatment of the Filipinos by many American soldiers, however, soon alienated them, resulting in a renewed insurgency against the Americans.

Initially, the guerrillas made the mistake of attempting to fight a major battle, but they lost thousands while inflicting only fifty-nine deaths on the Americans. This battle resulted in the Americans growing over-confident, and the insurgents reverting to true guerrilla warfare. In June 1899, in an ambush of four thousand American troops, the guerrillas inflicted very heavy casualties with only light losses. Having learned, too, that an army that isn't there cannot be defeated, the guerrillas were careful to merge with the population. In addition to allowing the guerrillas to 'hide in plain sight', this helped alienate the population from the Americans, as guerrilla atrocities against American soldiers were countered by indiscriminate American atrocities, a process which worked to the advantage of the guerrillas, driving the population into the guerrilla fold.

The Americans were too ponderous to catch the guerrilla forces, as the populace gave early warning of the approach of American troops. Becoming ever more adept at guerrilla warfare, the insurgents hit American supply lines and cut their telegraph wires.

In 1900 Arthur MacArthur, the father of Douglas MacArthur and himself a Congressional Medal of Honor winner during the Civil War, was put in command in the Philippines and almost immediately placed the islands under martial law and recruited local troops as scouts and counter-guerrillas. Under MacArthur's strong leadership, Brigadier Frederick Funston captured a rebel request for replacements and sent some of his Filipino scouts to infiltrate the rebel stronghold and capture Aquinaldo, the rebel leader. Such use of pseudo-guerrillas became a counter-insurgency art form during the campaign in Kenya against the Mau Mau and, particularly, in Rhodesia with the Selous Scouts. To follow up MacArthur's gains, in 1901 William Howard Taft was made civilian governor of the islands and began to establish civil government. Although hindered severely by the loss of Aquinaldo, the insurrection continued, but the Americans now took draconian action against any remaining guerrillas and established effective control of the population and regulation of the food supply, thus denying the guerrillas manpower and sustenance. To remove the base of guerrilla power, Taft took actions to win over the population, such as allowing the purchase of farmland at very reasonable rates. As a result, by 1903, the insurrection was basically over. The combination of removing the base of guerrilla support, denying them food and manpower, and removing their leadership had doomed this insurgency.

Conclusions

As the twentieth century dawned, many precepts which still hold true in countering an insurgency had begun to be developed. It was becoming apparent that to counter guerrillas, commanders had to be willing to be unorthodox, an idea which would be anathema to many professional soldiers. Funston's use of pseudo-guerrillas to capture Aquinaldo was unorthodox yet highly successful. Armies had to learn from each other's experiences. Tactics needed to be much more flexible to deal with guerrillas who would strike quickly and then fade back into the population. Extremely important, yet extremely difficult for many soldiers; those fighting a counter-guerrilla campaign needed to understand the local population and to gain their support against the guerrillas. By winning this support, a commander could eliminate a guerrilla army's supply depot, replacement depot, intelligence corps, transportation corps and signal corps at one stroke.

The need to study the experiences of others in fighting guerrillas was finally addressed in Major Charles Callwell's *Small Wars*, which appeared in 1896. This work, which offered tactical innovations based on previous successes and failures, would soon become the standard work on colonial campaigns and counter-insurgency warfare. It is still worth reading today by those preparing to face guerrilla warriors. Among Callwell's suggestions for fighting guerrillas are: harry them and give them no time for rest; divide the theatre into sections to control food and popular support; have highly mobile, self-contained counter-guerrilla forces ready to respond to attacks and to patrol against the guerrillas; gather good intelligence; and have self-reliant, competent junior officers. Although these suggestions were made near the end of the nineteenth century, they still hold true almost one hundred years later.

ROGERS' RANGERS' STANDING ORDERS

More than two centuries ago, during the French and Indian Wars, Major Robert Rogers formulated 19 standing orders for his Rangers. These same rules are applicable today for those acting as guerrillas or counter-guerrillas and are, therefore, reproduced here in their entirety, as still posted at the US Army Ranger School at Fort Benning:

1. Don't Forget Nothing.
2. Have your musket clean as a whistle, hatchet scoured, sixty rounds powder and ball, and be ready to march at a minute's warning.
3. When you're on the march, act the way you would if you was sneaking up on a deer. See the enemy first.
4. Tell the truth about what you see and what you do, there is an army depending on us for correct information. You can lie all you please when you tell other folks about the Rangers, but don't ever lie to a Ranger or officer.
5. Don't never take a chance you don't have to.
6. When we're on the march we march single file, far enough apart so one shot can't go through two men.
7. If we strike swamps, or soft ground, we spread out abreast, so it's hard to track us.
8. When we march, we keep moving until dark, so as to give the enemy the least possible chance at us.
9. When we camp, half the party stays awake while the other half sleeps.
10. If we take prisoners, we keep 'em separate till we have had time to examine them, so they can't cook up a story between 'em.
11. Don't ever march home the same way. Take a different route so you won't be ambushed.
12. No matter whether we travel in big parties or little ones, each party has to keep a scout twenty yards ahead, twenty yards on each flank and twenty yards in the rear, so the main body can't be surprised and wiped out.
13. Every night you'll be told where to meet if surrounded by a superior force.
14. Don't sit down to eat without posting sentries.
15. Don't sleep beyond dawn. Dawn's when the French and Indians attack.
16. Don't cross a river by a regular ford.
17. If somebody's trailing you, make a circle, come back onto your own tracks, and ambush the folks that aim to ambush you.
18. Don't stand up when the enemy's coming against you. Kneel down, lie down, hide behind a tree.
19. Let the enemy come till he's almost close enough to touch. Then let him have it and jump out and finish him up with your hatchet.

Whether it has been the US Special Forces hunting for Vietcong in Vietnam, the SBS or SAS setting out to raid Argentine positions in the Falklands, the Soviet Spetsnaz operating against guerrillas in Afghanistan, or Afghan guerrillas operating against Soviet Spetsnaz, Rogers' rules have retained their validity.

2 GUERRILLA WARFARE ENTERS THE TWENTIETH CENTURY

As the Industrial Revolution progressed, so did the vulnerability of modern armies to irregular warfare against their ever more sophisticated logistics trains. A perfect example was the Boer War in South Africa, where the Boers, expert with rifles and accustomed to living off the land, proved elusive foes for the British. Initially, the Boers, organized into 'commandos', a term Winston Churchill would borrow for his élite raiding forces of the Second World War, fought a somewhat conventional war. In this they were unsuccessful as the British, under Field Marshal Lord Roberts and Maj-General Lord Kitchener, with great difficulty pushed through to capture Pretoria, the Boer capital.

During the advance, the Boers tore up railway tracks and sniped very effectively with their Mauser rifles, eventually tying down half of Roberts' troops protecting his lines of communication. Having noted these successes, the Boers turned to full-scale guerrilla warfare after Pretoria's fall. Under such leaders as Jan Smuts and Louis Botha, the Boers lived off the land, and in the Orange Free State and Transvaal disputed the British claim to have won the war by raiding at will. Had the British been willing to give the Boers partial home rule, the conflict could probably have been settled at this point, but the government in London remained inflexible, thus hardening Boer resistance.

Left in command after the departure of Lord Roberts, Kitchener made use of his experience against guerrillas in Egypt and the Sudan, and divided the area of operations into sectors, building blockhouses to guard bridges, railway lines or other important installations in each sector. Eventually, barbed wire was strung between the blockhouses. Having established area control, he then used flying columns to carry out sweeps within areas for Boer irregulars. To deny the commandos the support of the populace, many civilians were moved into concentration camps, and farms were burned in a food denial campaign. Eventually this combination began to wear the Boers down. However, the Boers, tough frontiersmen and expert marksmen, late in the campaign were tying down 450,000 British troops with a force of about 20,000. Their intimate knowledge of the country and how to live off it, combined with their accuracy with the rifle gained from years of shooting for meat, made the Boers a particularly effective guerrilla force. An important lesson to be drawn from the Boer successes is that though urban guerrillas may seem formidable to governments by being active nearer the seat of power, rural guerrillas more familiar with firearms and capable of living off the land are far more difficult to contain and subdue.

During the latter part of the nineteenth century, French rule in Indochina was faced with an insurgency. Fortunately for France, General Hubert Lyautey proved a soldier who understood both the political and military aspects of counter-insurgency. He pacified territory to deny the insurgents support, while using mobile columns to isolate them. Later in Madagascar, Lyautey would again use the same methods successfully. Realizing that insurgencies need both a political and a military solution, he would often recognize the leadership potential of conquered insurgent commanders, incorporating them into his colonial government as administrators, thus gaining a subordinate supported by the people and turning an opponent into an ally.

Based on previous successes, Lyautey was sent to Algeria, where he agreed to take over the counter-insurgency campaign on the condition that he be given total military and civil control. Rather than using punitive expeditions against raiders from Morocco, as had previously been the norm, he set out to pacify tribes one at a time. Their support won, they would then act as a buffer against brigands. This technique would later be known as the 'oil slick' strategy, based on the idea that French influence would slowly spread until it permeated an area. Militarily, Lyautey relied on light, highly mobile columns to respond to any guerrilla incursions. Realizing, too, that intelligence is an absolute necessity in defeating guerrillas, he developed a strong intelligence service and used propaganda to praise the benefits of French rule. To support his intelligence and propaganda aims, French troops were ordered to treat the local populace fairly and considerately, thus contributing to winning their support.

As areas came under French control, Lyautey built forts, of the type familiar to fans of movies such as *Beau Geste*, to exert control. By 1907, his methods had proved so successful in Algeria that Lyautey had moved into Morocco, employing the same techniques. So effectively did Lyautey pacify and rule that, even denuded of troops during the First World War, he managed to prevent any major insurrections.

One of the most effective counter-guerrilla warriors of the early twentieth century, Lyautey was very individualistic. His system would only work with another officer as forceful and visionary as himself. Much can be learned from Lyautey's successes though, particularly the importance of combining military and political acumen in fighting a popular insurgency.

One guerrilla war of the early twentieth century is of interest primarily because it illustrates the need for a good base of support and also because it shows how some guerrilla movements can begin with political aims but degenerate into banditry. IMRO (Internal Macedonian Revolutionary Organization) was active in fighting against the Turks for Macedonian independence during the late nineteenth and early twentieth centuries. However, though at times the movement did control substantial areas within Macedonia, there was never realistically any chance of gaining independence. Instead, the group became involved in Balkan politics, attempting to secede and ally themselves with Bulgaria, but finally retreating into Bulgaria to become bandits specializing in bank robbery, the drug trade and other criminal activities.

Because of its proximity to America, and the involvement of various Americans, the Mexican Revolution was noteworthy for various reasons other than its purely guerrilla aspects. Guerrilla activities had taken place sporadically against governments of Mexico from the 1880s on, but the revolution really began in 1910 after President Diaz's re-election, when guerrillas in support of his opponent Francisco Madero began mounted raids on Chihuahua. One of these guerrilla bands was commanded by Pancho Villa, who soon had a force of five hundred mounted raiders under his control. The fighting proved bloody on both sides, since the government – which largely represented the interests of an oligarchy controlled by a few hundred important families – treated the guerrillas as bandits rather than soldiers. The revolutionaries, on the other hand, in conflicts against the army killed the officers but allowed enlisted personnel to join them.

In 1910 Emiliaro Zapata began organizing a peasant rebellion based on land reform. In less than a year he had 3,000 peasant guerrillas armed with captured Army weapons. Soon, government troops and the hated Rurales held the towns of the state of Morelos, while guerrillas controlled the countryside. Though most of the Rurales were tough, they were from other states and did not know the area well enough to track the guerrillas, thus granting the insurgents freedom of movement. Additionally, local villagers sympathetic to the revolution gave the insurgents access to good intelligence.

By 1911, guerrillas under Orozco were gaining ground in the north, while those under Zapata were gaining in the south. As a result, President Diaz was toppled, but Madero soon proved inept and unwilling to undertake real land reforms, causing Zapata to continue the revolution, based on a demand for the redistribution of land. He gained thousands of followers. A punitive expedition to Morelos by the government alienated the peasants even more. The one exception to the prevailing ineptitude in countering the guerrillas was General Felipe Angeles, who waged an effective campaign but received little support from his superiors.

Having proved a failure, Madero was assassinated and replaced in 1913 by General Huerta, who proved an even less effective leader. His strategy soon became one of holding only the towns and railway lines, leaving the countryside to the guerrillas. Pancho Villa, on the other hand, though no intellectual and having little understanding of the overall issues of the revolution, was astute enough to use his 8,000 troops on public works projects for the benefit of the peasants when not fighting, thus consolidating their support. Villa also realized the importance of mobility for a guerrilla army, and used trains to transport his forces. Unfortunately, this also restricted him to the railway lines.

By 1914, both Villa and Zapata were advancing on Mexico City, but neither was really capable of ruling the country, so the capture of the capital would have had little more than symbolic meaning. Not having clear-cut goals, other than Zapata's platform of land reform, the two guerrilla leaders continued to thrash about the countryside, destabilizing the government but not really offering an alternative. In early 1916, Pancho Villa raided across the border into the USA, leading to a punitive expedition under General Pershing being sent south into Mexico, but since the guerrillas enjoyed strong local support, this expedition really did little good. Eventually, Venustiano Carranza, who had become president in 1915, consolidated his power by buying off Villa and assassinating Zapata.

The fact that neither Villa nor Zapata had an established political programme, other than destabilizing the government, inhibited the effect of their insurgency. However, their control of the countryside and wide popular support were both classic aspects of successful guerrilla campaigns. The US punitive expedition would be hard to term a counter-guerrilla effort, since its objectives were never really defined and its successes were negligible. Moving into another country to engage in counter-guerrilla activities, hard enough with the support of the local government and population, is virtually impossible without it.

Although the First World War saw the dawn of

modern technological warfare, in two of its secondary theatres it also gave scope for classic guerrilla campaigns, both in support of conventional military aims.

In German East Africa, Lt-Colonel Paul von Lettow-Vorbeck proved himself to be one of the most capable guerrilla warriors of all time, with a systematic campaign to tie down British forces and prevent their being sent to the western front. Prior to his taking command of the German East African forces, Lettow-Vorbeck had seen irregular warfare at first hand, campaigning against the Hottentots, and had astutely realized its possibilities for an outnumbered force such as his attempting to support a war raging far to the north. His first success came when the British tried to occupy East Africa; Lettow-Vorbeck's troops inflicted fifteen hundred casualties for a loss of only sixty-nine troops.

Flaunting this success, Lettow-Vorbeck set out to lure British forces in quantity against him. Small guerrilla forces of two Germans and eight askaris, native troops, operated from the foothills of Mt Kilimanjaro, raiding bridges, railway lines, etc. Simultaneously, Lettow-Vorbeck recruited and trained white settlers and natives until he had a force of about fourteen thousand in the field. He overcame his shortage of arms in classic guerrilla manner by raiding the British. In 1915, too, a German blockade runner got through with additional weaponry. Still, his troops had to become self-sufficient, even making their boots from antelope skins.

As Lettow-Vorbeck improvised and recruited, the British found themselves committing substantial resources to track him down. Reasoning that the Boers should be able to counter Lettow-Vorbeck, a large South African contingent under Jan Smuts was sent against him. However, the Boers found fighting in East Africa very different from their home in South Africa, falling prey to sickness, which sorely depleted their ranks. Despite the numbers sent against him, Lettow-Vorbeck remained in the field throughout the war, eventually tying down up to 160,000 British troops, as well as contingents of Portuguese and Belgian troops sent from the neighbouring colonial possessions of those countries.

Belying the traditional view of the Prussian soldier as inflexible, Lettow-Vorbeck proved a master of improvisation and flexibility. He showed a marked aptitude at winning the loyalty of native troops, and made good use of his knowledge of Africa and how to wage a guerrilla campaign there. Realizing that he was far away from the primary theatre of the war, Lettow-Vorbeck perceptively concluded that he could best help the German war effort by pulling as many British troops as possible into East Africa. Incensed at his ability to elude them, the British obligingly continued to send troops against him, pouring massive amounts of money into the campaign.

Far more famous, but in actuality less skilled as a guerrilla warrior, was T. E. Lawrence, 'Lawrence of Arabia'. Lawrence began the war as an intelligence officer in Egypt, where, though very junior, he suggested to senior officers the advantages of fomenting an Arab revolt against the Turks. Lord Kitchener, the Secretary of State for War and a counter-guerrilla campaigner himself, agreed. With some prodding from the British, such a revolt did break out in 1916, when Husein, the Sherif of Mecca, captured the holy city from the Turks. Lawrence, who spoke Arabic, accompanied Ronald Storrs, a diplomat sent to meet with Arab leaders. Lawrence secretly evaluated the various leaders he met and decided that Feisal was the best leader for an Arab revolt. Lawrence also decided that due to Arab traditions, personalities and capabilities, a guerrilla war was the most effective use of Arab resources.

Upon his return to Cairo, he recommended that support be given to Feisal, a recommendation which was accepted with Lawrence being sent as the liaison with the Arabs. Lawrence himself had virtually no background in guerrilla warfare, and even had to undergo a crash course in demolitions before joining Feisal's forces. However, Lawrence did grasp the basic hit-and-run nature of guerrilla warfare, which was particularly well suited to the desert raiders he had to work with, and soon raids were being carried out against the Turkish lines of communication. Once again making a virtue of necessity, Lawrence realized that the nomadic nature of the Arabs made it unnecessary for them to control territory; instead they concentrated on lightning strikes against supply and communication lines, to isolate Turkish garrisons without fighting any major battles. Nevertheless, the Arabs still managed to inflict 35,000 Turkish casualties, and effectively eroded their will to fight.

More importantly from the point of overall strategy in the Middle East, by tying down large numbers of Turks the Arab revolt helped General Allenby take Palestine. Lawrence's strengths as a guerrilla leader were his ability to speak the language and understand Arab customs, and a philosophical understanding of the temperament of the Arabs, which allowed them to function most effectively as raiders. Special forces troops sent since then to raise guerrilla forces in support of conventional military operations have learned from Lawrence's revolt: the OSS, SOE and US Special Forces have all stressed the importance of linguistic knowledge and the ability to assimilate into other cultures for those charged with training guerrillas. The Turks, on the other hand, did not seem to learn or to be able to adjust. For example, a light, fast-moving force armed with machine guns could have done a lot to counter Lawrence's irregulars, but the Turks never fielded such a force. Neither did the Turks use propaganda effectively to convince the Arabs that as fellow Muslims they would be more trustworthy than the British.

Both Lawrence and Lettow-Vorbeck are noteworthy because they helped pursue their countries' wartime goals by raising guerrilla forces and using them to divert assets from the major war effort. In the Second World War such use of guerrillas would become even more formalized and effective.

Taking advantage of Great Britain's preoccupation with the First World War, the Irish began their Easter rising in Dublin in 1916. Although the initial rebellion was quickly quelled, the rebel leaders were hanged and thus became martyrs – a commodity guerrilla movements always find invaluable. Discontent continued to grow in Ireland, resulting in the formation in 1919 of the Irish Republican Army (IRA). By 1920 guerrilla warfare had begun in earnest, with 176 police and 54 soldiers killed, and another 251 police and 118 soldiers wounded. Police stations, military barracks, tax offices, post offices and other government buildings were attacked, culminating in an IRA show of force one night when they destroyed 315 Royal Irish Constabulary barracks.

In addition to direct attacks on the police, the IRA began a psychological campaign against the RIC by socially ostracizing members, which combined with the increasing danger resulted in more resignations and fewer recruits. To help counter this erosion of morale among Irish security personnel, a constabulary was recruited in England from ex-soldiers, which became known as the 'Black and Tans' because of its uniform colours. An Auxiliary Division of the RIC was also recruited in England. The advantage of these outside recruits was that they were less likely to be sympathetic to the Irish cause, and less likely to be influenced by social considerations; however, they were also outsiders without local knowledge.

Emergency powers were granted allowing arrest and detention without trial, and by 1921 full martial law was in force in many of the southern counties. Despite these wide-ranging powers though, the Black and Tans and Auxiliaries remained conventional soldiers, little able to deal effectively with a popular guerrilla movement. Out of frustration they treated civilians harshly, thus driving many into the IRA camp. Their movements made them easy targets for ambushes as well, a skill the IRA soon perfected. Bitterness and atrocities grew on both sides, resulting in the commitment of more troops by the British during 1921. Within the British government, suggestions that barbed wire, blockhouses, massive roundups of the population and other methods used during the Boer War should be implemented were opposed on political grounds, particularly since the IRA enjoyed wide support among the many of Irish descent in the United States. The population of Great Britain was tired of the terror, too, pointing up once again that successful guerrilla campaigns often rely heavily upon public opinion within the target country and around the world to erode the will to continue the counter-insurgency. British will did not survive the assault, and in 1921 the partition of Ireland into north and south was agreed upon.

In various parts of the world dissatisfied soldiers from the First World War continued to operate as guerrillas, in some cases bandits, for years after the war, much as mercenary bands used to roam Europe in the aftermath of the wars during the Middle Ages and Renaissance. Perhaps most noteworthy were the Freikorps in Germany, who functioned as an anti-Communist force throughout much of the country, and in Upper Silesia carried out a guerrilla campaign against the Poles. Many veterans of the Freikorps would join the burgeoning Nazi Party, too, in many cases acting as urban guerrillas during its campaign to destabilize the government and other political parties.

The Nazis came to power partly because they were viewed as a counter-force to Communism, which was seen as a threat in Europe, following the Russian Revolution in 1917. During the Revolution, dissident groups – often really bandits – carried out what could be termed guerrilla warfare, but Lenin attempted to form a cohesive Red Army as quickly as possible in an attempt to exert government control and put down the counter-revolutionary forces which were rising throughout the country. It was often in those parts of the country controlled by counter-revolutionaries – the Whites – that Red guerrillas were most effective, as they cut the vital railway lines and harassed the often disaffected White Armies.

The Russian Revolution is perhaps most significant in the history of guerrilla warfare for the commitment of the Communist Internationale – the Comintern – to supporting wars of liberation around the world. The Russian Revolution was also an important influence on Mao Tse-Tung in China, who was destined to become one of the most important theorists of guerrilla warfare of all time, and the subject of a later chapter in this book.

The French formed their Foreign Legion during the nineteenth century, and as part of their colonization of Morocco, the Spanish followed suit with their own Spanish Foreign Legion, the Tercio, in 1920. Although the Tercio would gain a sound reputation for courage and tenacity over the next half century, most of the Spanish Army of the 1920s was poorly equipped and trained, certainly not recommendations for entering a counter-guerrilla war. Nevertheless, that is exactly what happened as the Abd-el-Krim brothers raised a revolt against the Spanish in the Rif, the mountainous region on the northern coast of Morocco, across from Gibraltar. In May 1921 the first attacks by the guerrillas inflicted extremely heavy casualties on the unprepared Spanish. Initial success also caused various tribes to join the Rif rebellion.

Over the next weeks, the guerrillas virtually routed the Spanish and retook the Rif, killing an estimated fifteen to twenty thousand Spanish troops in the process. These initial successes were primarily the result of the Berbers' effective use of mobility to hit the Spanish in their static positions. When the Spanish launched their reconquest the guerrillas fought ferociously, making use of the mountainous terrain. Even though the Tercio and the locally recruited Regulares acted as the cutting edge of the Spanish assault, it still failed. As industrial powers have often done when confronted by insurgencies throughout this century, the Spanish then attempted to substitute technology for good light infantry and began bombing villages, thus alienating the populace even more and giving additional support to the Abd-el-Krims. Mining or oil interests have sometimes found it to their advantage to support insurgencies, and this was the case with the Rif rebellion, where British, German and Dutch mining interests gave financial support to the Abd-el-Krims in the hope of gaining concessions after a victory. Some of this money was used to purchase artillery and aeroplanes, not usual weapons for guerrillas.

By 1924 the only portion of Spanish Morocco actually controlled by the Spanish was the ground their forts occupied, and the war was growing ever more unpopular in Spain. In the autumn of 1924, the Spanish Army began retreating to its inner line of blockhouses, which were located one-quarter mile apart. Seizing the opportunity, the guerrillas inflicted over fifteen thousand casualties during the withdrawal and, in effect, virtually defeated the Spanish. However, they then made the mistake of overestimating their capabilities, and attacked French troops on the French side of the Rif. Initially, they scored successes here as well, forcing the Spanish and the French to offer them autonomy in the Rif. Having now expanded their aims to control all of Morocco, they refused, thus forcing the Spanish and French to join forces. In September 1925 the two powers launched a pincer offensive against the Riffian guerrillas. Pushed back from all directions, the senior Abd-el-Krim brother, his forces suffering from lack of food, asked for peace talks, but the French and Spanish ignored him, forcing his surrender to the French in 1926, though some guerrilla actions, endemic among the Berbers, continued until the 1930s.

The Abd-el-Krims had proved once again that nomadic mountain tribes make exceptionally good guerrillas, particularly if they hit savagely and quickly. However, the very rugged terrain that makes such guerrillas hard to engage is not normally agriculturally productive. As a result, a food denial campaign can be particularly effective against such irregulars. The fact that guerrilla leaders let their ambitions exceed their capabilities may also have doomed what could have been a successful insurgency had they been satisfied with their initial goal, the independence of the Rif.

Although the use of aircraft as a punitive measure in the Rif proved counter-productive for the Spanish, the RAF did use aircraft effectively during the 1920s in the Middle East against various guerrilla bands. RAF flights were used for intelligence-gathering and also to project power in Iraq and on the North-west Frontier in India, where insurgents would have their villages bombed and their herds scattered. Such methods seemed to work against insurgencies which weren't really too serious, but would have been of doubtful value otherwise. In fact, although the British faced various independence movements throughout their colonies during the 1920s and 1930s, none really erupted into serious guerrilla warfare.

The US Marines, on the other hand, seemed to be involved constantly in counter-insurgency operations in Latin America. Realizing that effective local constabularies would normally be the best counter-insurgency forces, in the Dominican Republic the Marines helped form and train the *Policia Nacional*. In this small country another effective expedient proved to be the rounding up of males for identification by informers of any guerrillas. The problem with this system, of course, is that informers are of dubious reliability and may really be settling personal scores. This was a problem with the Phoenix Program in Vietnam, which often undermined its own effectiveness and credibility. Another effective tactic in the Dominican Republic was offering amnesty to guerrillas. This tactic has proved valid again and again in counter-insurgencies, as it allows the disillusioned to leave a guerrilla movement and also provides ready sources of intelligence about the guerrilla movement. Finally, during 1914–24 the Marines formed counter-guerrilla units from those who had suffered guerrilla depredations. These forces often proved relentless in tracking the guerrillas, and proved quite effective due to their local knowledge.

A better-known counter-guerrilla campaign by the Marines took place in Nicaragua. Initially, the Marines were sent to prevent a civil war and to supervise elections. However, Augusto Sandino – who would give his name to the later Sandinistas – formed a guerrilla band and began a guerrilla war based on his experience of fighting in Mexico with Pancho Villa. The fact that Nicaragua is so mountainous and had few roads made it particularly suitable for guerrilla warfare. Sandino knew the countryside well and enjoyed wide support among the peasants. The guerrillas frequently tried to ambush the Marines, but a combination of fire discipline and air support saved the Marines from really heavy losses. Once again the Marines formed a local constabulary, the *Guardia Nacional*, which along with the Marines carried out aggressive patrolling, particularly at night. That was the stick; the carrot was an offer of a ten-dollar reward for each guerrilla who accepted amnesty and turned in his rifle. In addition to the other benefits of an amnesty, this system helped deprive the guerrillas of arms.

Still, though the Marines helped contain the insurgency, Sandino remained at large for five years and was never captured by the Marines. The

Guardia was first trained by the Marines, then later officered by Marines until deemed ready to operate on its own. Eventually, after the Marines had left, the Guardia lured Sandino to Managua and killed him. Two important outcomes of this campaign were that the Somoza regime took power and Sandino became a hero for other Latin American guerrillas.

Despite the fact that the Spanish had proved particularly adept at guerrilla warfare during the Napoleonic Wars, the Spanish Civil War saw only scattered action by guerrillas, though any reader of Hemingway's *For Whom the Bell Tolls* would certainly assume guerrilla warfare played a much greater role. Some Republican guerrilla units were active against the Nationalists, particularly in the mountains, but the fact that the Republicans were, theoretically at least, the lawful government probably kept them from using guerrillas more. The best of the Nationalist troops were the Tercios, under Franco, who had been brought in from Morocco, and the Republicans needed to concentrate on forming an effective counter-force to contest control of the cities. Finally, the very unsophistication of the Spanish Army meant that it did not have long, complex supply lines which would have been vulnerable to guerrilla warfare. That many fighting for the Republican cause were irregulars is true, but they were not normally engaging in guerrilla operations.

The 1930s also saw an Arab insurgency in Palestine against Jewish settlement. At one point, Arab insurgents controlled much of the country, but the British Army imposed curfews, set up road blocks, carried out raids into rebel territory, and rounded up potential troublemakers. These moves, along with concessions to the Arabs on Jewish immigration, helped turn the population against the insurgents and deprive them of their base of support. The formation of Jewish counter-guerrilla forces by Orde Wingate, later to achieve fame as a guerrilla warrior during the Second World War, created an effective counter-force to the remaining guerrillas. As a result, by the outbreak of the Second World War the insurgency had largely run its course.

Conclusions

Though guerrilla warfare was still viewed as somewhat of an aberration by most professional soldiers, the twentieth century prior to the Second World War saw the development of certain tactics by both guerrillas and guerrilla fighters which would be of lasting importance. The experiences of Lawrence and Lettow-Vorbeck, for example, proved that insurgencies raised in support of conventional military operations could provide a very effective adjunct, tying down large numbers of enemy troops and preventing them from being deployed against conventional forces. This idea led to the development of the OSS and SOE during the Second World War. The period was also one of

▲ Colonel Jose Millan Astray, the founder of the Spanish Foreign Legion

training for some who would effectively use guerrilla warfare during the Second World War. Wingate's experiences in Palestine, for example, helped prepare him for his Chindit campaign against the Japanese. The experiences in the jungles of Latin America, even if the Marines did not at the time have a fully developed plan for counter-insurgency operations, did help prepare the Corps for its later operations in the jungles and for future counter-insurgency operations.

Writing about the subject of guerrillas during this period, the German Arthur Ehrhardt made a salient point when he noted that modern mechanized armies would advance so rapidly that their supply lines carrying crucial fuel and spare parts would become especially vulnerable to attack, particularly by motorized guerrilla units. The Special Air Service used exactly such units to attack the extended German supply lines in the Western Desert during the Second World War. The industrialized nations also learned, during this period, that public opinion could be turned against the authorities in an extended guerrilla war. Just to give two examples, in the Rif rebellion and in the Irish insurgency, public opinion at home influenced the conduct of the counter-guerrilla campaign. More sophisticated international interlocking of economies also made guerrillas more effective, as they could now attack economic targets (e.g. Middle Eastern oil production) and exert a far-reaching effect.

THE SPANISH FOREIGN LEGION

Though not as well known as the legendary French Foreign Legion, the Spanish Foreign Legion gained its own reputation for toughness and courage during Spain's colonial period in North Africa. Founded in October 1920 by Lt-Colonel Jose Millan Astray Terreros for service in Morocco, the Legion originally consisted of three Bandaras (battalions). While still called a 'foreign' legion, throughout its history the Spanish Foreign Legion has drawn at least ninety per cent of its strength from Spain, and there is a very active veterans' network throughout Spain. Millan Astray – whose courage would become legendary as he was wounded numerous times in combat, losing an eye, an arm and a leg, yet continuing to serve – had as his second in command Major Francisco Franco. One of Major Franco's first duties was the establishment of a Legion depot at Dar Riffien, which was soon the finest in the Spanish Army. The Legion drew highly motivated recruits through its aura of adventure, and also because it offered the highest pay in the Spanish Army.

Millan Astray developed a special creed for the Legion, which combined Catholic mysticism with the virtues of comradeship, bravery, loyalty and willingness to die. The latter was deemed extremely important, and the Legion battle cry was 'Viva la Muerte!' (Long live death!). Legion discipline was rigorous, but so was the life in Morocco.

The Spanish Foreign Legion first saw action in June 1921, against the Rif rebels. Suffering heavy casualties spearheading Spanish counter-offensives, the Legion recruited replacements and formed the 4th and 5th Bandaras in late 1921. Millan Astray was seriously wounded twice leading attacks, as were many other Legion officers who led from the front. In November 1922, the 6th Bandara was formed, then in June 1923 Franco took command of the Legion. Under Franco's leadership, the Legion continued to build a sterling combat record, acting as a

▼ Legionnaires of the Spanish Foreign Legion on patrol; their weapon is the CETME assault rifle *(Spanish Foreign Legion)*

rearguard at Xauen during the withdrawals of August–October 1924, and holding the fortress to gain time for others to pull back, then leaving straw dummies in Legion uniforms on the parapets while they made their own withdrawal. This and other operations during the period had been designed to remove the Spanish Army to defensible lines, and were highly dependent on the legionnaires to hold positions while other troops were pulled back.

In February 1925 Franco was promoted to full colonel, then his command was expanded as the 7th Bandara was formed that May, followed shortly by a squadron of mounted lancers. In 1925 the Legion also became known as the 'Tercio' after the famous Spanish combined musket/pike formations of the Renaissance, who had been the greatest soldiers of their day. Now organized into two Legions, the Tercio was deployed with one Legion at Melilla and a second at Ceuta. The lancers remained directly under the control of the colonel commanding the Legion, to carry out escort and reconnaissance duties.

After the attack by the Riffian rebels on the French in April 1925, a joint operation against the Abd-el-Krims was launched in September 1925. On 8 September the 6th and 7th Bandaras under Colonel Franco took part in landings at Alhucemas Bay, spearheading the operation and driving the Riffians from the heights overlooking the beaches. In the overland portion of the operation, the 2nd and 3rd Bandaras also acted as spearheads for the relief of the fort of Cudia Tahar. By 2 October the Abd-el-Krims' capital had fallen, the Legion having been in the forefront of the operation throughout. In partial reward for the Legion's excellent showing, Franco was promoted to Brig-General in February 1926, becoming the youngest general in the Spanish Army at thirty-three. His former mentor, Colonel Millan Astray, resumed command of the Legion.

The Legion helped mop up the remaining insurgents over the next few months, then Millan Astray was promoted to Brig-General himself in June 1927, now leaving the Legion for good, having fought in sixty-two actions with it. His heart always remained with the Legion, however, and when Millan Astray died he was buried with his Legion sidecap on his coffin. During the Rif Rebellion, the Legion had sustained over 8,300 casualties, including 2,000 killed, but had

▶ A Spanish Foreign Legion recoilless rifle and its crew *(Spanish Foreign Legion)*

inflicted far heavier losses on the enemy. As part of overall military reductions, the 7th and 8th Bandaras and the lancers were disbanded in December 1932.

The Legion saw its first service in Spain proper in October 1934, when legionnaires were brought in to put down a miners' revolt in Asturias. Leftist sentiment continued, however, resulting in a left-wing government being elected by a narrow margin in February 1936. Although unrest was brewing in Spain itself, it was some Legion Bandaras in Morocco that first revolted against their government, in July 1936. They were soon joined by a full-scale revolt in Spain proper. Realizing the most effective troops Spain possessed were in Morocco, and that they owed him substantial personal loyalty, Franco took command of the Army of Africa and airlifted the 5th Bandara to Spain to help hold Seville. Over the next month the remainder of the Legion arrived in Spain to fight against Republican forces.

Throughout the Spanish Civil War, the Legion was in its traditional position at the vanguard of assaults. Often taking villages from Republican forces with bayonet charges, the Legion spearheaded the march on Madrid. Twelve new Legion Bandaras were formed between September 1936 and April 1938. To combat the Republican tanks, a Legion Tank Bandara was formed, then early in 1938 this was expanded to a tank group. Other heavier units including anti-tank and flamethrower companies were formed as well. Although the International Brigades which fought on the Republican side are better known, many foreigners served on the Nationalist side as well, often in the Bandaras of the Legion. When the Civil War finally ended in April 1939, the Legion had been in over three thousand actions and had suffered over 37,000 casualties.

At the war's end, the Legion was reduced to eleven Bandaras and returned to Morocco. Terminology was changed once again, too, as the entire Spanish Foreign Legion was now known as the Legion, with three Tercios as sub-units. Each Tercio now had a Heavy Weapons

Insignia worn by members of the Spanish Foreign Legion Special Operations Unit, which specializes in counter-insurgency

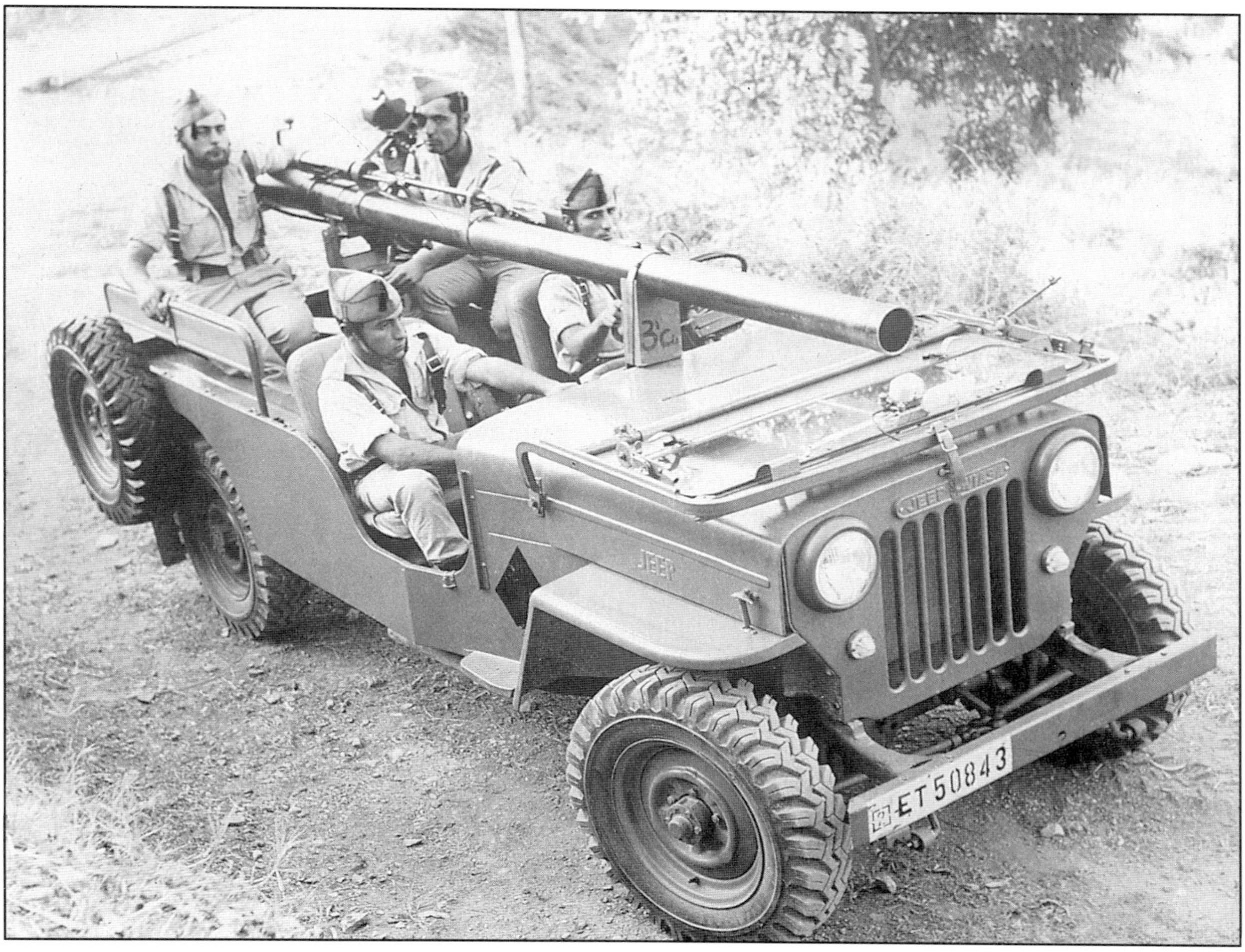
ET 50843

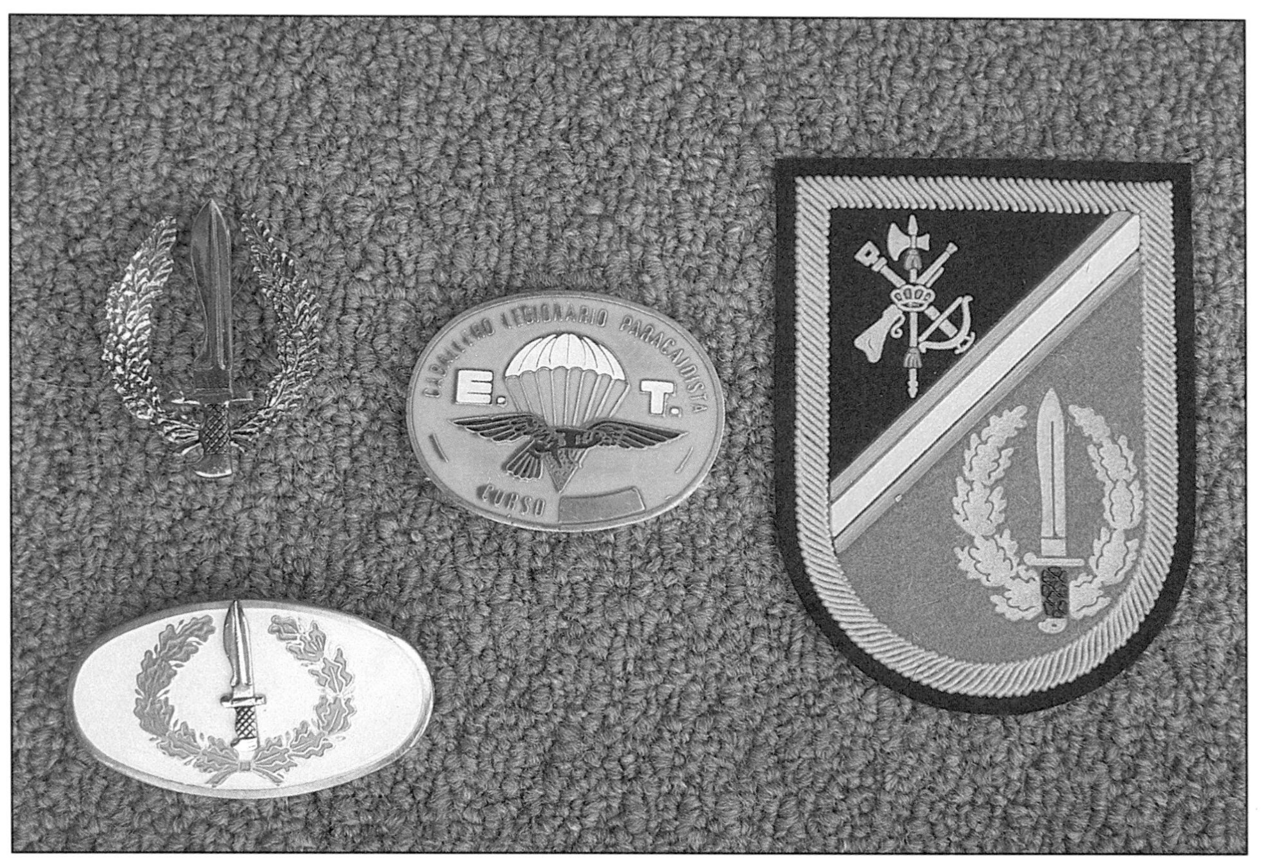

LEGIONARIO PARACAIDISTA
E. T.
CURSO

Mixed Group with artillery, anti-tank and AA companies.

In honour of Spain's past military glories, beginning in 1943, each Tercio was named after a military hero of the sixteenth or seventeenth century, the 1st becoming the 'Gran Capitan', the 2nd the 'Duque de Alba' and the 3rd the 'Don Juan de Austria'. Although the 10th and 11th Bandaras were scheduled for disbandment in 1947, instead they were joined by the 12th in 1950 to become the 4th Tercio, 'Alejandro Farnesio', at Villa Sanjurjo.

Morocco gained its independence in 1956, but Spain retained enclaves at Ceuta, Melilla and Ifni. Ifni included the Spanish Sahara in the south, and to protect this area, the 13th Independent Bandara was formed, in July 1956. In response to attacks by the extremist Istiqlal groups in Ifni and the Sahara, the 2nd, 4th and 6th Bandaras were sent to reinforce the 13th. Then, on the night of 22–23 November 1957, 2,500 members of the 'Saharan Liberation Army' launched attacks throughout the area. Initially the Legionnaires held the capital at Sidi-Ifni, then with reinforcements began counter-insurgency operations and aggressive patrolling throughout the Spanish Sahara, in February 1958. As in the Rif Rebellion, the rebels also attacked the French positions in Morocco, resulting in joint operations with their counterparts from the French Foreign Legion against the Liberation Army, resulting in its defeat.

In August 1958, Tercios 3 and 4 were assigned to the Sahara and renamed the 'Saharan Tercios'. Each was organized into two Bandaras, a light armoured group and a motorized artillery battery. In 1966 the two light armoured groups were renamed the 1st and 2nd Light Saharan Groups, and the next few years saw their equipment upgraded to include Panhard armoured cars, AMX-30 tanks, and Panhard M-3 APCs.

In 1961 the 1st and 2nd Tercios moved to Melilla and Ceuta. With the Saharan responsibility ending, the 13th Bandara was disbanded in 1969; then in 1976 Spain left the Sahara completely, resulting in the disbandment of the 4th Tercio as well. The remaining three Tercios were then deployed at Melilla, Ceuta and in the Canary Islands.

In 1986 foreigners not already serving in the Legion were banned from joining its ranks, though foreigners already serving could remain. Along with the Spanish Airborne Brigade, the Spanish Legion now acts as the primary Spanish rapid deployment reserve. Legion strength was about seven thousand as of late 1987, still including a few hundred foreigners, organized into four Tercios, each of two Bandaras. There is also a Legion Special Operations Bandara with airborne qualified personnel and a cavalry unit. The Special Operations unit still trains assiduously and realistically in a counter-guerrilla role, normally spending ten months of the year in the field on realistic operations.

As the Spanish Legion nears its seventieth anniversary it still gives Spain a highly credible counter-insurgency force, one that combines tough, realistic training with a strong sense of unit identity and a proud martial tradition, a combination which makes the motto 'Legionarios a Luchar, Legionarios a Morir!' – 'Legionnaires to the Fight, Legionnaires to the Death!' – one that should strike fear into Spain's enemies.

3 PARTISANS, GUERRILLAS AND OTHER IRREGULARS IN THE SECOND WORLD WAR

The continued development of technological warfare, while making armies more sophisticated, also made them more logistically dependent. As a result, the vast territories rapidly conquered by the Axis became fertile ground for guerrilla warfare. Innovations such as the aeroplane, parachute, shortwave radio and submarine, all contributed to the Allied ability to support guerrillas, while compact explosives and clandestine weapons specifically designed for guerrilla warfare made equipping the guerrilla easier. To all of these introductory statements, however, must be added the caveat, theoretically, as in practice, that guerrilla movements often were extremely hard to supply and often depended on obsolete weapons if they had weapons at all.

Fortunately for the Allies, the Germans and Japanese often created their own enemies by imposing harsh regimes in conquered lands and by their own arrogance. It then fell to Great Britain, the USA and the Soviet Union to fuel nationalistic anti-German feelings with propaganda, advisers, supplies and even the occasional provocation. As a result, in Britain the Special Operations Executive (SOE) was formed with the mission, according to Churchill, of setting Europe ablaze with sabotage and resistance, though this order proved a bit optimistic. SOE was emulated by an American organization, the Office of Strategic Services (OSS), with the same basic mission, though the OSS also had an intelligence-gathering role, carried out in Britain by MI6.

Before the outbreak of hostilities, the British had published two pamphlets, *The Art of Guerrilla Warfare* and *Partisan Leader's Handbook*, setting forth the basics of guerrilla warfare. A few officers, including Lt-Colonel Colin Gubbins, who would head SOE, had also shown a serious interest in guerrilla warfare, but most professional officers disliked any mention of irregular warfare, feeling it just wasn't 'playing the game'. As a result, SOE was formed under the Ministry of Economic Warfare, rather than the Ministry of Defence. Likewise, the OSS was a 'civilian' agency, though most of its operatives held military rank. Both took the rather pragmatic view that any group fighting the Axis was worthy of support, a view that in some cases will be seen to have contributed to the post-war glut of guerrilla wars.

▼ Members of the British Commandos were trained to function as surrogate guerrillas carrying out raids on occupied Europe *(IWM)*

EUROPE AND NORTH AFRICA

Semantically, the Winter War between Finland and the Soviet Union in 1939 may not have been part of the Second World War, but in actuality it certainly was, particularly since the Red Army's poor showing may have influenced Hitler to invade Russia. One reason the Finns fared so well against the numerically superior Soviets was their excellent use of the Finnish terrain to launch hit-and-run raids by ski troops. Playing a key role in this organized guerrilla warfare were Finnish Civic Guards, local militias equipped only with small arms but intimately familiar with the countryside, which they used to maximum effect.

In the wake of Dunkirk, Great Britain prepared for the possibility of losing London and other metropolitan areas to a German invasion. It was planned that resistance should continue if this happened, based on the 'Auxiliary Units', a clandestine resistance movement formed and in place in the countryside, particularly in Scotland, where rough terrain and the Scots' long history of forming close-knit groups offered fertile ground for a guerrilla movement. The large number of retired military officers in Scotland offered a good pool for recruiting local resistance leaders. Gamekeepers were recruited as scouts and snipers, miners as saboteurs and postmen as intelligence-gatherers. From Yorkshire to Cornwall, resistance cells were formed and equipped with special radios and weapons caches.

Though the invasion never came, the resistance cells did serve the very useful purpose of allowing Colin Gubbins and others who would work with SOE to gain practical experience at forming a resistance organization. Winston Churchill himself set an example for the country as he worked marksmanship practice with his personal weapons into his busy schedule, and preached his 'Each one kills one!' philosophy for dealing with a German invasion.

Once SOE actually began developing underground movements, or working with those which had developed on their own, German-occupied Norway assumed an early importance due to the Allied fears of German progress towards an atomic bomb. As a result, the Norsk Hydro Elektrisk plant, which produced the heavy water necessary for nuclear research, became a top priority target. The Norwegians had been forming their own underground army, the Milorg, but initially a British and Norwegian commando force was sent against the plant. When this attack and bombing sorties proved unsuccessful, however, local guerrillas carried out perhaps the most successful sabotage coup of the war against the heavy water plant and associated transport.

It became apparent early in the war that the terrain of a country would play an important role in the effectiveness of its resistance movement. Poland, Holland, Czechoslovakia, Belgium, Denmark and France particularly did not have terrain

▶ Welrod silenced assassination pistol developed during the Second World War for the OSS and SOE *(Danish Resistance Museum)*

▶ Armoured car built by the Danish Resistance for use during the liberation of their country *(Danish Resistance Museum)*

▼ Underground arms workshop of the type developed by many European Resistance movements during the Second World War *(Danish Resistance Museum)*

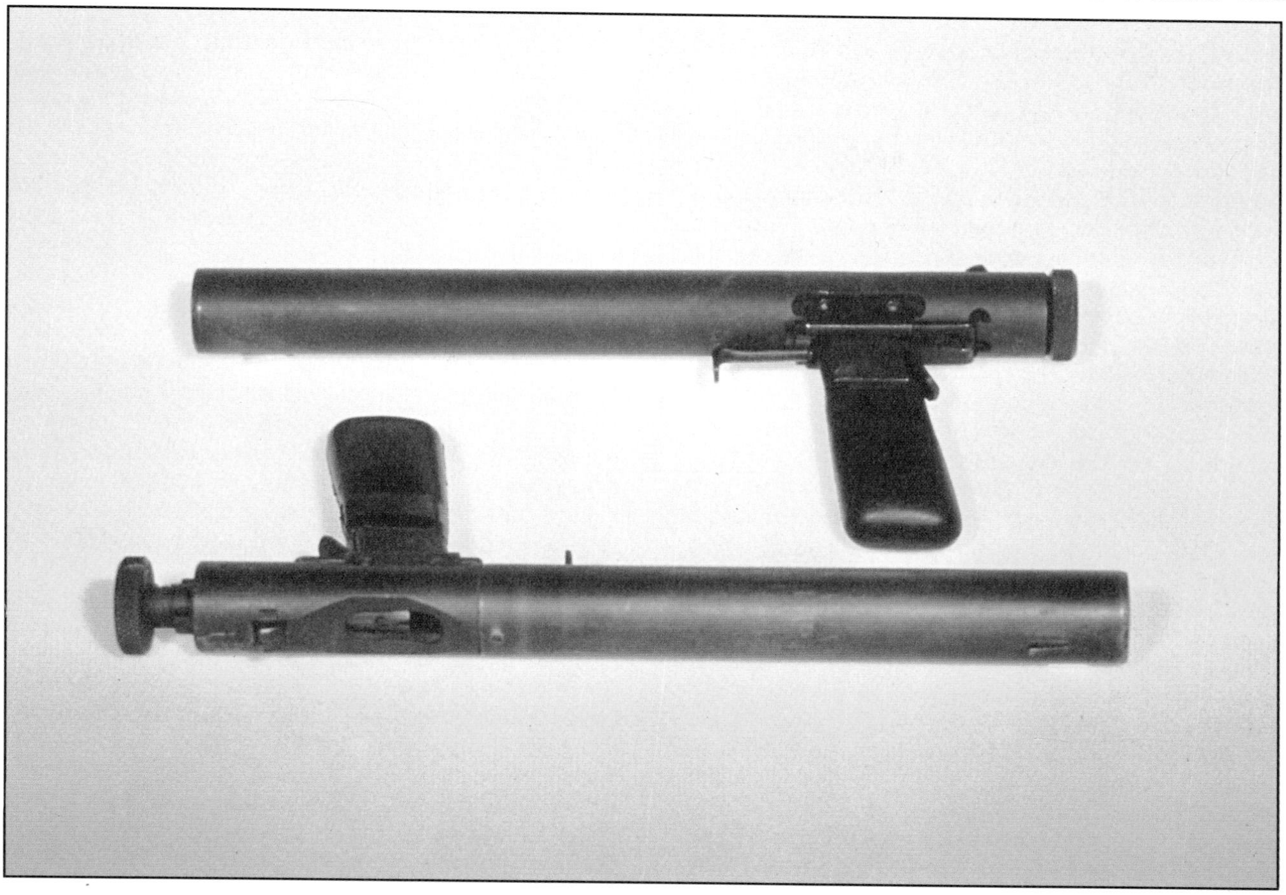

conducive to supporting guerrillas, though the Ardennes in Belgium, the Carpathians in Poland and Czechoslovakia, and the Alps in France offered some scope for this. Denmark and Holland especially contained virtually no rugged country in which to hide guerrilla bands. Norway offered great open spaces, but the climate made outdoor survival difficult. Parts of Italy, Yugoslavia, Greece, Albania and the Soviet Union, on the other hand, were perfect for irregulars. Though ambushes and sabotage are the guerrilla activities most often associated with European resistance movements, intelligence-gathering and aiding Allied airmen and POWs to reach freedom were even more vital, early in the war.

The initial shock of the German invasion, and the civilian tendency to let life return to normal, kept early resistance rather minimal in Western Europe, but the combination of harsh German occupation policies, German arrogance and conscription of the local population for the German Army or forced labour, together with the deportations to concentration camps, soon created a climate for the nascent resistance. The most effective organization for creating guerrilla forces in occupied Europe was not SOE, the OSS nor the NKVD; it was the SS!

Among the first occupied nations to resist Hitler were the Poles, where the Home Army formed by General Rowecki was subdivided into provincial, area, section and outpost commands, each organized into staff, diversionary action platoons and combat platoons, each numbering about fifty men. As German repression increased, active underground presses helped build on dissatisfaction to generate recruits for the guerrillas. The Home Army carried out acts of sabotage as well until the fall of France, after which, realizing they were in for a long war, General Sikorski's government in exile called for a cessation. Although Polish guerrillas in the forests fought a vicious war – including mailing the genitals of murdered Germans to their families in Germany, as a rough form of psychological war – it is the urban fighting which took place in the Warsaw Ghetto that is most often associated with resistance in Poland. Warsaw's Jewish urban guerrillas fought with few weapons but with backs-against-the-wall determination, beginning on 18 April 1943. The primary lesson to be learned from the Warsaw Ghetto uprising today is that sewers, rooftops, basements and the other warrens within a large city can make highly effective guerrilla hiding places – but for a limited time, and assuming the willingness to undergo the total destruction of the city.

The resistance in Czechoslovakia illustrates two important points about guerrilla warfare. First, in forming underground organizations, it is useful to build on established groups who already know and trust each other. The Czech resistance built partially upon the Falcon Gymnastics Organization for the OSVO resistance circuit. The Czech resistance and/or SOE have been cynically credited with the realization that sometimes an occupier must be goaded into atrocities to arouse the public. Thus, when the Czech resistance assassinated Reinhard Heydrich, head of the Gestapo in Czechoslovakia, they triggered the Nazi destruction of the village of Lidice, which served to awake many Czechs to the realities of German occupation.

In literature, the French Resistance is by far the best known, although it encountered many problems, not the least of which was widespread collaboration. Additionally, there was not one, but two primary Resistance organizations, one led by de Gaulle, the other by Giraud. After Germany invaded the Soviet Union, Communist guerrillas also became extremely active in France, having the advantage of an effective cell organization already in place. Yet another hindrance to the formation of an effective Resistance was France's division into Vichy and occupied zones, which gave the Vichy French the illusion of self-determination. As the war progressed, de Gaulle's BCRA (*Bureau Central de Renseignements et d'Action*) achieved primacy, but though SOE worked with the BCRA they also sent their own independent agents into France. Later, the OSS would work closely with the BCRA as well.

As in other occupied countries, the German policies of curfews, hostages, forced labour and conscription all contributed to increased French willingness to resist. No doubt food shortages were a particular incentive as well among the gastronomically militant French. In its efforts to counter growing resistance, the German Abwehr was able to locate some cells or individual agents through radio direction or infiltration. The French collaborationist *Milice* had some success as well, based on their local knowledge, but they were soon so detested by the population that they proved ineffective, even a hindrance in the counter-guerrilla role.

After the Allied landings in North Africa, the Allies not only gained additional potential agents to infiltrate back to France, but the Germans created greater scope for resistance, by occupying Vichy. By early 1943 the FTP – *Franc-Tireurs et Partisans* – claimed to be carrying out about 250 attacks, killing 500–600 Germans per month. Like most figures relating to successes on either side in guerrilla wars, these must be viewed with caution; however, they are indicative that active French guerrilla warfare was increasing as the North African invasion and German losses at Stalingrad began to show German vulnerability.

Railway sabotage certainly increased to the point where 20,000 German railway workers had to be imported and the SS used to guard the French rail system. Reportedly, between June 1943 and May 1944, over 1,800 locomotives were destroyed or damaged. These attacks prior to the Normandy landings increased during the spring of 1944 and the targets included railways, telephone lines, roads, and other parts of the German logistics

▲ British Commandos preparing to set off on a raid against the coast of occupied Europe *(IWM)*

net in France. One Resistance circuit, 'Armada', specialized during 1943 in destroying locks and other installations along the waterways, thus slowing the barge traffic supplying the German war machine. This same circuit then turned to the electricity generators and pylons serving French industry.

One area where the Maquis proved particularly strong and played an important role was on Corsica, the rugged terrain and tradition of banditry both contributing to a successful Resistance.

Resistance activities in mainland France built towards a crescendo as the long-anticipated Allied landings approached. During June, for example, over one thousand railway lines were cut, hampering German reinforcement of their units on the beaches. So successful were these attacks that it took some German divisions weeks to reach the battlefront. Just before and after the landings, Jedburgh teams, with a combination of OSS and French Resistance, and SAS jeep raiding teams, were parachuted into France to co-ordinate targets and provide intelligence for the Allied armies breaking out of the beachhead. Once Patton's Third Army had broken out, the Resistance mission shifted from destroying bridges or other key logistical points to holding them and preventing their destruction, thus speeding the Allied advance. Members of the Resistance also operated behind Allied armies, helping mop up any remaining Germans and rounding up collaborators, many of whom were executed on the spot.

During the period when the French Resistance was receiving arms drops, over 400,000 weapons were parachuted in. Only a fraction, of course, reached the guerrillas, but even those weapons captured by the Germans had at least the minimum psychological value of making the Germans wonder how many drops they had missed. Acts of resistance often resulted in the deaths of French men and women, sometimes brutally under Gestapo torture; these martyrs helped harden resistance in many others.

Although the Soviet propaganda mechanism was quick to turn the partisans into people's heroes, initially the Germans met few likely partisans other than local Communist officials. In fact in many parts of Russia the Germans were welcomed as liberators. Despite pre-war plans to develop a comprehensive strategy involving partisans and specialist airborne troops to operate behind enemy lines, the Soviet Union was actually poorly prepared for guerrilla warfare, partially out of a reluctance to arm the peasants. However, shortly after the invasion, plans were formulated to begin guerrilla warfare. On 3 July 1941 Stalin

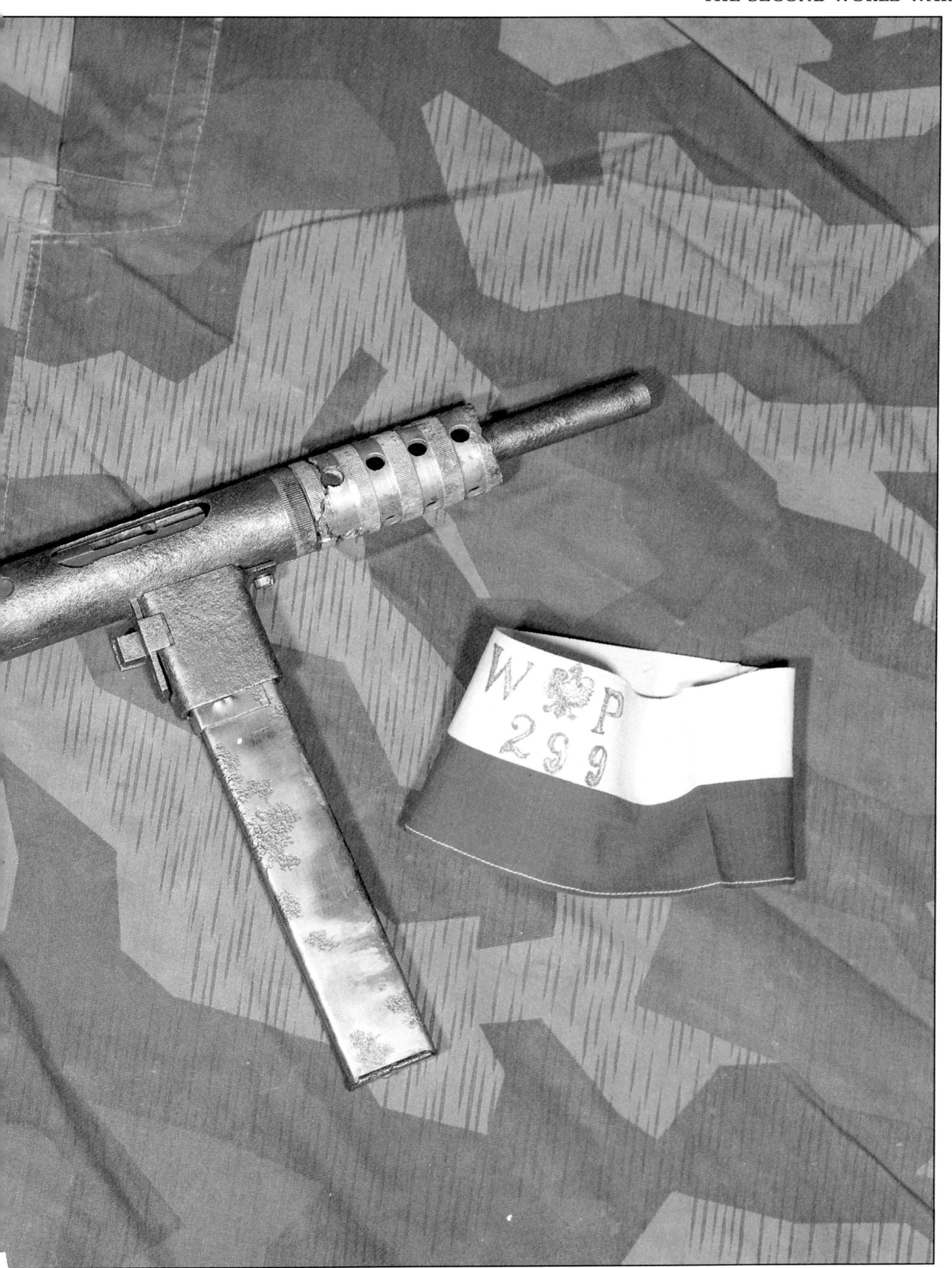
W P
299

▲ Soviet paratroopers such as these often joined the partisans, after a jump, and helped organize and lead them *(IWM)*

made his famous radio call for guerrilla action against the Germans, which actually had less immediate effect in the Soviet Union than in other occupied countries of Europe, where local Communists answered his call to action with increased partisan activities. July also saw the formation of a Red Army command specifically to organize partisan warfare. As is frequently the case in the Soviet Union, a second agency also became involved, the NKVD being charged with forming partisan bands as well, though their true task may have been to ensure that partisans maintained a proper Communist outlook. The NKVD also formed specialist assassination and sabotage units later in the war to function somewhat as the British SAS; these were the forerunners of the current KGB Osnaz units. Both the Red Army and the NKVD trained selected individuals to parachute in to recruit and train partisans; once again these were akin to SOE or OSS teams, with similar missions. Another policy which was to evolve in the wake of Soviet airborne operations was that airborne troops dropped off target, or surviving after a parachute raid, should form partisan bands or join local partisans. This policy helped infuse very high quality fighting manpower into the Partisan movement.

Although much of western Russia is not very well suited to guerrilla warfare, the Pripyat Marshes did lend themselves well to supporting some of the earliest guerrilla bands operating behind the German lines. Even those partisans who found good operational areas still had to face the Russian winter, however, never easy even under peacetime conditions. Once again, the greatest impetus to the formation of guerrilla units was the Germans themselves and their harsh occupation policies. As the tide began to turn in favour of the Red Army in late 1942 and early 1943, too, the fear of reprisals against anyone who had not opposed the Germans influenced many to join the partisans. So harsh were conditions in the German POW camps that some prisoners collaborated and formed anti-partisan forces serving the Germans, while still others escaped and joined the partisans. Though life with the partisans was harsh, Germany's systematic genocide against the Slavs made it seem more palatable when the other choice was death.

◀ Version of the Sten gun produced in underground workshops by members of the Polish Resistance during the Second World War *(AMI)*

A great difficulty in partisan camps was lack of medical treatment, so volunteer doctors – mostly female – were parachute-trained and dropped to the partisans. Local air superiority now made possible supply missions and personnel drops to the partisans. The Partisan movement was becoming more systematic by late 1942. *The Partisan's Handbook* had been published, and guerrilla training camps were operating behind German lines.

The Wehrmacht had entered the Soviet Union with specialist security divisions which operated behind the advancing armies to guard their supply lines. However, the very size of the Soviet Union and the growing number of partisans soon proved these measures inadequate. Also in place were the *Einsatzgruppen* with members of the SD, Gestapo and SS. These units were concerned principally with exterminating undesirables, such as commissars, and were unproductive from a counter-guerrilla point of view, since they stimulated hatred within the populace. The partisans soon became so numerous and confident that they raided German supply depots, got food from villagers, and planted their own crops and kept herds of cattle.

Some local German commanders grasped the fundamentals of counter-guerrilla warfare better than others. One tactic which proved successful was the formation of pseudo-partisan bands, which would infiltrate and then slaughter groups

of partisans. This same method would later be used very effectively in Kenya and Rhodesia. Units formed from Cossacks made particularly vicious anti-partisan forces. More conventional, but still effective, were highly mobile *Jagdkommandos*, which hunted down the partisans, and the tactic of clearing security zones on each side of railway lines. In those cases where the Germans supported local anti-Communists, they often achieved good counter-guerrilla results. Had the Germans been willing to tone down their oppressiveness it is probable that many partisans would instead have become German allies. Partisans made good use of propaganda, though, to publicize German atrocities and used selective assassination against the Germans, and particularly against collaborators.

The Germans found that major, multi-divisional counter-guerrilla sweeps proved effective, but the manpower needed for such operations precluded their use normally. The Soviet Union's huge distances made such operations difficult since the partisans always had a new area to begin operations in. As the Red Army went on the offensive, many troops previously used for security duties were sent to the front, resulting in increased scope for partisan attacks on German supply lines.

Depending on the terrain, some partisans operated from fixed bases in the forests, while others functioned as roving bands. Still, however, the most effective partisans were normally those bands composed of Red Army troops operating behind the lines, or with a strong contingent of paratroopers or other regular soldiers. As partisan units grew they often received radios by airdrop, with which to co-ordinate their operations with the Red Army.

In addition to being good gatherers of intelligence, the partisans waged their campaign against railways, bridges, roads, enemy vehicles and enemy supply depots. Special demolition charges, including one which would cut a rail line in 150 places at once, were developed to ease their task.

The Soviets made highly effective use of their own guerrillas in countries they hoped to occupy after the war. They had their own Poles, Hungarians and even Germans ready to operate in those countries during the Soviet advance. The Soviets were also realists about the future occupation of Poland and other countries, allowing the Polish Home Army to be decimated by the Germans, fighting for Warsaw, so they would not be able to offer cohesive resistance against the Soviets when they moved in.

The most successful guerrillas in Europe were not those in the Soviet Union, however, but in Yugoslavia, where the mountainous terrain offered excellent scope for partisan operations. Additionally, the sea coast could be used for infiltration, and much of the population was combative by nature, with a long tradition of banditry and guerrilla warfare. Already by mid-1941, many guerrilla bands were operating in the mountains, though divided along ethnic and political lines. Initially, the group best known in London and Washington was the Chetniks under Kosta Pecanac, a Serbian First World War guerrilla leader; however, he was soon collaborating with the Germans, and was replaced by General Draza Mihailovich.

Initially less well known, but far more effective, however, were the Communist partisans under Josip Broz (Tito). Ironically, early in the guerrilla campaign, even the Soviets supported the Chetniks rather than the partisans. Occasionally the two groups formed a fragile alliance for operations against the Germans, but for the most part they were more interested in fighting each other. Ignorant of what was really happening in the Yugoslavian mountains, SOE initially supported the Chetniks, who by 1942 were working with the Nazis against the partisans. However, as SOE teams finally managed to reach both Tito and Mihailovich, and then communicate with London about Chetnik collaboration, support was eventually switched to Tito.

Part of Tito's success can be attributed to aggressiveness in attacking the Germans, but his forces were also well organized into political cadres, 'shock divisions', guerrilla bands and part-time guerrillas living in villages or towns. So powerful did the partisans become that the Germans launched massive offensives to surround them in the mountains and destroy them. Though the partisans suffered heavy casualties, they still used the hackneyed but effective guerrilla strategy of dispersing, exfiltrating and reforming. In forming anti-partisan forces in Yugoslavia, the Germans found that both horse cavalry and Alpine troops proved effective.

Actually, the partisans preferred to attack the Italians rather than the Germans, since they were more likely to run, abandoning their weapons.

By spring 1944 Tito had over two hundred thousand men in the field, whom he committed to cutting German railway lines to hamper the shift of reinforcements to Normandy or Italy where Allied troops would be advancing. So successful were partisan operations that at the peak they were tying down nine German and ten Italian divisions; when Italy was knocked out of the war, even more German divisions.

Much of the partisans' success can be attributed to Tito, who grasped the basic concepts of waging guerrilla warfare. The well-disciplined partisans did not loot, paid for their food and always tried to evacuate their wounded. As a result, their morale was high and they had broad support from the population. Even during retreats, the partisans would go over to local counter-attacks, thus keeping their fighting spirit. The Germans realized the importance of Tito, and attempted to bomb his cave headquarters and to kill or capture him using a raid by SS paratroopers.

As the Germans began their long retreat back to Germany, the partisans harried them, inflicting additional casualties and also liberating their own country, an important factor in regard to the relative independence from the Soviet Union achieved by Yugoslavia. Yugoslavia's partisan war had proven particularly effective because Tito grasped the importance of keeping popular support, the fact the Communist partisans were based on an already existing cell system, they had long-range goals, their discipline was strong and they kept their mobility.

The guerrilla situation was even more confused in Greece, where internecine struggles abounded. Once again the Communist group, ELAS, was the best organized. Others included EDES, EKKA and AAA. EDES, the Republican group, and ELAS were the premier fighting groups, though as in Yugoslavia they often spent as much time fighting each other as the Germans. In 1942, an SOE mission did manage to get ELAS and EDES to work together long enough to cut rail lines carrying supplies to the Afrika Korps for six weeks. By autumn 1943 guerrillas, mostly ELAS, were in control of about two-thirds of Greece; as in Yugoslavia, this had a political as well as a military impact. As ELAS strength grew, they fought more against EDES and less against the Germans, conserving their manpower for the future struggle for Greece after the German withdrawal.

As part of Operation Noah's Ark in September 1944, ELAS and EDES both attacked the retreating Germans to hinder their withdrawal, but both held back strength to battle each other, ELAS being more guilty of such malingering than EDES. As soon as the war ended, ELAS began an attempt to take over the country, refusing to disarm, and ended up fighting against the British as well as EDES.

In Albania also there were multiple guerrilla organizations, with the Communists pre-eminent. The Albanian guerrillas were known for being particularly savage, leading to a no-quarters guerrilla/counter-guerrilla war. Despite the intramural fighting, however, the Greek guerrillas managed to tie down six German and twelve Italian divisions, while the Albanians tied down five Italian divisions, then four German divisions after the Italians left the war.

One of the most important lessons to be learned from the various Balkan guerrilla campaigns is the importance of political as well as military knowledge for those recruiting or fighting guerrillas. SOE and OSS both proved naïve about political considerations, and were much less effective as a result.

After the Italian surrender, many members of the Italian Army formed anti-German partisan groups, before they could be disarmed. These groups were often joined by Allied POWs who had been freed or had escaped from camps in Italy. Best of the Italian guerrillas, however, were former members of the Alpini, who took to the hills in Yugoslavia and aided the partisans. Communist guerrillas in Italy as always had their own agenda, hoarding arms drops not for use against the Germans but for use in a post-war struggle for the 'liberation' of Italy. However, the Communists did aid the Allied invasions by striking at German communication lines in support of Operations Anvil and Overlord.

Conclusions

European Guerrilla warfare in the Second World War proved particularly effective in Yugoslavia and particularly ineffective in the Low Countries and Scandinavia, with the exception of the raids against German heavy water production. Power struggles between resistance groups for post-war control certainly contributed to this, as did terrain limitations in many parts of Europe. Nevertheless, guerrillas did tie down substantial German resources which might otherwise have been used to help counter Soviet advances or the Allied landings.

▶ Member of the French Special Air Service working with the French Resistance during the Second World War

The most effective guerrillas in the European theatre of the Second World War were in actuality the regular irregulars of such special behind-the-lines units as the OSS Operational Groups, the Special Air Service, the German Brandenbergers or *Jagdverbände*, or the Soviet Guards Minelayers (forerunners of today's Spetsnaz). When these groups linked up with local partisans, as with the SAS in France just after the Normandy invasion or the Soviet special forces working with partisans, they often proved particularly effective.

The German attempts to counter guerrillas often hardened rather than lessened resistance. The fact that in August 1942 SS head Himmler had been put in charge of all anti-partisan activities certainly legislated for brutality rather than

creativity or flexibility. Hitler's 'Commando Order' of October 1942, setting forth the death penalty for raiding troops, also raised the stakes for those carrying out behind-the-lines operations, and also probably guaranteed the death of far more German troops in retaliation, both during and after the war. The deaths of more and more civilian hostages in reprisal continually increased the pool of sympathizers for the resistance movements.

In France and Holland particularly, some counter-guerrilla officers were very successful in playing the *Funkspiel* (radio game) to turn or capture agents. Major Giskes of the Abwehr was especially deadly in Holland, luring some forty-nine SOE parties on captured radios and eventually

◀ Organized military raiding units such as this patrol of the Special Air Service proved the most effective 'guerrillas' of the Second World War *(IWM)*

arresting over four hundred agents or members of the Resistance, thus effectively crushing much of the guerrilla movement in Holland. The Germans used informers extensively to gain information about the Resistance, though frequently this led to the arrest of personal enemies of the informers rather than members of the Resistance. In France, the German intelligence agencies did have some notable success at infiltrating *agents provocateurs*.

Drawing on the experiences of those German officers who were effective at countering guerrillas, the May 1944 publication *OKW Regulations for the Fighting of Bands* stressed the adoption of guerrilla methods to fight them. Those German commanders showing the flexibility to use this tactic were often highly successful. German ski troops living in the wild and using their mobility over the snow proved very effective, for example, on counter-guerrilla operations. Food denial operations often proved effective, too, particularly in Russia where guerrillas were forced to forage for food rather than fight, or to steal from villages, thus alienating the population.

Rather than developing really effective counter-guerrilla forces, however, the Germans would often pull divisions or regiments from relatively quiet sectors and carry out massive anti-partisan operations. Prior to Operation 'Zitadelle' (the gargantuan tank battle at Kursk), for example, the Wehrmacht carried out five massive sweeps in May and June 1943. These sweeps inflicted a substantial number of partisan casualties, but then the partisans faded away and within weeks were inflicting as much damage as before. Meanwhile, the activity had delayed the beginning of the very operation they were meant to secure the supply lines for.

The basic German strategy in most occupied countries was to hold the lines of communication and strategic points (i.e. mines, cities etc.), while only occasionally launching operations to harry the partisans. Since they were primarily concerned with draining resources from occupied countries, this strategy proved workable, if not optimum. It did, however, deny them most of the population resources, and allowed resistance to germinate and grow – in Yugoslavia, particularly, becoming an army. From the point of view of post-war Europe, Communist guerrillas learned many

SAS OPERATIONS IN EUROPE IN SUPPORT OF THE PARTISANS

The Special Air Service is so closely associated with operations against Rommel's airfields and supply lines in North Africa that it is easy to forget their service in Italy, Greece, France, Belgium, Holland and Germany itself. Although the SAS worked with OSS and SOE agents, Jedburgh teams and Resistance cadres, they remained a uniformed military formation, though still subject to Hitler's Commando Order if captured. Although the SAS teams worked with guerrillas helping to train them, or raiding in conjunction with them, they remained far more amenable to command and control and, hence, proved more reliable.

The SAS performed with their usual high degree of professionalism in Italy and Greece, but they were deployed most frequently and most effectively in France. As Operation Overlord approached, the parachute-qualified SAS was assigned to the British 1st Airborne Division, although for special operations they reported directly to SHAEF. On such missions they were dropped in small raiding parties behind the enemy lines. Once a mission was completed, the SAS parties either tried to make their way back through the lines to join advancing Allied troops, stayed put until the advances got to them, or received resupply by air and continued to operate behind the lines.

In co-operation with French and later Dutch Resistance groups, bases were established in forested or mountainous areas near likely drop zones. From these bases the SAS teams would operate over hundreds of miles, raiding and disrupting German supply and communications lines. The largest SAS bases were established in the good guerrilla country of Brittany, the Forest of Orleans, the Grand Massif, the Forest of Chatillon, near Poitiers and near Vosges. From D-Day until the German surrender, in France, Belgium, Holland and Germany 2,000 SAS troops saw action and accounted for 7,733 dead or seriously wounded enemy, 4,784 prisoners, 700 motor vehicles destroyed or captured, 7 trains destroyed, 33 trains derailed and 164 railways cut; all for losses of only 330 SAS. The SAS was also influential in the capture of 18,000 Germans at Issoudun, when they helped block all escape routes. Another important contribution of the SAS was intelligence, including information which led to the RAF bombing eleven petrol trains, twelve ammunition dumps, a flying-bomb site,

lessons about insurgencies which influenced their view of the struggle for Europe and the world.

An interesting lesson learned in France and other occupied countries was that for guerrillas to be effective, arms caches should not be centralized but each guerrilla should have his or her own weapon. Post-war Norway has done away with any type of central firearms registration for this very reason, so that arms caches which would be used by guerrillas cannot be easily located, while the Swiss system based on each soldier keeping his weapon at home appears excellent, should that country ever have to wage guerrilla warfare.

In discussing the success or failure of German counter-guerrilla tactics, it is interesting to note the Germans' own last-ditch attempt to form a guerrilla movement, the 'Werewolves'. Otto Skorzeny and his *Jagdverbände* had shown that the Germans could carry out irregular warfare quite well, but the excellent road system in Germany, which allowed rapid Allied movement around the country, combined with the large number of Germans who had grown disillusioned with the Nazi system, kept the Werewolves from ever really gaining a foothold. The benevolent Allied occupation policies short-circuited the likelihood of a serious German resistance as well.

Interestingly enough, when Otto Skorzeny, Germany's most famous irregular warrior, was being tried for war crimes, one of the witnesses in his defence was Gp-Captain Yeo-Thomas, the famous 'White Rabbit' of the Resistance, who realized better than most that the rules of regular warfare do not apply to irregular warfare.

Writing after the war, the German General Blumentritt hypothesized that the reason the Germans never really formed an effective guerrilla movement themselves was that it was alien to the basic concept of order that is typically German. Perhaps; if so, this same theory might help explain why the Germans did not prove particularly effective at fighting guerrillas either, since they had little understanding of this type of warfare. Certainly, the biggest single lesson to be learned from the German experience is that harshness in government can create a climate where guerrillas can function and thrive, particularly where an occupying or governing force is spread so thin that control cannot be exerted through force on more than a small portion of the population at any one time.

two enemy air bases, one SS barracks (resulting in three hundred SS dead) and one radio station. Twice they also located their arch-enemy Rommel's HQ and pinpointed it for bombing, thus disrupting the co-ordination of the German defence of France.

The earliest planned use of the SAS in support of the Normandy landings was to have been the dropping of a few dozen men, along with hundreds of dummies, on Calais to help reinforce the German belief that the main invasion would take place there. It was decided late in the planning, however, that just dummies dropped at various locations would create enough confusion, and the SAS was reserved for other tasks. Shortly after D-Day, the first major operation, Houndstooth, took place near Dijon. On 6 June 1944, 144 SAS troops were parachuted in, along with supplies and jeeps. They blew up numerous railway lines, hampering the transport of German troops and supplies to Normandy, took more than 100 German prisoners and killed or wounded 220 Germans, as well as spotting targets for the RAF.

Other important SAS operations included Bulbasket, launched on 6 June 1944 and involving fifty men near Chateauroux; Garn, on 14 June 1944, in which fifty-eight men in jeeps drove all around the German rear areas between Rambouillet and Chartres, attacking truck convoys and blowing up railway lines; and Cooney, when eighteen three- to six-man parties were dropped on 7 June 1944 between St Malo and Vannes, where they proceeded to harass communications and blow up key installations. The latest of the SAS operations was Amherst, which began on 6 April 1945. At that time the Germans were retreating through Holland, and the SAS was assigned to keep pressure on them so that they could not form a coherent defence. A secondary mission was to protect key bridges and airfields, so that these would not be destroyed by the retreating Germans. As SAS operations went, this was a short one, scheduled to last only seventy-two hours. Seven hundred men were dropped in nineteen different locations, and in the subsequent fighting accounted for almost seven hundred enemy dead, wounded or captured, with only ninety-three SAS casualties.

Though not as large in terms of men involved as some other forays, nor as successful in enemy killed as some, perhaps the mission best illustrative of the employmentof the SAS in Europe was Wallace. Eventually turning out to be the deepest SAS jeep penetration in France, Wallace started with the American

▲ Members of the Special Boat Service such as these often worked with the guerrillas in the Balkans *(IWM)*

◀ Members of an SAS Jeep raiding party of the type that operated in Europe just prior to and after the Allied landings in Normandy *(IWM)*

breakout at Avranches. Twenty SAS jeeps, each equipped with oversized petrol tanks, giving them a range of up to nine hundred miles, and five Vickers .303 machine guns, were airlifted along with their three-man combat crews to Rennes airfield. The commander of Wallace was Major Roy Farran (whose book *Winged Dagger* is one of the best about the SAS during the Second World War).

Avoiding primary roads and staying on country lanes, this column headed through occupied territory for the SAS hidden base established in the forests near Chatillon. Unfortunately, a short time after entering German territory they encountered a German panzer division and, though they gave a good account of themselves against heavy odds, they lost thirteen jeeps. Luckily, most of the men escaped in the remaining jeeps. Upon finally reaching the base near Chatillon they joined forces with a small group of SAS men who had been operating from it for more than a month. Now having a combined strength of ten jeeps (more jeeps had been parachuted in) and sixty men, this raiding party ventured out of the forest daily to mine roads, knock out trucks and attack German radar posts. In another favourite SAS manoeuvre they quietly approached a German HQ at night and began firing on it with a three-inch mortar.

Later, in co-operation with local Maquis, Farran's group staged ambushes on larger German supply convoys, before moving on to a new area of operations. Eight more jeeps having been dropped (unless they had actually seen the drop, the French refused to believe the jeeps had come in by air and kept thinking the SAS were scouts for an approaching Allied division or army), an attack was launched against the town of Chatillon, in which more than a hundred Germans were killed.

The SAS party was then ordered to move towards the Belfort Gap where the Germans were retreating from the Third and Seventh Armies, so they left the Chatillon area. Along the way they continued to destroy fuel dumps and attack any targets of opportunity that turned up. Whenever their much-abused jeeps broke down, French mechanics who were working in German motor pools would be contacted by the Resistance and would sneak out with German spare parts to jury rig repairs. Finally, after more than a month behind enemy lines, this SAS group linked up with the Seventh Army, which they supplied with much useful information.

During Operation Wallace, and more than forty other major operations, air drops of supplies were a prerequisite for success, and the RAF consistently came through with everything from new boots in requested sizes to jeeps and six-pounder anti-tank guns. Many weapons were already containerized for drop to the Resistance, thus a twenty-four-container drop might include: 19,800 rounds of 9mm Parabellum ammo, 38,006 rounds of .303 ammo, 1,116 field dressings, 240 empty Bren-gun magazines, 124 empty Sten gun magazines, 145 lb of explosive with detonation equipment, 4 PIAT anti-tank launchers, 125 PIAT bombs, 40 Gammon grenades, 8 Bren-guns, 10 Sten guns. Drops would be varied to fit specific needs in weaponry, ammunition or food. Air support was not without its problems. Allied fighters normally strafed anything that moved on the roads behind the German lines, including the SAS jeeps, but eventually by flying the Union Jack from their aerials and igniting yellow smoke canisters when Allied planes approached, they avoided most such attacks. A certain number of their resupply drops also went astray, causing hours of searching – normally at night – to remove any trace which might arouse German suspicions. Most drops were arranged by radio, but the SAS parties also had pigeons, which were also used to carry back intelligence maps they had sketched.

It soon began to seem as if the SAS was liberating France on its own. In Brittany, French members of the SAS raised forty thousand Maquisands who openly rebelled against the Germans, while in Central France, ninety members of the SAS were tying down an entire SS division on security duty. But the operation which most endeared the SAS to the French occurred when five SAS men in two jeeps came upon an SS unit at Les Ormes preparing to execute twenty villagers in reprisal for Resistance activity in the area. Charging in with Vickers guns blazing, the SAS rescued eighteen of the Frenchmen and destroyed two trucks and a staff car, while killing sixty Germans.

Although raids carried out by the SAS destroyed equipment and killed Germans, their greatest value was psychological. Even hundreds of miles behind their own lines the Germans could not feel safe, and many thousands of troops who could otherwise have been opposing Patton, Hodges or Montgomery were instead searching for the SAS. German logistical units in these areas functioned less efficiently, too, due to extra guard duty and extra security measures in fear of SAS attack. The SAS reputation was such that it was used to help force the surrender of the German garrison in Norway, and the assignment of the SAS to hunt down war criminals, particularly those who had enforced the 'Commando Order' against their comrades, no doubt hastened the capture of some wanted Nazis.

The successes of the SAS proved that highly-trained guerrillas operating in support of general strategic aims of conventional forces can be extremely valuable diversionary and intelligence-gathering forces. By remaining mobile in their operations, and with wide support among the population, the SAS proved to be almost the perfect guerrillas during the liberation of Western Europe. Although the SAS mission since the Second World War has more often been counter-guerrilla operations, the regiment maintains its raiding capability to this day.

GUERRILLAS AGAINST JAPAN

In their arrogance the Japanese managed to out-Nazi the Nazis, turning fellow Asians – in most cases anxious to be free of white colonial rule – from potential allies into avid anti-Japanese guerrillas. Initially, rapid Japanese advances and the perceived collapse of the colonial powers precluded resistance movements, with the exception of a few hard-core troops who refused categorically to admit defeat and took to the hills instead. As were the Germans in the Ukraine, the Japanese were welcomed as liberators by many fellow Asians. Retarding resistance, too, was the reluctance of Great Britain and some other colonial powers to arm the native peoples such as those in Malaya, for fear arms would be used in revolt against their colonial masters rather than against the Japanese.

One exception to the general lack of preparation for guerrilla warfare in the Pacific was on the part of the Australians, who had established their Coast Watcher programme to provide stay-behind intelligence sources in New Guinea, Papua and the Solomon Islands. Although the Coast Watchers normally did not carry out typical guerrilla activities, assisted by local natives loyal to them personally they provided excellent intelligence about Japanese fleet and air movements.

The Australian Independent Companies – similar in mission to the British Independent Companies which were forerunners of the Commandos – proved particularly effective at guerrilla warfare on the island of Timor. Of course, these Australians had had excellent training from the likes of Michael Calvert, who would later help reform the SAS, and F. Spencer Chapman, whose book *The Jungle is Neutral* is still a classic text on guerrilla war in the jungle. Though all the Australian Independent Companies performed yeoman service, it was 2/2, composed primarily of tough men from the outback, which would prove one of the most effective guerrilla forces of the war.

In December 1941, 2/2 had been sent to reinforce the Dutch on Timor as part of 'Sparrow Force'. After most of 'Sparrow Force' surrendered in February 1942, members of 2/2 retreated to the mountainous interior to fight very effectively as guerrillas, staging mortar raids, ambushes and other hit-and-run assaults, then fading away when pursued by the numerically far superior Japanese. The Australians continued to carry out vigorous patrols of the island, constantly moving and maintaining the mobility essential for successful guerrilla operations. In fact, they rehearsed again-and-again packing and moving on, so that when it was really necessary it came as second nature. When the Japanese did try to send long-range patrols after them, the Australians would wait until the Japanese were exhausted, and then ambush them. A standard tactic practised by 2/2 members, useful for guerrillas or any other deep penetration unit, was the setting up of rallying points at which to meet after dispersing either when attacking or under attack.

Later in their guerrilla campaign, the men of 2/2 began teaching guerrilla tactics to local natives who had proven loyal, and arming them. Other reinforcements came when 2/4 Independent Company landed from the sea. Eventually, the Independent Companies were pulled out when it was decided to bypass the island and mop up resistance later, but in the thirteen months the Australians had carried out their guerrilla war they had killed about fifteen hundred of the enemy, while losing only forty of their own men. More importantly for the overall thrust of the war in the Pacific, they were tying down an entire Japanese division of fifteen thousand veteran troops which could have been used elsewhere, including Guadalcanal.

On Timor and on other islands, harsh Japanese occupation policies, which included physical abuse of the natives and demeaning acts such as making them bow to any Japanese soldier, were creating much resentment. Often these natives would become good Allied intelligence sources, or would act as scouts for Allied forces who landed on the islands. On Guadalcanal, for example, many locals guided the Marines. General Vandegrift, commanding the Marines on Guadalcanal during the early stages, was obliged to contemplate the possibility of being overwhelmed by the Japanese, and planned to take to the high ground as guerrillas rather than surrender. Later in the campaign, Vandegrift used Evans Carlson's Marine Raiders for jungle penetration missions to flank the Japanese. Carlson, it should be noted, had learned guerrilla tactics from a master – Mao Tse-tung in China.

The guerrilla campaign, if it can really can be called a campaign, in the Philippines was drastically different from the resistance in occupied Europe. Before the fall of the Philippines, some US and Filipino troops took to the jungle rather than surrendering, particularly on the island of Luzon. From the beginning these guerrillas received willing assistance from the population, based on the fact that General MacArthur and the Americans in general were popular, and that Philippine independence had already been promised by the United States.

Based on American or Filipino officers who had avoided capture, and with local leaders, various guerrilla movements sprang up throughout the 7,100 islands that make up the Philippines. Eventually, at least fifty guerrilla groups emerged, including those formed of Filipino Communists who, like their counterparts in Europe, rose in opposition to Fascism, as personified by the Japanese. Known as the *Hukbalahap*, the Communists were extremely well organized, and will turn up in a later discussion of the post-war Huk Rebellion.

Some of the smaller islands had small cells of a dozen or fewer guerrillas; the major bands appeared on the larger islands of Luzon, Leyte, Samar and Mindanao. Initially, some 'guerrilla groups' were in fact bandits, preying upon the local population. In some cases, the real guerrilla forces were able to gain support by hunting down these bandits, or at least warning them off.

Many of the guerrilla leaders had served in the American or Philippine Army, a fact which helped them organize their resistance effectively and efficiently, though shortage of weapons was a problem, solved in some cases by establishing jungle weapons and ammunition factories. By 1943, however, contact between the guerrillas and Australia had been achieved, and US submarines began bringing in arms.

Among the most important guerrilla leaders was Lt-Colonel Ruperto Kanglear, who had escaped from a Japanese POW camp and led the guerrillas on Leyte. On Mindanao, an American, Colonel William Fertig, led the guerrillas, while another American, Captain (later Colonel) R. W. Volckmann, led the guerrillas on Luzon.

Against Kanglear's forces on Leyte, the Japanese made effective use of informers for a time, but the guerrillas soon eliminated these. The Japanese launched sweeps in an attempt to capture the guerrillas, but these normally proved futile. As their frustration grew, the Japanese grew harsher in their treatment of the population, generating sympathy for the guerrillas. Some villagers decided to fight, rather than be taken prisoner and mistreated by the Japanese. So widespread did the resistance grow that eventually the Japanese virtually surrendered the interior of Leyte to the guerrillas.

On Mindanao the guerrillas hit immediately and dramatically at any informers, to discourage collaboration. Despite having 150,000 troops on Mindanao and using dogs to search for guerrillas, the Japanese had little success at capturing Fertig's irregulars. The Japanese problem was that in essence they were combating the entire population of the island, including the fierce Moros – the same Filipino Muslims the United States had fought at the end of the nineteenth and beginning of the twentieth centuries.

▼ The $1.71 FP-45 'Liberator' pistol distributed by the Allies to resistance groups, particularly in Asia

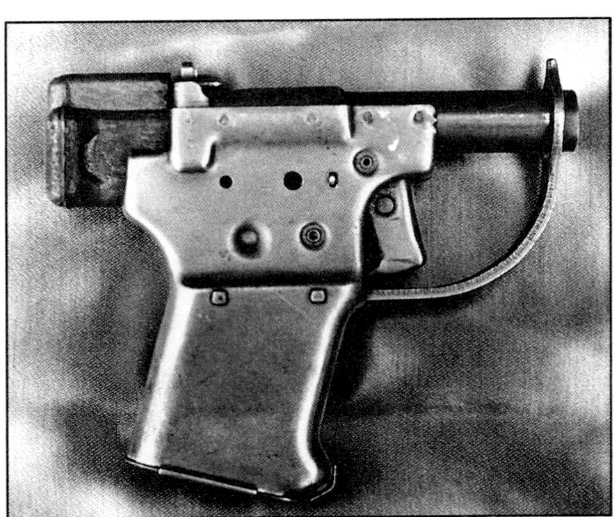

Because of their widespread support, food was never a problem for the guerrillas on Mindanao, and Fertig made good use of mobility, moving his HQ frequently and trusting his scouts to warn of impending attack. The guerrillas made excellent use of their local knowledge not just to scout but also to ambush ambitious Japanese patrols and then fade away.

On Luzon Volckmann also learned early that he had to deal ruthlessly with collaborators, and that once agents of the Japanese had either been killed or frightened off, the guerrilla movement could grow.

One of the problems the guerrilla movement faced in the Philippines was jurisdictional disputes among the various leaders, but MacArthur's staff solved this by roughly dividing responsibility along pre-war Philippine area command lines, a solution that worked well since most of the guerrilla leaders had served in one or more of these commands. MacArthur also resisted the impulse to commit the guerrillas to symbolic but futile raids against the Japanese, which would only have resulted in retaliation against the population. Instead, he used the guerrillas primarily as an intelligence organization prior to the reconquest of the Philippines. Thus at the end of January 1945 when the Americans landed, twenty thousand guerrillas ready to act as scouts greeted them. In a classic use of irregulars, guerrillas assisted in the liberation of Allied POWs from Cabantuan prison camp, in conjunction with members of the Rangers and the Alamo Scouts, between 28 and 31 January 1945.

The combination of Japanese maltreatment of the population – this was repeated throughout the Pacific – plus the knowledge that the Americans intended to grant them independence – had kept the Filipinos waiting for MacArthur's return. Together with MacArthur's intelligent husbanding of guerrilla resources, thus preventing really extreme Japanese counter-guerrilla measures, the blueprint for a successful, if relatively low-key, movement was created. An interesting point worth noting for later reference is that many of the veterans of the guerrilla movement assumed positions of power in the post-war government and army, and were thus well acquainted with guerrilla methods when they had to face the Huk Insurgency.

Of all the countries invaded by the Japanese, in few were they welcomed as warmly as in Indonesia, where the population had grown restive under Dutch rule. Yet again, however, Japanese soldiers managed to create a resistance through their own arrogant disregard for the feelings of the local population. The Japanese, in fact, helped unify the Indonesians in their hatred of them, and indirectly caused the creation of the nationalist movement which was eventually to force the Dutch from Indonesia now that their fallibility had been shown by the Japanese.

Thailand had given support to the Japanese and thus maintained a nominal independence. By 1944, however, there was some OSS infiltration of that country, and by 1945 there was a budding guerrilla movement. The collapse of the Japanese war effort, however, precluded its becoming really active.

In nearby Indochina, Vichy France, nominally Germany's ally, had allowed Japan virtually to occupy the country, though French troops had not been disarmed. Nevertheless, some Frenchmen in Indochina supported de Gaulle's Resistance and were prepared to aid the OSS in planning a guerrilla campaign in Indochina. The OSS soon realized that the most effective basis for resistance was Ho Chi Minh's Viet Minh, but the French refused to work with these Communists. In 1945, when the Japanese finally tried to disarm the French garrisons, some went meekly into captivity, but others, including some French Foreign Legion units, resisted and began fighting as guerrillas. The OSS, meanwhile, despite French opposition, was actively supporting Ho and Giap, who by 1945 had 10,000 irregulars under arms and were receiving substantial US aid. As did many of the Communist guerrilla movements in Europe, the Viet Minh seized the opportunity offered by the power vacuum at the end of hostilities and moved to gain control of Vietnam. Though their attempt failed, they did manage to capture large stockpiles of surrendered Japanese and French arms, stockpiles which would be used in their guerrilla war against the French.

To some extent the Japanese conquest of the Pacific, particularly Malaya, was based on the precepts of guerrila warfare. Using well-trained jungle divisions, the Japanese hit quickly and used surprise and deception to aid their assault. The British, on the other hand, were ill prepared for an attack on their fortress at Singapore from the jungle. Number One Special Training School in Singapore had initially been established to train stay-behind parties, and had instructors such as Spencer Chapman; however, the local Commander-in-Chief saw no need for such irregular forces. As a result, when the Japanese took Malaya, SOE found itself with few likely agents in the area. The readiest source of recruits, in fact, proved to be the Malayan Communist Party, which SOE began arming. A few British troops had taken to the jungle, including Spencer Chapman, who worked with the Communist guerrillas attacking targets of opportunity. The Communist Malayan Peoples Anti-Japanese Army, which will be heard of again during the Malayan Emergency, was well organized into eight regional groups, each with patrols of about a hundred men, broken down into sections of eight to ten. Once again, the Communist cell structure lent itself well to guerrilla warfare by limiting the amount of damage an informer could do. Informers were not all that common, however, partly due to party loyalty, and partly due to special 'traitor-killer' units within the MPAJA.

For the most part the Communist guerrillas in Malaya proved quite dedicated. The first SOE liaison team arrived in May 1943, but regular air drops did not start until November 1944. As a result, while Malayan guerrillas caused a certain amount of damage against the Japanese, they primarily husbanded their resources to prepare for the post-war struggle for Malaya.

In Burma, the hill tribes offered a particularly suitable group of potential guerrillas. During the British retreat across Burma, in fact, Karens armed by the SOE helped screen for the British forces, then became guerrillas. Other guerrillas were drawn from the Shan, Kachin and other hill tribes. General Slim was astute enough to analyse the defeat in Burma and conclude that, to retake the lost ground, Allied troops had to be able to fight in the jungle, using flanking attacks and indirect approach. As a result, he started an intensive training programme for the troops under his command.

A rather eccentric officer named Orde Wingate, who had experienced guerrilla warfare in Palestine where he had trained Jewish counter-guerrillas, and later in Ethiopia where he had commanded a good force of irregulars known as 'Gideon Force', joined Slim and began working on forming a long-range penetration force to operate in the Japanese rear. In actuality, Wingate was planning on introducing a mixed group to act as guerrillas behind the Japanese lines. Known as the Chindits, Wingate's force was inserted, had some brushes with the enemy, and blew up a few railway lines, but militarily was not really much of a success. As a morale-builder in Great Britain, the Chindits proved a real boon.

Wingate won support for a second Chindit expedition. This time, Wingate was to have three brigades - two to be airlifted in and one to infiltrate overland - to be committed in support of a major offensive by Slim's forces in early March 1944. Wingate himself was killed in an air crash, however, on 23 March, though the operation continued until May, mostly as small unit semi-guerrilla actions in the Japanese rear.

The Americans launched a similar deep penetration raiding mission by the 5307th Composite Group, known as Galahad Force or more commonly as 'Merrill's Marauders'. Operating in support of Chinese troops under General Stillwell, who were advancing south, the Marauders proved poorly acclimatized and conditioned for the operation, and suffered accordingly. The fact that they were well supported by the Kachin irregulars trained by the OSS helped protect their flanks and gave them reliable scouts. Both the Chindits and Marauders proved the value of aerial resupply for such raiding forces, both relying heavily on support from the air. The 8,500 Kachins raised by about five hundred members of the OSS harassed the Japanese flanks during the reconquest of Burma, scouted for Stillwell's forces and proved a good source of intelligence. Other tribes working with SOE, especially the Chins and Karens, provided intelligence and carried out raids as well. The most successful guerrillas fighting the Japanese were, in fact, probably these Burmese hill tribes, partly because of their inaccessible operational base in the highlands, and partly because of the effective organization and training given them by the OSS and SOE.

Conclusions

In countering guerrillas, the Japanese did very little right. Although they had very mobile light infantrymen who were at home in the jungle, these were usually busy fighting the US Marines or other Allied troops, and could not be spared for counter-guerrilla operations. Through arrogance and a complete lack of understanding for the native peoples of South-East Asia and the Pacific, the Japanese themselves created many of the guerrilla movements they had to contend with. The Pacific war reinforced many of the lessons of the European war in regard to operations behind enemy lines. Well-trained regular forces such as the Australian Independent Companies proved invaluable, since they combined effective military organization and tactics with the mobility and harassing tactics of the irregulars. MacArthur's use of the Philippine guerrillas as an existing force still helped tie down substantial numbers of Japanese troops, provided accurate intelligence to the Allies and offered a ready source of irregular light infantry when the reconquest began. OSS Detachment 101 also showed what a force-multiplier troops trained in raising guerrillas could be.

OSS DETACHMENT 101 AND THE KACHIN RANGERS

Among the greatest successes of the OSS was Detachment 101 in Burma, which raised and trained effective irregulars and offered a pattern for the future development of the Army's Special Forces – along with the CIA, a direct OSS descendant.

In the first months of 1942, the Japanese terrorized the Kachins of northern Burma, burning villages and mutilating Kachins as souvenirs of their advance. Many Shans, traditional enemies of the Kachins, aided the Kempi Tai (the Japanese Secret Police) in their campaign of terror against the Kachins, while other Burmese helped the Japanese as members of the 'Burmese Independence Army'. The British Army fled west towards India, leaving only a few remnants of some Kachin levies and scattered stragglers behind Japanese lines, as well as a few missionaries, mining engineers, planters and other westerners. One missionary, Father Stuart, had worked among the Kachins and would eventually become a guerrilla leader with Detachment 101.

In the USA, the COI, predecessor of the OSS, formulated plans for operations in Burma by Detachment 101 under Captain Carl Eifler, who not only had to recruit his unit, but also had to convince General Joseph Stillwell to allow it to operate in his command area. Members of Detachment 101 had received training in such skills as hand-to-hand combat, combat shooting, demolitions, communications and guerrilla tactics, including as a realistic final exam a simulated attack on a heavily guarded installation in the US or Canada.

Detachment 101 was officially activated on 14 April 1942, sailing on 28 May; Eifler had flown on ahead. In transit, the OSS men received Chinese lessons and lectures on India and South-East Asia. By 15 July, most of the OSS men were in New Delhi, where they received British briefings on Burma. Although General Stillwell still opposed OSS operations in his area, Eifler flew to Chungking and finally got a reluctant commitment from Stillwell for Detachment 101 to operate in Burma for three months.

The OSS men established their base at an Assam Tea Company facility near the Burmese border, using the cover of a malaria research station. The base was operational by October, and members of 101 began recruiting guerrillas among Burmese who had fled to India. Because of the pressure to produce rapid results, Eifler knew he had to get agents into Burma by the end of 1942. Thus, many of these first recruits were former members of the Burmese Army, especially those with British fathers and Burmese mothers. 'Able Group', as the initial group of twelve agents was called, received training in weapons, demolitions, lockpicking, forgery, hand-to-hand combat, communications, codes and other clandestine skills from Detachment 101; simultaneously, the OSS operatives learned about Burma from their recruits.

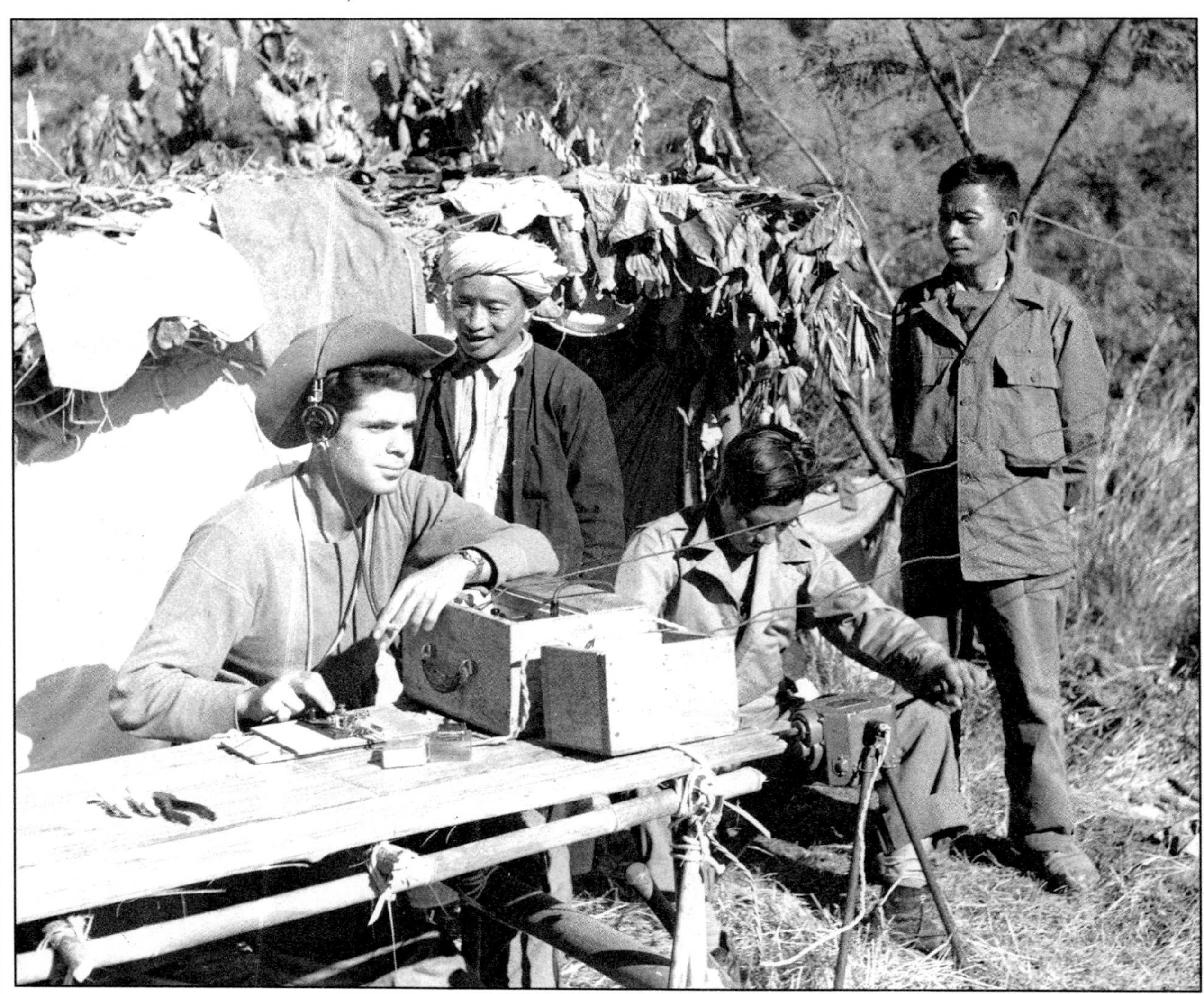

▲ OSS radio team assigned to the Kachin irregulars in Burma; such teams often included Navaho codetalkers, since the Japanese could not understand this Indian language even if messages were intercepted *(US Army)*

Prior to Able Group's commitment, Eifler had compact, long-range radios fabricated for them. Among initial Detachment 101 contacts in Burma were Naga headhunters from whom they learnt tribal customs. Then in early 1943, Able Group infiltrated through Japanese lines to sabotage roads and railways and make initial contact with the Kachins, especially any already fighting the Japanese. Other Detachment 101 members were infiltrated to establish a forward base within Burma.

Scattered Kachins had already begun carying out sporadic guerrilla operations against the Japanese, but it was up to Detachment 101 to organize, arm and train the Kachins to create an effective guerrilla force. As soon as Detachment 101 agents began operating in Kachin teritory, young Kachins started volunteering to fight the hated Japanese. Americans and Kachins soon found an affinity for each other, allowing them to form an affectionate and effective partnership.

Detachment 101 members not already parachute qualified (original members had received parachute training, but some recruited locally had not) and their guerrillas received jump training in early 1943. In return for Air Transport Command aid in giving this training, Eifler made arrangements to help rescue ATC pilots flying 'The Hump' who went down in northern Burma. In Europe and Burma, air crew rescue proved a useful guerrilla mission. A bonus for parachute-trained young Kachins was that their arrival from the sky seemed to make them especially sexually desirable to local Kachin girls.

Able Group and two 101 agents jumped into the Koukkwee Valley in January 1943, and commenced operations from the valley. On their first sabotage mission, they covered 100 miles in two days to blow up a Japanese railway bridge. After operating for four months, due to the possibility of having been compromised by Shan informers they were ordered to exfiltrate by walking out, often boldly strolling into Japanese garrisons and stealing rice during the trek.

Throughout 1943, Kachin recruitment multiplied as Detachment 101, augmented by new arrivals from the States, trained and led groups of Kachins on intelligence-gathering missions and ambushes against the Japanese. Now experienced guerrillas, Able Group veterans led their guerrila bands. In March 1943 a group was inserted into the Lawksawk Valley, but all were lost. Most others were successful at establishing bases throughout the Kachin areas of north-western Burma. The largest Kachin Ranger unit under Duwa Htaw Naw numbered over a thousand men, but operations were normally carried out by units of fifty to sixty. As Detachment 101's guerrilla forces grew they were assigned the strategic mission of harassing Japanese supply lines to support the hard-pressed defenders of India.

The OSS agents realized they had to win the Kachins' trust before leading them into battle. For example, in one case the local duwa (leader) was nursed back to health from a malaria attack, thus sealing a bond between him and the Detachment 101 man who had nursed him. The OSS men who lived and worked with the Kachins adopted their customs, ate their food, drank their liquor and made love with the attractive Kachin girls (sexual freedom being accepted among the Kachins, so this caused no problems). So fond were the Kachins of their American friends that three or four would assign themselves as bodyguards and refuse to leave their adviser's side.

The Kachins not only proved to be formidable raiders, but were also adept raw intelligence gatherers, providing invaluable data about Japanese movements. Japanese prisoners lifted out for interrogation proved another valuable intelligence source after Detachment 101 acquired its own light planes in 1941. Operating from makeshift airstrips in support of the guerrillas, 101 pilots included Eifler himself, and a former Flying Tiger. When Detachment 101 moved into new areas, hidden airstrips for their supporting light planes were built as a high priority.

▲ Kachin irregulars trained by the OSS to operate in Burma *(US Army)*

The building of the Ledo Road through the Naga Hills gave the Kachin Rangers another mission, acting as a screening force ahead of the engineers. By late 1943, the Kachin Rangers were such a highly skilled guerrilla force that, notwithstanding the great publicity Orde Wingate's Chindits were receiving, small Detachment 101 units were really hurting the Japanese far more.

Early in 1944, Ray Peers, who had taken over as CO of Detachment 101, replacing Eifler, had his work cut out for him as General Stillwell asked him to step up behind-the-lines sabotage and scouting in preparation for an Allied offensive to retake Burma. As part of the offensive, Kachin guides were to be assigned to Merrill's Marauders. At this point, the number of Kachins operating behind Japanese lines had grown to the point that OSS had established four forward bases to decentralize control.

Setting booby traps and ambushes, the Kachins harassed the Japanese withdrawing ahead of Stillwell's advancing Chinese troops and Merrill's Marauders. Some of these ambushes accounted for hundreds of dead Japanese. Railway lines along the Japanese logistical network were also blown up to inhibit reinforcements and resupply. On another occasion when the Japanese had surrounded Merrill's Marauders, Kachins broke the encirclement. Kachin scouts assigned to the Marauders proved invaluable, leading them over little-used trails to seize Myitkyina Airfield, at one point during the advance a fourteen-year-old Kachin guide pushed on even though bitten by a krait, a deadly snake, an indication of Kachin toughness and dedication.

Stillwell was so impressed with the Kachins' contribution to the Marauders' advance that he decided to have one Kachin flown out to be decorated. When Stilwell asked the Kachin how he kept track of the Japanese he had killed, the warrior calmly dumped a sack of ears in front of Stillwell and told him to divide by two. The Detachment 101 men present explained to the astonished Stillwell that they considered it a great stride forward to have persuaded the Kachins to collect ears instead of entire heads!

The Allies may have been ready to go on the offensive, but the Japanese retained substantial striking capability, and during a major Japanese offensive in February 1944, the Kachins harassed supply lines and attacked the Japanese flanks to slow their progress.

Prior to Wingate's second Chindit operation the Kachins provided intelligence and Detachment 101 radio operators and Kachin guides accompanied the Chindits, then stayed in the area after the Chindits returned, to form new Kachin guerrilla forces. In spring 1944, retreating Japanese took vengeance on many Kachin villages, causing even more Kachins to join the fight against the Japanese. Aiding the 'Hearts and Minds' Campaign, OSS doctors tended sick and wounded Kachins as well as leading local guerrilla operations.

The Kachins were used to hunt down Japanese who had taken to the jungle as the Allied forces pushed into Burma, though the Kachins were not known for bringing in entire Japanese prisoners. When strategically important Myitkyina finally fell, the Kachins killed more than a thousand Japanese who were trying to retreat through the jungle.

By late 1944 more than ten thousand Kachins were under arms, with some individual units numbering up to one thousand. Though very loyal to the Americans, the Kachins didn't get along well with the Chinese troops they were ordered to support in the Golden Triangle. Seeking revenge against the Chinese for acts against the Kachins, the Rangers often set ambushes for them, though the Detachment 101 men ostensibly tried to discourage such acts against 'allies'. On at least one occasion, in retaliation against a warlord who had raided Kachin villages, Kachin raiders crossed into China. In truth, the OSS men justifiably considered the Chinese pretty useless. Though they disliked them, the Kachins normally provided assistance to Chinese units on operations. As the Allies advanced further into Burma, the Kachins, roughly trained in basic cartography by their OSS advisers, helped map the areas ahead of the advance. Continuing their duties as intelligence gatherers, scouts and guides, late in 1944 and early in 1945, the Kachins screened for the Mars Task Force during its advance to retake the Burma Road and reopen the supply line to China. By early 1945, however, Kachin strength allowed them to capture towns such as Ismailong without the support of conventional troops.

The Burma Road had been reopened by March 1945, and many Kachins had now moved south to operate ahead of British troops advancing across the Chindwin towards Mandalay. Once again the Kachin forte proved to be ambushing the retreating Japanese. As opportunities to kill Japanese increased so did Kachin recruitment; thus by 20 March 1945, when Mandalay finally fell, 10,500 Kachins in seven battalions of about 750 men each and various smaller raiding and intelligence-gathering units were serving under Detachment 101.

Some Kachin units were disbanded in April 1945, following the reconquest of northern Burma. A few battalions fought on until June, then on 12 July 1945 Detachment 101 was officially deactivated.

The Americans who served in Detachment 101 were a very special breed, unconventional as those leading irregulars often are. Some were eccentrics such as Carl Eifler, who kept a pet bear to wrestle with while commanding the unit. Others, such as Father Stuart, were men of God who took up arms to protect their flock – the Kachins. In all cases, though, those who were successful at leading the Kachins into battle had first to understand their customs. This often meant eating such things as raw monkey brains, or paying homage to the nats, the local gods which could wreak havoc if angered.

By creating an effective guerrilla force from the Kachins, the men of Detachment 101 had an influence out of all proportion to their size, establishing the principle of force multiplication which would form a basis for the Special Forces and setting traditions still carried on by their successors in the green berets.

4 THE CHINESE REVOLUTION AND MAO'S THEORIES OF GUERRILLA WARFARE

Perhaps no guerrilla campaign in history has had the same impact on other countries and other peoples as the Chinese Revolution. The mere fact that the world's most populous country fell to a guerrilla army sent reverberations throughout Asia and the West, and Mao's systematic guerrilla campaign, codified in his writings, became a blueprint for other guerrilla campaigns, often continents and oceans away.

The Chinese Communist Party did not initially begin with an organized guerrilla campaign; instead it began in the traditional Marxist manner – organizing trade unions to gain power for the workers. At the same time the CCP began organizing rural peasants into associations with similar goals. Mao Tse-tung himself began with these peasants' organizations, and by 1926 had become Chairman of the Peasants' Associations. In 1927, when Chiang Kai-shek cracked down on the Communists, Mao along with other CCP leaders went into hiding and formed local groups of Red Guards and Peasants' Insurrection Corps as an armed resistance.

By the end of the 1920s, with strong support and intelligence from local peasants, these armed units were using a rudimentary form of guerrilla warfare in hit-and-run raids against landlords and local warlords. Chiang did not really take the Communist threat seriously enough to launch a concerted campaign against them; nor, considering his power struggle against other warlords, is it likely that he could have completely exterminated the Communists anyway.

Although Mao's formal writings on guerrilla warfare were still some years in the future, prior to 1930 he had helped formulate five basic needs of a liberation/guerrilla movement: support of the masses; strong party organization; a strong Red Army; favourable terrain, including a sanctuary; and economic support. He also established four simple yet astute tactical rules: if the enemy advances, retreat; if the enemy halts, harass him; if the enemy avoids battle, attack him; if the enemy retreats, follow him. These concise precepts were simple enough to be understood by the lowest peasant in the movement, yet were profound enough to work against Chiang's massive but inept forces. One other fundamental precept of the Communists from the beginning was basic sanitation, such as boiling water. As a result, Red Army members would remain healthy and able to withstand the hardships of their campaigns.

Initially Mao's forces lacked arms and warm clothing for the rugged winter in their Chingkang Mountain sanctuary. They were held together, however, by their belief in what they were fighting for. In 1930, the Central Committee of the CCP ordered attacks on southern Chinese cities, but after initial successes the Communists were badly defeated at Changsha and were forced to the hills once again to regroup. This failure against the cities convinced Mao that a guerrilla campaign based on the peasants and the countryside – a People's Revolutionary War – was the proper route to winning China. This plan met with opposition from many members of the Central Committee, as it was contrary to standard Communist ideology basing power on the workers.

Now beginning to take the Communist threat more seriously, Chiang started a bandit-suppression campaign, but the Communist forces refused to do battle except when they could lure the Nationalists into an ambush, or otherwise engage on their own terms. Then, in 1931, Chiang had to deploy many of his troops to counter the Japanese invasion of Manchuria, leaving a Red Army now sixty thousand strong in control of Kiangsi Province and substantial portions of surrounding provinces. Over the next two years, Chiang launched two additional campaigns against the Communists, neither being particularly successful. Then, in October 1933, with German advisers the Nationalists began a massive sweep to remove peasants from their villages, then established blockhouses in a strategy similar to that used by the British in South Africa against the Boers. Denied his base of support and source of intelligence and food, Mao withdrew and began the famous Long March, covering the six thousand miles to Shensi Province in the north. During this year-long fighting withdrawal, the Communists combated warlords, hostile tribes and Chiang's troops, as well as traversing harsh and inhospitable terrain. Of 130,000 who began the Long March, only 30,000 completed it, but this complement now formed a loyal inner circle bonded by their accomplishment and by having established a legend which soon grew in the minds of the peasants. Along the route of the Long March, Mao had left small cadres in likely areas to recruit and agitate.

By February 1936 the hardened Red Army was back in action in Shansi Province. In response, Chiang sent 150,000 troops north, but their lack of success plus his poor showing against the Japanese invaders combined to erode his credibility. At this point, Mao offered to form a united front against the Japanese, but Chiang refused. One of Chiang's local commanders, however, actually took Chiang prisoner to force him to come to an accommodation with the Communists for the purpose of countering the Japanese invaders. As a result, an uneasy alliance was established, though Chiang still left hundreds of thousands of troops in position against the Communists. Mao, too, felt the fight against Japan was only a prelude to the fight against Chiang's Nationalists.

Mao had been formalizing his theories of People's War, and incorporated his practical experience along with his theories into his work, *Guerrilla Warfare*, in 1937. Among his most basic ideas was that mobile war and guerrilla war complement each other, and that morale would prove the decisive factor in a protracted war. Mao propounded his three phases of guerrilla warfare:

First Phase: The guerrillas, strategically weaker, could at times be tactically superior, in which case they would use hit-and-run tactics and fight to capture weapons. This phase stresses organization and consolidation of base areas and the recruitment and training of volunteers.

Second Phase: During this phase the guerrillas and their enemy would be strategically stalemated as the guerrillas equipped and trained a conventional army in preparation for phase three. Increasing acts of sabotage, particularly against military and police outposts, would be carried out, large portions of the population would be indoctrinated, and areas of the country would be taken over as liberated areas.

Third Phase: As the guerrillas went on the strategic offensive, they would carry out open warfare with powerful conventional forces to drive the enemy from the area.

Mao conceived of different phases occurring simultaneously in different provinces, as the revolution progressed at different paces. Although Mao's famous statement that 'power comes out of the barrel of a gun' has frequently been quoted, he still felt that combat had to be subordinated to overall political goals. Unlike many generals, in fact, he understood that military action's only justification was to achieve a political goal.

Within the Red Army discipline was rigorous, but self-imposed, thus giving the troops a particular ability to endure hardships, and great moral strength. Strong self-discipline also aided the Communist strategy of honest and fair dealing with the local population, which Mao viewed as the ocean in which the guerrilla army – like fish – could swim. Enemy captives were treated fairly and considerately as well, resulting in an unwillingness on their part to fight to the death, and a readiness to defect from their corrupt commanders.

Another point Mao considered in his analysis of guerrilla warfare is how guerrilla units are formed. He conceived of various types of formation: the people rising to fight an oppressor; regular army units fighting as guerrillas; a mixture of regulars and spontaneous guerrillas; local militias; enemy deserters; and former bandits.

Basic guerrilla organization, according to Mao, must remain simple and flexible. Within the Red Army the basic unit was a squad of nine to eleven men. Two to four squads comprised a platoon, two to four platoons a company, two to four companies a battalion, and two to four battalions a regiment. Guerrilla units had the following missions: 1. exterminate small enemy forces; 2. harass large enemy forces; 3. attack enemy lines of communication; 4. establish bases in the enemy rear; 5. force the enemy to disperse his strength. Many of the tactics Mao formulated were based on the centuries-old writings of Sun Tzu and were primarily based on the strategy of indirect approach, using surprise and deceit to attack while the enemy is on the move. Most of all, Mao stressed that guerrillas should not try to hold ground.

Although Mao's precepts for guerrilla warfare were, no doubt, important in welding the Red Army into an effective fighting force, the traditional corruption and ineptitude of Chinese government aided the Communists as well, giving the peasants no hope except the People's Liberation Movement. While the Red Army fought the Japanese they continued to institute reforms in the areas they controlled, thus gaining support and allowing them to move into additional areas. The Japanese were so hated, too, that those fighting them – and the Communists were doing a better job than the Nationalists – were bound to be popular. Against the Japanese, the Red Army used the same guerrilla tactics which had proved successful against the Nationalists. One Japanese general, Tada Hayao, proved somewhat effective against the Red Army by building a ring of forts to contain them and digging ditches alongside roads and railways for defence. Additionally, he built highways through communist-controlled areas to carve up guerrilla strongholds and allow his troops to move rapidly against the guerrillas.

In August 1940 Mao launched his 'Hundred Regiments Offensive', cutting railway lines, derailing trains, blowing up bridges, destroying forts, and killing many thousands of Japanese soldiers. By 1941, however, the Japanese had blunted this offensive. Soon, both Chiang and Mao were husbanding their resources for the battle for China after the defeat of Japan, which both felt the United States could accomplish. Mao still made gains during this period, though, as corrupt senior Nationalist officers stole money intended for supplies, forcing the Nationalist Army to live off the peasants and creating discontent.

An attempt was made to form anti-Japanese guerrilla units from among Nationalist forces, under Commander M. E. Miles of the US Navy (and later OSS), but the involvement of Chiang's corrupt head of secret police, Tai Li, prevented this effort being really successful, except as another way of lining Nationalist pockets with gold. Members of the OSS and other Americans who worked with Mao and his troops, on the other hand, were extremely impressed, but lacked the political clout to overcome the Nationalist lobby in Washington and get substantial aid for Mao. Among the reasons why General Stillwell was eventually replaced in China, in fact, was his support of American aid to Mao's forces in the fight against Japan. His replacement, General Wedemeyer, took the line that co-operation between Chiang and Mao against the Japanese was undesirable if it meant US aid going to the Communists. Partly as a result of US vacillation on this subject, renewed fighting broke out between the Nationalists and Communists in the autumn of 1945.

On paper, Chiang was in a far better position, having three times the number of troops and massive US aid. It must be borne in mind, however, that the quality of Nationalist troops was poor in most cases, and most US aid was being siphoned off by corrupt members of Chiang's regime. Chiang refused, though, to face the venality of his government and come to grips with the reforms that had to be made.

Therefore, as the Japanese surrendered, the Communists gained control of much of northern China, as well as substantial quantities of Japanese arms. Despite the ability the Communists now had to interdict his supply lines, Chiang insisted on sending his best troops to Manchuria and the major cities of northern China. In anticipation, Mao had already sent an army to Manchuria under Lin Piao, one of his best generals. With the tacit assistance of the Soviets, who had moved into Manchuria after their belated declaration of war against Japan, the Red Army managed to seize most of the Japanese arms dumps in Manchuria, which were used to arm members of the local population recruited to their cause.

By March 1946 extensive fighting was taking place in Manchuria between Communists and Nationalists, with the latter being forced into enclaves in a few major cities. Though George C. Marshall had gone to China from the USA to attempt mediation, he found Chiang still unwilling to listen to reason, and unwilling to accept the fact that he could not defeat the Communists militarily. While holding only the heavily garrisoned major cities in Manchuria and northern China, the Nationalists contrived to be excellent recruiters for Mao as the civilian victims of their brutality swelled the Red Army ranks. By late 1946, too, large numbers of Nationalist troops – at times entire divisions – were defecting to the Communists.

Now in control of virtually all of Manchuria and northern China, with the exception of the beleaguered Nationalist enclaves, in the autumn of 1947 the Communists switched over to the offensive. But as the situation worsened, Chiang became even more resistant to the idea of massive political, military and social reforms.

After isolating and then eliminating the remaining Nationalist garrisons in the north, Mao's forces began increasing pressure on the garrisons in central and southern China. Finally, at the battle of Hsuchow, Chiang's remaining major forces in the north were decisively encircled and defeated, leaving the Nationalists with a tenuous hold on a defensive line at the Yangtze during the winter of 1948–9. Then, in April 1949, Mao's army flooded across the banks of the Yangtze, submerging the Nationalist Army. In October, Mao declared the People's Republic of China, and in December Chiang, now facing a Communist Army of over four million, fled to Formosa.

In the United States, politicians of the Joe McCarthy stamp attributed Chiang's defeat to a sellout to the Communists, rather than admitting Nationalist incompetence and corruption and, most importantly, the wide support for and popularity of the Communist forces.

Conclusions

By far the most important conclusion to be drawn from the Chinese Communist victory is that popular revolutions have a very good chance of success. This was true in America in 1776, in France in 1789, and in China in 1949. Counter-guerrilla warfare is difficult if the regime is so corrupt and inept that the people view virtually any government as better than the current one.

Mao is justly viewed as the sage of guerrilla warfare, but what must be understood is the fact that his greatest strength was the ability to look at the reality of China and design a strategy fitted to the terrain, the political situation, and the people. By emphasizing the guerrilla as a people's soldier, Mao ensured that a substantial portion of the massive population of China would become the logistics system and intelligence service of the People's Liberation Army. His precepts for guerrilla warfare are profound in their very simplicity; the best strategy and tactics normally are.

It is entirely logical that many guerrilla wars – wars of national liberation, if you will – in Latin America, Asia and Africa have followed Mao's blueprint very closely. It is a simple blueprint to follow, and there have been lots of corrupt regimes which helped convert apathetic peasants into guerrilla warriors. Middle-class Americans or Europeans may not understand what makes a Communist insurgency appealing, but destitute peasants certainly can. Mao's concept of People's War seems to have been designed for them, while America's ideas of democracy seem to have been designed for the junta ruling them. To a peasant concerned about his next meal, understanding the balance of payments and his country's international debt situation may be rather difficult; understanding a few precepts of guerrilla warfare and a simple ideology tailored to the peasant's world view is less so.

MAO'S STRATEGIC PRINCIPLES AND EIGHT REMINDERS

Officers of the People's Liberation Army had to learn ten strategic principles, often known as the Ten Commandments, by heart, while all members of the PLA had to learn the Eight Reminders by heart. Although translations vary, the principles and reminders are worth repeating for anyone interested in insurgency - or, even more so, in counter-insurgency.

The Ten Strategic Principles

1 Strike first at isolated, scattered groups of the enemy, then later strike at concentrated, powerful groups.

2 Take first the small and medium-sized towns or cities and control the countryside, then later take the large cities.

3 The primary objective is not to take and hold places, but to annihilate the enemy's fighting potential. Taking and holding cities or places results from this annihilation, but it may be necessary to fight many times before the cities are finally taken.

4 Always, in every battle, concentrate superior forces to encircle the enemy completely and annihilate him, letting none escape. If the conditions so indicate, strike the enemy with smashing blows by concentrating forces against his centre and one or both flanks, smashing him in parts so that our forces can be transferred to smash another part. Do not fight a battle of attrition unless gains outnumber losses. Though we may be inferior in numbers as a whole, we can achieve local superiority to win each campaign, eventually outnumbering the enemy and destroying him.

5 Do not fight unless you are well prepared, and do not fight unless you are sure of victory. Attempt to win every engagement.

6 Promote and reward bravery in battle. Do not fear sacrifice, fatigue or constant combat. Be willing to fight several engagements in succession with little rest.

7 Attempt to destroy the enemy while he is on the move, while still being willing to attack positions and seize strong points or bases from the enemy.

8 When attacking cities seize those strong points and cities which are weakly defended or where circumstances allow it. Wait until strong enough and conditions are favourable, then seize the strongly defended cities.

9 Replenish our arms and manpower by capturing those of the enemy; men and material for our army are gained at the front.

10 Use the intervals between campaigns for rest, regrouping, retraining, or training new troops, but such periods should not be too long because the enemy should not be allowed breathing space to recover.

The Eight Reminders

1 Be polite to the people
2 Be fair in all dealings
3 Return everything borrowed
4 Pay for everything damaged
5 Do not bully the people
6 Do not damage crops
7 Do not flirt with women
8 Do not ill-treat prisoners

5 THE POST-WAR WORLD: FIGHTING CONTINUES IN GREECE, THE PHILIPPINES AND IN PALESTINE

As has been seen during the last two chapters, most of the Communist guerrilla groups which were active during the Second World War had aspirations for post-war control of their countries. In some cases, these groups disbanded and were satisfied with becoming a leftist opposition, while in other cases they launched a new guerrilla campaign against the recognized government, resulting in full-scale civil war. In Palestine, on the other hand, the Jews fought a guerrilla campaign to force the British to grant independence to a Jewish state, a campaign which had some of its origins in the Second World War and the German atrocities against the Jews.

GREECE

As described earlier, ELAS took advantage of the power vacuum at the end of the Second World War to attempt to seize control of Greece. In northern Greece, the Communists were in contact with Albanian and Yugoslavian Communists, who had successfully wrested control of each country. However, lacking Mao's astuteness about waging an insurgency, ELAS began open warfare too soon. Even though they had forty thousand troops in the field, divided into a northern and southern army, the British Army of occupation was too experienced and well equipped for them, and by January 1945 had driven ELAS from Athens and other populous areas. Once again lacking Mao's insight about the importance of popular support, ELAS took thousands of civilian hostages during their withdrawal, garnering widespread hatred in the process.

In February 1945 ELAS was officially disbanded, many of its guerrillas turning in at least their more outdated arms. The Communist Party of Greece, KKE, was legalized, and some ELAS officers were incorporated into the regular Greek Army. Many guerrillas, however, refused to disband and remained a force in being in the mountains, while KKE infiltrated the infrastructure of the Greek government and agitated for change in the face of rampant inflation and other post-war ills. The fact that the British still occupied parts of Greece also offered KKE propaganda fodder. The Greek government, weak and irresolute at this point, did not take decisive action against KKE or ELAS, as the latter expanded by sending recruits into Yugoslavia and Albania to rearm and retrain.

In March 1946, ELAS, with little real popular support, boycotted the elections and began a new campaign of raids against villages. By summer the 'Republican Army', as ELAS's 'teeth' units were now called (composed primarily of those fighters returning from Albania and Yugoslavia), moved from raiding villages to killing village policemen, local officials and others who supported the government, and taking hostages to force villages to support them. As a result, the police and area administrators centralized their operations for security, thus cutting themselves off from the people.

The government over-reacted at this point, with virtual right-wing death squads, the closure of left-wing newspapers, and other repressive measures. These acts alienated some of the non-Communist population and gave KKE a sound basis for propaganda. By ignoring guerrilla depredations in the countryside – viewing this as banditry rather than insurgency – large areas of rural Greece were lost to government control. The government did try some useful counter-moves, such as arming selected villagers as local militias, but they were not given adequate training to counter guerrilla hit-and-run tactics.

Late in 1946 the government finally admitted they were facing a major insurgency and committed the Greek Army to this struggle, although its command structure was creaky and unresponsive, and its troops were poorly trained and poorly equipped. Nevertheless, guerrilla ranks were eroded by a government amnesty policy which resulted in hundreds of Communist defections, thus giving the government good intelligence on the guerrillas.

By early 1947 the Communists, now known as the Democratic Army of Greece (DSE), had about seven thousand fighters in the field, occupying much of northern Greece. Their numbers continued to grow, doubling by summer 1947, and tripling by the end of the year. Meanwhile, in Athens and other populous areas, the KKE used a secret assassination and intimidation wing (OPLA) to eliminate its enemies. By mid-1947,

KKE and DSE strength had almost peaked, at fifty thousand active underground members and perhaps a quarter of a million sympathizers. Problems were arising with their allies in Yugoslavia, Bulgaria and Albania, however, as all three began to show a desire to acquire portions of Greece for themselves. Then in February 1947 the British withdrawal from Greece was announced, followed in March by the United States' announcement of massive aid.

The next month the Greek Army launched a particularly successful campaign, while the government made a crackdown on Communists who had infiltrated the fabric of government, business and the press. Still, Communist strength under the military leadership of Markos Vafiades grew as recruits were fed into the 250-man battalions of the Democratic Army for the move into central Greece.

In December 1947, KKE announced the formation of a 'Free Democratic Greek Government', with a plan to use Konitsa as its capital, but the Democratic Army was unable to capture it, losing 1,200 men in the attempt. In addition to their manpower losses, the Communists obviously lost prestige as well, though they launched a propaganda campaign comparing themselves to the Greek fighters for freedom against the Turks in the nineteenth century.

In addition to facing an improving Greek Army, the KKE found agitation among the people growing more difficult as US economic aid was used to improve agricultural production and for building projects, thus improving the lives of a good portion of the country's citizens. With the increased US military aid, particularly air support, the Greek Army was even more successful in 1948. Better equipment helped the Army overall, but specially trained commando units, skilled at counter-insurgency operations in the mountains, proved particularly invaluable. The local gendarmerie, now armed with automatic weapons and mortars, could more effectively defend villages, too. As the Greek Army became more effective, the poor training of many of the Communist military leaders became apparent, as they proved incapable of extracting themselves when surrounded.

Fighting from the Vitsi Mountains, Vafiades still remained a formidable foe, especially since his forces could infiltrate back and forth into Yugoslavia, Albania and Bulgaria. Although the government's measures in some cases were rather repressive, the KKE was no better, many atrocities being committed by members of the DSE. With the lack of willing recruits, Vafiades was forced to conscript villagers, thus losing one of the greatest guerrilla advantages - dedicated fighters with high morale through a common cause. More and more, in fact, about the only willing recruits were from the northern Slav minority, recruits who proved to be a disadvantage in that their appearance immediately identified them to the Greeks as 'outsiders'.

Late in 1948, Vafiades was forced by Nikos Zakhiardis, the Secretary General of the KKE, to abandon the strategy of guerrilla warfare. The DSE now attempted a conventional war against the Greek Army. In January 1949, Zakhiardis replaced Vafiades as military commander.

The Greek government had now begun population relocation in some parts of the mountains, to deny DSE sources of food, intelligence and recruits. During the winter, guerrilla problems increased as the Greek Army, with warmer clothing and better equipment, could continue campaigning despite harsh conditions in the mountains. Finally, in July 1949 Tito closed the border with Yugoslavia, making it much more difficult for the guerrillas to receive aid. Under its very able general, Alexandros Papagos, by July 1949 the Greek Army had harried the Communists to the point where they sued for peace, the leadership withdrawing from the country. During the years of strife the Communist casualties numbered 84,000.

Conclusions

Initially, the Communist guerrillas had the advantage of three countries sympathetic to their cause just across the mountainous border. This granted not only a safe haven, but also a ready source of weapons and medical treatment. The guerrillas, however, made many mistakes in their treatment of the population and, as a result, did not gain true popular support for their insurgency, nor could they capitalize on the initial government inefficiency. Once the government began creating militias, offering amnesty for those willing to cross over, and providing security to isolated villages, the Communists were in dire trouble. Add the mistake of switching over to conventional warfare at the point when the Greek Army was growing stronger every day, and it is easy to see why the KKE and its armed units were defeated. Of special note in the victory is the will of the Greek government and people to fight against the Communists, an obvious but not always present prerequisite to defeat an insurgency.

Unfortunately for future US policy in combating insurgencies, the US Army concluded from the Greek Army's success that conventional arms were the best means for defeating guerrillas, while such factors as the lack of broad-based support for the Commmunists were not really appreciated.

THE PHILIPPINES

At the end of the Second World War the Philippines faced massive economic problems, as well as the need to overcome the political fragmentation caused by splits between those who had actively been part of the guerrilla movement and those who had, at least tacitly, worked with the Japanese. When Manuel Roxas, a collaborator in many people's minds, became president, even more polarization occurred. An additional problem, which had persisted for hundreds of years, was the oligarchy of rich landowners who virtually controlled the country. Drawing upon the widespread dissatisfaction, especially among the peasantry, the Communist Huk guerrillas began to push for land and political reforms, though initially diverse views among the Huks themselves concerning how a revolution should be pursued and the American military presence restrained them from open warfare.

Originally, the Huks worked within the political system, winning some seats in the Philippine congress, but through political manoeuvring not being seated, because their reform platform presented a threat to the major landowners. Though Huk appeal to the have-nots was strong, initially they faced a problem among the highly religious Catholics, who viewed Communism as a Godless philosophy which they instinctively distrusted. Deprived of electoral status, the Huks now took to the hills to dig up buried weapons and prepare for armed conflict.

At most about ten per cent of the peasants really supported the Huks, but most of the remaining ninety per cent were neutral, and certainly were not avid supporters of the government. The Huks were organized into regional commandos, which were then broken into squadrons. These were the primary combat units. Part-time guerrillas were members of the Barrio United Defence Corps, while the National Peasants' Union (PKM) formed a political and logistical support arm. Using the cry of land reform and appealing to their nationalism, the Huks wooed the peasants. Initial successes against the military and police enhanced their prestige and won support. Traditionally, guerrillas strike first at isolated police or military outposts; so did the Huks, who also used assassination and torture selectively against local political opponents.

The army and police, still reorganizing after the war, did not respond well, often resorting to widespread repression, which as is usually the case backfired and gained recruits for the Huks. The Philippine Constabulary, the militarized national police force which carried much of the initial counter-insurgency burden, was hamstrung since the government did not pass an emergency powers act, thus they had to release detainees within seventy-two hours. As a result, out of frustration, they often beat detainees as object lessons, whether they were guilty or innocent!

The Communists continued to gain recruits and to ambush the police and military, provoking increased brutality on the part of the security forces. The Philippine Army, re-equipped and advised by the US Army, was much improved, but it was designed to fight a conventional war and was too ponderous for a counter-guerrilla campaign. A favourite Army tactic was the use of the 'zona' to seal off and screen hostile villages. Since the hated Japanese had used this same technique, it was almost guaranteed to alienate large segments of the population. To exacerbate matters, many soldiers used the zona as an excuse to rape and plunder. Using their very effective propaganda organization, the Political, Economic, Intelligence and Research Association (PEIRA), the Huks quickly turned the zona into a *cause célèbre*.

On large-scale search-and-destroy operations by the Army, the guerrillas normally received advance warning and dispersed easily, thus rendering the Army impotent. Such was the situation in 1949 when Elpidio Quinino was elected President, instituting an even more corrupt and incompetent regime. As a result, by 1950 the Army or constabulary could only enter many areas of Luzon in force with weapons pointed at the populace. They viewed and treated the peasants as enemies and were viewed accordingly by the peasants. So much in control of central Luzon were the Huks that it became known as 'Huklandia'. Army tactics were reckless, and often resulted in innocents being killed. Army checkpoints along the roads alienated the peasants, too, since they were time consuming and often used as toll-gates by the soldiers.

Effective from the military point of view, but giving the Huks a propaganda victory, were the 'Nenita' units, which worked much as the US Phoenix Program would in Vietnam, identifying and then assassinating Huk leaders. The multiplicity of intelligence-gathering agencies within the security forces was a problem which caused poor information co-ordination.

The Huks visited the Barrios with highly effective propaganda teams seeking food donations and, therefore, making the people feel part of the fight, though on occasion they did use intimidation in the villages. In practice they fell somewhere between Mao's precepts for dealing with the peasants and the harshness of the Greek insurgents. Though by 1949 the Huks appeared to be on the road to victory in the Philippines, there were some serious disagreements within the Huk leadership over how to expand the insurrection.

Fortunately for the government of the Philippines, the decision to expand operations led to increased Huk use of terror, including the murder of the widow of former President Quezon, an act which alienated much of the population. As the tide of public opinion began turning against them, in 1950 the Huks launched an all-out campaign against police and military posts. The military was learning, though, and now used small, mobile patrols which harried the guerrillas, got to know villagers, and garnered local intelligence. Areas of high guerrilla activity would be saturated with

◀ A key morale issue in counter-insurgency wars is the ability to evacuate the wounded rapidly *(Larry Dring)*

these small patrols, resulting in many successful contacts.

The real turning point was the appointment of Ramon Magsaysay as Minister of National Defence in 1950. A former guerrilla leader himself during the war, and from peasant stock, he knew how the peasants thought and how the guerrillas fought. He immediately began broad reforms of the military, stressing that the peasants must be protected and made to believe that the government represented them. Many corrupt or inept officers were replaced, and the Army was trained to be responsive to the people. The zonas and free-fire zones were eliminated, and civil affairs officers were assigned to Army units to work with the local people. Soon the soldiers who had previously taken the people's food were replacing that taken by the Huks, and winning hearts and minds accordingly. As the peasants began to trust the Army they began supplying the troops with timely intelligence on Huk movements and locations. Huk prisoners were now treated better, too, resulting in more intelligence from them and more of them willing to come over to the government cause. Amnesty programmes combined with large rewards for Huk leaders also denuded the Communist ranks.

Drawing on some of the Huks who had come over to the government side, Force X was formed as a pseudo-guerrilla force which could infiltrate guerrilla areas. This force not only proved adept at ambushing Huk parties, but also at gathering intelligence about which village officials were collaborating with the Huks. Occasionally, some of the pseudos would be 'captured' by police and put in jail, where they would gather even more information, and Huk ammunition supplies were adulterated with rigged ammo which would explode in the gun.

The expansion of the small patrol concept proved particularly effective, fifteen- to twenty-man long-range patrols with automatic weapons moving deep into Huk territory to ambush and raid the Communists in their previously safe areas. Using a strategy of constant pressure, relentless pursuit, surprise, mobility, sound intelligence and good operational security, these units and others soon had the Huks on the run throughout Luzon. The government instituted an EDCOR plan which helped eliminate the Huks' primary platform by instituting land reform and offering land to peasants willing to resettle on Mindanao. Additionally, when not in combat, the Army began helping with community development projects.

Within a year and a half, Magsaysay had brought the insurgency under control and gained the trust of the people. When he was elected President in 1953, he instituted further reforms, resulting in the surrender of Luis Taruc, the Huk commander, in 1954. By that time Huk strength had fallen from about twelve thousand to two thousand, and the counter-insurgency campaign had been won.

Conclusions

The campaign against the Huks offers some excellent counter-insurgency lessons. First, the appeal of the Huks to a large segment of the population was based on a recognized social ill, the need for land reform. Against that the Huks faced certain disadvantages, including the strong Catholicism of the Filipinos, their basic pro-Americanism, and the lack of outside support for their insurgency. The initial incompetence of the Philippine government and security forces in dealing with the problem actually made the Huks appear more successful than they really were, since by their own repressive actions the constabulary and Army alienated the population.

Particularly noteworthy is the importance one man with an understanding of the problem and the willingness to take drastic action can have. Ramon Magsaysay was definitely the right man at the right time. In addition to his reforms of the Army which gained the peasants' trust, his use of pseudo forces and long-range patrols both proved particularly effective. Magsaysay, too, understood the correct mix of military force and civic action in fighting a counter-insurgency war, first to remove the guerrilla power base, then eliminate them piecemeal. One of the most effective post-war counter-guerrilla campaigns, the fight against the Huks offers extremely important lessons for anyone fighting a counter-insurgency war.

PALESTINE

Jewish refugees had been drifting into Palestine for centuries prior to the granting of the British Mandate over that land in the wake of the First World War. As a result, there was increasing conflict between Arab and Jew, resulting in the Arab uprising discussed earlier. The British tried to mediate between the two, but normally managed to satisfy neither. Then, in 1939, Neville Chamberlain's White Paper limited Jewish immigration to Palestine to 15,000 per year, severely curtailed the ability of Jews to purchase land, and called for an Arab state in Palestine with a Jewish minority. Though they found these stipulations distasteful, most Jews in Palestine bided their time, realizing there was widespread opposition to the idea of a Jewish state, and not wanting to alienate their friends in Britain and the USA.

The Jews in Palestine had a defence force known as the Haganah, which had been expanded during the Arab Rebellion of 1936–9. More élite shock troops were formed in 1941 as the Palmach,

initially for service in Syria. In fact, during the war, 32,000 Jews from Palestine would serve in the British Army. After the war, many of these veterans would serve in the Haganah or Palmach. In 1937 there was the formation of a party which was more militant than the Jewish Agency, which semi-officially represented Jewish interests. Known as the Irgun, this group was led by David Raziel, who wrote texts on weapons usage, studied military tactics to prepare himself for conflict, and gave small arms training to Palestinian Jews. Initially, the Irgun was primarily concerned with smuggling in refugees, but in 1939, in retaliation for Arab attacks, it launched a terror campaign against Arabs in Palestine.

An even more militant group than the Irgun, Abraham Stern and his followers, the Fighters for the Freedom of Israel (usually known as the 'Stern Gang'), broke from the Irgun in 1940. During the war the Stern Gang opposed helping the British, and assassinated British, Arab and Jewish policemen, or other opponents of a Jewish state. Raziel was killed fighting for the British in 1941, while Stern lost his life to a policeman's bullet in 1942. Menachem Begin replaced Raziel in 1943, and David Friedman-Yellin took over the Stern Gang.

In January 1944 the Irgun and the Stern Gang formed an alliance to fight against the British mandate and for an independent Jewish state. The Stern Gang increased its attacks on the opposition, while Begin developed a strategy based on the assumption that destroying British prestige in Palestine would also destroy British rule. Begin was astute enough to realize that after the war Britain was going to be far more concerned with the Soviet Union than with Palestine. The sympathy of American Jews, particularly in light of revelations about Hitler's 'Final Solution', was considered another factor in their favour.

The murder in Cairo in November 1944 of Lord Byrne, the British Minister of State, caused the Jewish Agency and the Haganah to disavow the more militant fringe, helping the police round up three hundred Irgun and Stern Gang members. This co-operation continued until May 1945, when the British were asked to create a Jewish state and to allow unrestricted immigration of Jewish refugees. Constant delays by the British government caused the Haganah to begin smuggling refugees once again, however, and to realign themselves with the Irgun and Stern Gang.

On 31 October 1945 the Haganah announced the formation of the Jewish Resistance Movement, and carried out a series of over 250 raids on Palestine's lines of communication, breaching railway lines in more than 150 places, sinking three police boats, damaging the Haifa oil refineries, and hitting at various other targets. The incidents increased in late December, the Irgun raiding two police headquarters and an arms dump, killing nine soldiers in the process. The British reacted harshly, in January 1946 instituting the death penalty for membership of terrorist organizations. The British faced problems not only within Palestine, though, for the USA was calling for increased Jewish immigration, as well.

Sabotage continued, culminating in June 1946 with the destruction of twenty-two RAF aircraft at one airfield. In response, the British ordered the arrest not just of militants, but of moderate members of the Jewish Agency as well. Documents implicating the Haganah in previous acts were also seized. In revenge, the Irgun bombed the King David Hotel, killing ninety-one and wounding forty-five. At this point, world opinion shifted against the Jews, but the British military commander quickly changed that by issuing a set of non-fraternization orders that sounded as if Himmler had written them. The Jews quickly publicized these rules, diverting attention from the King David Hotel atrocity.

In August 1946 the British sealed off Tel Aviv with twenty thousand troops and searched every building, taking eight hundred people into custody. Many were able to slip through, however, and the operation alienated many moderate Jews who had been inconvenienced. The new British Colonial Secretary was more sympathetic to the Jewish cause, however, so once again the Haganah dissociated itself from the extremists. The poor intelligence available to the British, and the number of sympathizers for the Irgun and Stern Gang, made the job of British security forces particularly difficult, even so.

In frustration, the British began using corporal punishment on suspected terrorists, but the Irgun responded by kidnapping two British soldiers and giving them eighteen lashes. Basing their response upon the Biblical 'eye for an eye' philosophy, the Irgun were widely applauded for their reaction. The British then hanged a young militant named Dov Gruner, turning him into a martyr. World attention, however, kept the British from implementing really harsh measures against the militants, yet the measures they did take were abhorrent enough to alienate most of the population; the British security forces found themselves in the classic no-win situation. The high cost of the Second World War also meant that the country could barely spare the resources to deal with a costly campaign in Palestine.

In reprisals for Gruner's death, in March 1947 there were widespread attacks on British installations, eighty soldiers being killed or wounded in one day alone. The declaration of martial law which followed still did little to deter the terrorists, but it did widen the gap between the British authorities and the Jews. In July the British hanged three more terrorists, whereupon the

◀ Parachute insertions allow small highly trained groups of counter-insurgency troops to ambush guerrillas deep in 'safe' areas *(US Army)*

Irgun kidnapped two British soldiers and hanged them. Violence was begetting violence. When the UN finally recommended partition, the British gladly agreed to end their mandate, on 15 May 1948. Months before then, however, the Irgun and Stern Gang had turned their attention to fighting the Arabs. Israel, formed to some extent on the basis of acts of terrorism, has itself become a prime target of terrorists, often using the exact tactics the Irgun or Stern Gang had used against their enemies.

Conclusion

The Jewish guerrilla campaign in Palestine offers a good example of certain aspects of guerrilla warfare which can greatly inhibit a counter-insurgency campaign. There are times when sympathetic ethnic or religious groups in another country can adversely affect a counter-insurgency campaign. The power of American Jewry was always a factor in British counter-guerrilla operations, particularly since anyone using repressive measures against Jews in the early post-war years would face comparisons with the Nazis. The British find themselves, to a certain extent, facing some of these considerations today in Northern Ireland due to the large American Irish population.

The British will to hold Palestine had been severely eroded, too, by the economic and human depredations of the recent war. Most British soldiers were of the opinion that if Jews and Arabs wanted to kill each other, that was their business; the morale of the troops reflected this viewpoint. Finally, the very fact that Palestinian Jews had undergone great hardships to settle in Palestine normally united them in their cause, if not always their methods. This made them formidable opponents.

6 WAR IN FRENCH INDOCHINA

Ho Chi Minh had founded the Indochinese Communist Party in 1930, then after the 1941 Japanese invasion had founded the Viet Nam Doc Lap Dong Minh Hoi (League for the Independence of Vietnam), normally abbreviated to Viet Minh. In the fight against Japan, and early in the anti-colonial campaign against the French, the Viet Minh had more a nationalist character than purely Communist. During the guerrilla war against Japan, Ho and his military leader Vo Nguyen Giap had received substantial aid from OSS Detachment 404, a medic from which can probably be credited with saving Ho Chi Minh's life. The OSS men who worked with Ho and Giap had great admiration for their abilities, and found them very pro-American. To this day, in fact, debate exists about whether Vietnam could have become an Asian Yugoslavia, had the US supported Ho Chi Minh, rather than the French attempt to reassert colonial authority at the end of the war. With most of the French in Indochina collaborating with the Japanese, the Viet Minh had been the only real resistance during the war, and thus found themselves in a relatively strong position after the Japanese surrender.

At the end of the Second World War Joseph Stalin pursued a policy of supporting revolution in countries recovering from the war, while the West countered with the Truman Doctrine and NATO. As a result, the United States, Britain and other Western countries were to find themselves involved in brushfire wars around the globe. When the Viet Minh made their attempt to seize independence at the war's end, British Maj.-General Douglas Gracey, the commanding officer of the occupation forces, rearmed French POWs and surrendered Japanese, censored the press, declared martial law, and imposed curfews in the south of Vietnam, while in the north Chiang Kai-shek allowed Ho to seize Hanoi. In December 1945, Free French veterans of the war in Europe arrived to find a power vacuum they lacked the men to fill. In the North, particularly, the Japanese pull-out had left widespread starvation.

Taking advantage of discontent with the impending return of French rule, the Viet Minh offered a programme of tax reforms and education to woo the peasants, while other nationalist parties controlled scattered provinces. Viet Minh requests for 'voluntary contributions' soon replaced taxes. Ironically, the Viet Minh received little support from the Comintern, and in 1946 their greatest supporters were actually members of the OSS. As a result, the Viet Minh and French negotiated, both in an attempt to buy time. By making concessions to Chiang, the French finally got the Chinese to leave the North, then in March 1946 reached an agreement theoretically recognizing the Democratic Republic of Vietnam as a free state. As per the agreement, fifteen thousand French troops were allowed to replace the departing Chinese in the North, though on the understanding that they would train Viet Minh troops to take their place over a five-year period.

As it turned out, the militants in Ho's ranks opposed the agreement, demanding complete control immediately, while the French began regretting their compromise as they re-established control over the country. Incidents increased as the Viet Minh ambushed French troops, often provoking them into reprisals against innocent peasants. In the South, where French control was more secure, Nguyen Binh led the insurgency, while Ho and Giap continued to lead in the North. In a tailor-made propaganda victory for the Viet Minh, a French cruiser opened fire on throngs trying to flee Haiphong, killing six thousand civilians and injuring countless more.

On 19 December 1946 the Viet Minh attacked French garrisons, launching the First Indochina War. Though it would turn out that they acted prematurely, the Viet Minh already had about sixty thousand fighting men, forty thousand of them armed, plus another forty thousand in militia and paramilitary groups. Initially the French used the strategy which had proved effective in their earlier colonial wars, holding the cities and lines of communication, then dividing areas of operations into 'quadrillage' to be cleared with highly mobile troops. This was Marshal Lyautey's *tache-d'huile* or 'oil slick' strategy. This, however, worked best against scattered groups, while the Viet Minh proved too numerous and too cohesive for the French really to exert area control. The

◀ Tough Colonial Para in Indochina, armed with the M1A1 carbine and wearing the camo hat distinctive of the paras (ECP)

diverse nature of the French forces fighting in Indochina made it difficult for them to gain the confidence of the populace as well.

Still oriented to conventional war and tactics, in October 1947 the French launched Operation Lea in an attempt to seal off large areas of mountain and jungle in Tonkin. Fifteen thousand French troops were committed, with the primary mission of capturing Ho and other Viet Minh leaders, but though Lea inflicted heavy Communist casualties, the leadership escaped. Viewing the insurrection as strictly a military problem, the French failed to come to grips with the political reality that most of the population wanted independence. Instead of offering independence, the French brought back the figurehead Emperor Bao Dai.

Militarily, France followed the strategy of area pacification mixed with occasional attacks. Support at home was questionable even early in the campaign, as the government tilted towards the left and faced financial problems. To make the French situation even worse, the Chinese Communist victory in 1949 left a giant Communist power poised just to the north. General Revers, Chief of the French General Staff, recommended immediate evacuation of isolated garrisons along the Chinese border and building up the Vietnamese Army to help carry the combat burden and to gain wider popular support.

For the most part, however, French military and political leadership in Indochina refused to admit that Ho's movement was quite nationalistic in nature or had wide public support. Ironically the French, fresh from their own resistance against the Germans, could not see that their repressive measures were aiding the guerrillas and alienating the population.

Ho and Giap were well aware of Mao's three phases for waging guerrilla war, but had attempted to move directly into the conventional phase too early. French commanders, on the other hand, were not aware that the Viet Minh had moved back into the guerrilla warfare and consolidation phase by 1947. Using guerrilla tactics to keep the French off-balance and confined to population centres, Giap's forces controlled the countryside while he built an army capable of defeating the French.

Though the United States had originally opposed the reassertion of colonialism in Indochina, under Truman it supported French aspirations because of the simplistic view that the Indochina War was a battle against Communism, and because of the critical importance of France to peace in post-war Europe. As has previously been pointed out, the Indochina War was not just a struggle between Communism and French colonialism, however, since many of those fighting against the French were nationalists. Because of the proximity of China, and the prolonged presence in the area of Ho and Giap, the North was much more heavily Communist than the South, but even in Tonkin, many who fought with the Viet Minh were primarily nationalists.

The Viet Minh carefully organized the population into six interzones, subdivided into zones, provinces, districts, intervillages and villages. From these areas were drawn the fighting forces, including regulars, regional forces drawn from zones, provinces and districts, and popular forces drawn from intervillages and villages. Because of the importance of organizing from the ground up, particular effort was directed at winning over villages and hamlets, using propaganda to create an image of the Viet Minh as a people's party fighting a people's war. To enhance this image, Ho followed Mao's example and formulated rules governing Viet Minh dealings with the people. These rules included warnings against damaging property, breaking one's word, offending religion or custom, or acting contemptuously to the peasants. Instead, Viet Minh were adjured to help the people with their work, purchase commodities for them if they lived far from markets, teach reading and hygiene, and to study local customs; in all cases attempting to appear disciplined and diligent.

To organize the peasants, Committees of Resistance were formed in the 'liberated' areas, while in French-controlled areas a shadow government was established. Jungle workshops were established to produce armaments. Using mobility and surprise – two of the guerrilla's most effective weapons – the Viet Minh carried out raids to demoralize the French and to capture weapons. These raids often proved particularly effective, since local people supplied excellent intelligence about the strength and disposition of French outposts. The French, on the other hand, alienated the people, destroying villages or crops in clumsy clearing operations. In the South, which was more fully under French control, the Dich-Van, or assassination squads, used terror against officials who supported the French.

China's victory over the Nationalists in 1949 gave Ho the support he needed to move into the third phase of his campaign against the French, by beginning a major offensive in the North. Giap's assault on the Black River Valley outposts was aided by good intelligence, mobility and surprise, enabling him to overrun the French positions and separate the highlands from the Red River Valley. By early 1950 the French forts were isolated and their supply lines interdicted; then with fresh troops trained in China, Giap increased the pressure throughout the summer, forcing the French to retreat and killing six thousand troops, capturing enough weapons and equipment to equip an entire Viet Minh division in the process. During 1950, in a move towards all-out war, the Viet Minh formed a total of five divisions. Things were not going well at home for the French, as Communists launched strikes against docks loading Vietnam-bound supplies.

In January 1951, Jean de Lattre de Tassigny took command of both the civil and military

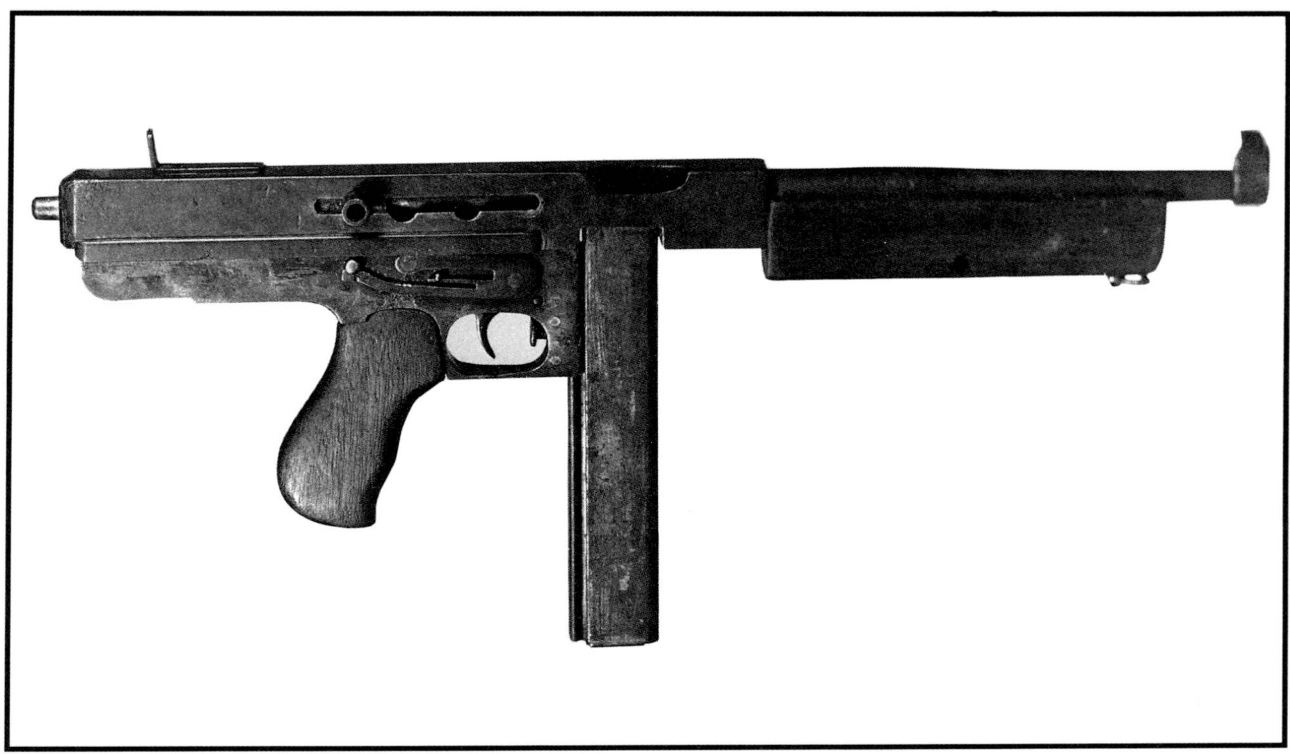

prosecution of the war. Such was his reputation that morale was immediately boosted among the fighting forces. The situation he faced in the North was dire, however. As a prelude to threatening Hanoi itself, Giap attacked Vinh Yen, luring a French Mobile Group into a costly ambush. Eventually, US-supplied napalm helped break the human wave attacks employed by the

▲ Jungle workshop sub-machine gun of the type made by the Viet Minh and later the Viet Cong; in this case a copy of the Thompson SMG *(West Point Museum)*

▼ The M1A1 Carbine, which was the standby of French paras in Indochina

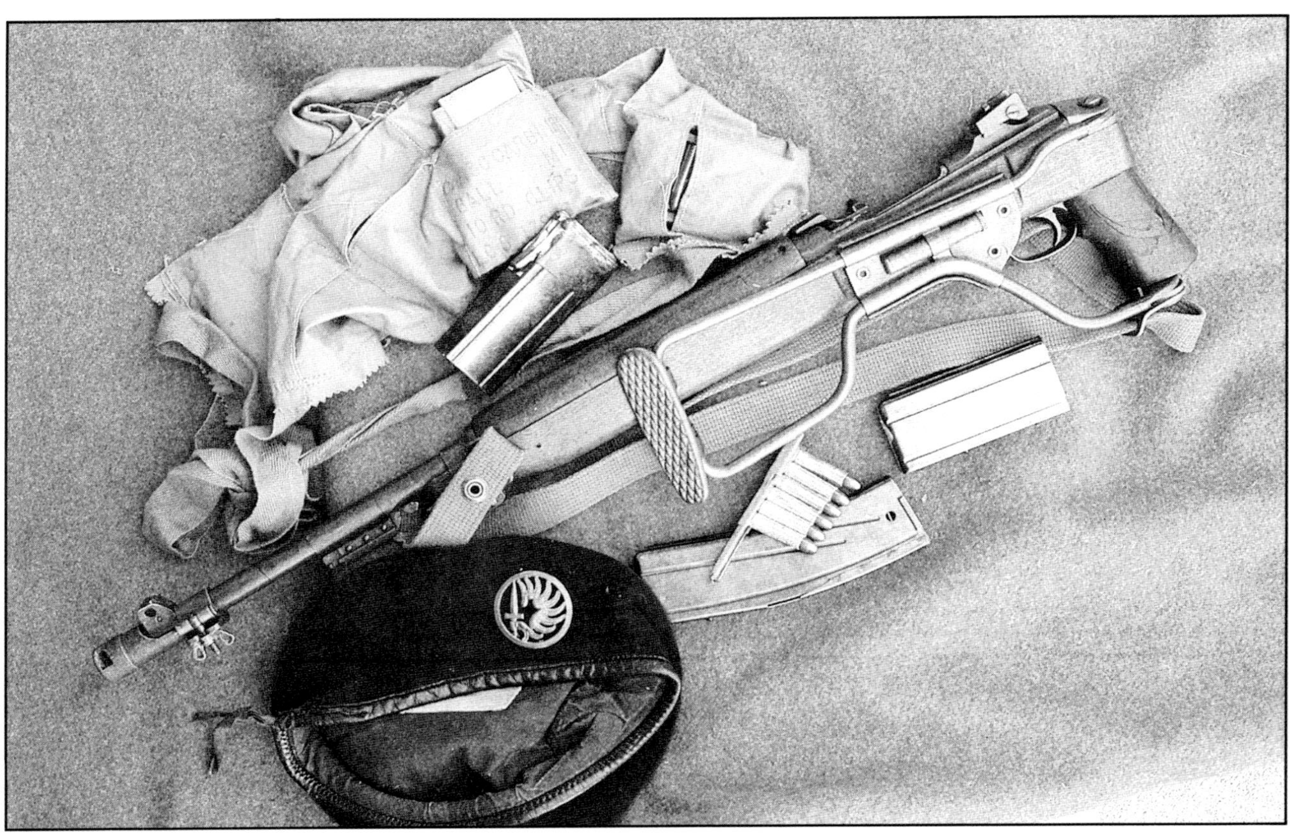

Viet Minh, enabling the French to gain a precarious victory and to inflict heavy Viet Minh casualties.

Giap showed great resilience, though, continuing to apply pressure elsewhere before pulling back in mid-June to rebuild his strength, prior to pushing into Thailand and Laos. While an additional boost to morale, the French success at Vinh Yen had the unfortunate result of making them over-confident in the use of conventional tactics. Though an inspired leader, de Lattre still virtually ignored the political aspects of the war and did not devise a method for countering Viet Minh popular support. Admittedly, he did push the development of a Vietnamese army, but his staunch anti-Communism blinded him to the true nationalist nature of the war.

Appreciating food denial as a valuable counter-insurgency tactic, de Lattre tried sealing off the key rice-producing Red River Delta with twelve hundred forts and blockhouses, while introducing mobile groups to patrol between these redoubts. Along with eight para battalions, these Mobile Groups would be the primary French mobile striking force for the remainder of the Indochina War. Realizing that waterways were another key supply route in Indochina, de Lattre formed special river assault units, the Dinassauts, as well. In an attempt to take the war to the enemy, he also formed the GCMA, which employed French special forces along with turned Viet Minh as the basis for local counter-guerrilla forces.

Throughout this period, US support was ambivalent; many Americans were strongly opposed to supporting the reimposition of colonial control, while others felt the fight against Communism must be supported everywhere. To make matters even more confusing, many Vietnamese were asking for US assistance in gaining independence.

Still failing to realize that the Viet Minh would fight only when it suited their purposes, de Lattre attempted to lure them into battle at Hao Binh in November 1951. Three para battalions jumped in and seized this area, theoretically a critical Viet Minh logistics centre, but Giap just bypassed the area. When ready to fight, Giap infiltrated troops and began interdicting French supply lines. Since the French were much more dependent on traditional logistics systems, Hao Binh now proved a supply nightmare. De Lattre was replaced by General Salan, due to illness, in December, leaving Salan with a deteriorating situation at Hao Binh, now surrounded. A task force had to fight its way in to evacuate the troops from Hao Binh, in the process using most of Salan's reserves and leaving the Delta open to infiltration.

▶ Members of the Colonial Paratroops after one of the many operational parachute jumps used in Indochina to give the counter-insurgency forces mobility *(ECP)*

By March 1952 Mobile Groups were even being used behind the French lines to keep open their lines of communication! In the process of patching up problem areas, the 'oil slick' strategy was being neglected. Some civic action was undertaken, and indigenous troops were successful in securing some areas, but, viewed as pawns of the French, they could really offer the people little or no political incentive to support them. Often, upper-class Vietnamese officers assigned to these units were incompetent and arrogant, thus alienating the local populace even more.

Lack of timely intelligence still plagued the French and prevented them from realizing that the Viet Minh had suffered extremely heavy casualties at Hao Binh and were losing ground in some areas, particularly Roman Catholic ones. As a result, Giap decided to strike into the 'softer' target of Laos, while rebuilding his strength. Once again, rather than saturation patrolling, relatively effective against guerrillas, Salan relied on the establishment of *Bases Aero-Terrestres* (isolated, air-supplied garrisons) along the Laotian border and in north-western Vietnam. Theoretically, these bases would exert French influence, draw Viet Minh attacks, and support the GCMA. Actually, they just tied down troops and drained air resources to keep them supplied. Still thinking in terms of a conventional war with 'lines', Salan launched Operation Lorraine against the Viet Minh supply lines. Once again Giap, however, reliant on coolies carrying supplies by foot or bicycle, simply rerouted his spartan logistics troops and ignored the French offensive, with the exception of committing two regiments to harass the French with guerrilla actions.

By late 1952, support for the war was eroding continually in both France and the USA. However, one very positive suggestion was made by the Vietnamese. Light indigenous units trained in counter-insurgency warfare were proposed, an excellent idea, but one hampered by a lack of French enthusiasm and of adequately trained or motivated Vietnamese officers. While the Vietnamese upper and middle classes avoided military service, most Vietnamese units still had a majority of French officers and NCOs; thus it was hard to convince the populace that it was 'their' army fighting the Viet Minh, who it should be noted had Vietnamese officers and NCOs. It was becoming more apparent as well that the 'de Lattre Line' with its nine hundred forts was really just sapping mobility and initiative, while controlling only the ground the forts actually occupied. Not only was the oil slick strategy not working, but Giap was expanding into central Vietnam, formerly a relatively secure area.

With great difficulty, Salan managed to hold Laos after a fight for the Plain of Jars, but though the Viet Minh had been forced back, they left cadres to work with the Pathet Lao. As General Navarre took command in spring 1953, he was faced with a dictate from France that there would be no further troop replacements; he would be forced to fight an ever-expanding enemy with ever-decreasing resources. An intelligence specialist, Navarre warned that the war could not be won. Of his 190,000-man expeditionary force, 100,000 were tied to static defensive duties, while of 500,000 men available counting Vietnamese troops, 350,000 held static positions. Despite this vast investment in garrison troops, of seven thousand villages in the strategic Red River Delta in May 1953, only two thousand were held securely by the French.

Navarre attempted to instil a more aggressive spirit in his troops. One of his methods was to insert his most mobile force, the airborne troops, on raids, but these were not decisive. Giap still refused combat except on his own terms. After the Korean cease-fire, the Chinese began supplying many captured arms to the Viet Minh, including artillery, which allowed the formation of a Viet Minh artillery division. Giap's new strategy was to stretch the French as thinly as possible, then pick away at strategic points which would inevitably be left vulnerable. However, as his strength increased, and French strength declined relatively, Giap was ready for a decisive battle.

Still tied to the idea of airheads deep in Viet Minh-controlled territory, and unwilling to admit that Giap now had the capability to invest such bastions, in November 1953 Navarre established a new series of airheads in north-western Vietnam, the largest at Dien Bien Phu astride the route to Laos. Instead of another push into Laos, Giap now decided to attack Dien Bien Phu in force. Secretly, he concentrated massive forces in the area, while coolies built supply routes and manhandled artillery for miles into position. Despite indications of increased Viet Minh activity, Navarre believed that Giap could not successfully besiege Dien Bien Phu, which could be supplied by air.

By 13 March 1954 when the Viet Minh attacked, 17,000 French troops were concentrated at Dien Bien Phu. Eventually, over 100,000 rounds of Viet Minh artillery would rain on to the fortress, while special Viet Minh assault units attacked and eliminated the outer defences and invested the airstrip, thus compressing the area into which supplies could be dropped. To counter French air superiority, guerrillas hit airfields, destroying planes and fuel on the ground, while Chinese AA gunners manned a bristling array of guns around the valley. As the situation at Dien Bien Phu worsened, some Americans even advocated using nuclear weapons against the Viet Minh, though fears of Soviet and Chinese reaction helped discourage this idea.

On 8 May 1954 the remaining defenders of Dien Bien Phu finally surrendered, 2,000 having died during the battle. Most went into captivity, including many North Africans who proved a fertile basis for the future insurgency in Algeria.

After having spent $11.5 billion and suffering 170,000 casualties, France was finally ready to concede defeat in Indochina. As a result, the North was ceded to the Viet Minh, with the demarcation line established at the 17th Parallel, pending elections to unify the country. The stage was now set for the Second Indochina War, as the United States was sucked in to fill the power vacuum left in the South by the departing French.

Conclusions

The Viet Minh victory in Indochina can be attributed to a combination of Ho' and Giap's astuteness, and the French lack of that quality. By playing down his Communism, and playing up the nationalist aspects of his insurgency, Ho won wide popular support. The French, on the other hand, in their attempts to reinstate an unpopular colonial regime, eliminated virtually all popular support. Had a really viable Vietnamese government, supported by an effective Vietnamese Army, been established, the course of the war might have been quite different.

While Giap showed excellent flexibility in adjusting to French moves against him, the French failed to realize that the initiative throughout the war remained with the Viet Minh. By tying up greater and greater numbers of troops in static garrison positions, the French will to fight was eroded, while Viet Minh mobility allowed them to strike at will. By sticking too much to the roads, the French virtually invited ambushes of their best mobile troops; the Viet Minh were glad to oblige. The French logistic system was overstretched at best, while the Viet Minh's reliance on coolies allowed them to adjust to the local situation. By establishing outposts far from supply centres, the French invited disaster after disaster, culminating in the fall of Dien Bien Phu. The presence of a giant ally to the north after the Communist victory in China gave the Viet Minh the added advantage of a safe haven and a ready source of supply.

Although some of the Foreign Legion and para units became skilled counter-guerrilla forces, for the most part the French remained oriented towards conventional war rather than counter-insurgency. Indochina is the classic example of how a failure to come to grips with the political reasons for an insurgency can doom any military effort to defeat the insurgents.

THE FRENCH COLONIAL PARAS IN INDOCHINA

The French did not send conscripts to Indochina, and the burden of fighting the war fell heavily on the professionals of the Foreign Legion and Colonial Paratroops. For the French, the term 'Colonial' as applied to paratroops and infantry meant they were intended to serve overseas in French colonies. This applies today to the 'Marine Paratroops'. Many paras serving in Lebanon, for example, were with RPIMa units.

Life was tough in the Colonial Paratroops, normal enlistment being for three years, mostly in Indochina. Two months of basic infantry training was followed by one month of jump school. After completing the first jump, the fledgling para was awarded the red beret of the Colonial Paras, which he wore with great pride. Failure to jump, on the other hand, was greeted with little compassion. Anyone refusing to jump was normally beaten by the NCOs as soon as the plane landed, then forced to run through the base area with a sign on his parachute harness reporting, 'I Am a Coward'. Many Colonial Paras were German Second World War veterans, while others were very rough individuals who had found the para recruiters before the law found them.

Standard strength and organization of a Colonial Paratroop Battalion called for about 540–50 men, divided into four Commando Groups. For clarity, it should be pointed out that the Colonial Paras had three separate designations in Indochina. Initially they were known as the BCCP (*Bataillon Colonial des Commandos Parachutistes*), then as GCCP (*Groupement des Commandos Coloniaux Parachutistes*), and finally as BPC (*Bataillon des Parachutistes Coloniaux*).

Attempting to use vertical envelopment to block Viet Minh escape routes, the French made over a hundred combat jumps during that conflict, over half by the Colonial Paratroops. By comparison, US forces made only one major combat jump in Vietnam. In fact, the French probably made more jumps than were made by all Second World War combatants. The need for rapid troop insertion to block enemy escape, or to seek and destroy, remained throughout the US tenure, but by then the helicopter had taken the place of the parachute.

The first combat jumps during the Indochina War were made by the French Special Air Service in 1946 and early 1947. This unit then evolved into the 1st BCCP. Although it preceded the first official jump by the Colonial Paras, Operation Lea in October 1947 is ▶

noteworthy because it illustrates why parachute troops proved so valuable in Indochina. Combining the drop of 1,137 paratroops with an armoured thrust to seize Viet Minh leaders, Lea was intended to end the conflict quickly by decapitating the Viet Minh dragon. The SAS paras performed their mission perfectly, landing directly on the Communist HQ so swiftly that they captured Ho Chi Minh's mail waiting on his desk, as well as important supply depots, but Ho and Giap, the two primary targets, escaped. Other airborne troops in this operation had the mission of seizing and holding bridges along the armoured route of advance. Most Viet Minh units in the operational area, however, managed to slip through the cordon, along with their leaders.

During the remainder of 1947 paras carried out sweeps in attempts to cut off Viet Minh units, forcing them to fight, but Giap refused to be drawn into battle. By late December that year, Viet Minh pressure had forced a French withdrawal from North Vietnam, except for some forts along the Chinese border. The next two years saw continued erosion of French control as more and more of the countryside fell under Viet Minh control. Using company-sized para insertions, the French tried to seize back the initiative, but even though the paras fought well when the Viet Minh would fight, this strategy did not prove very successful.

As the first half of the twentieth century came to an end, the Colonial Paratroops remained busy as one or two Commando Groups would be dropped to carry out raids, rescue POWs, reinforce positions under attack, or attack Viet Minh camps or depots. During 1948, for example, the Colonial Paras averaged one combat jump per month, spread among the 1st, 2nd and 5th BCCPs. In 1949 the Colonial Paratroops were assigned the same types of mission, though the initiative was obviously shifting to the Viet Minh, as nearly half the jumps were made to reinforce beleaguered outposts. Other jumps still involved raids, including one on 30 April that year by 196 members of the 5th BCCP to capture members of the Viet Minh leadership. As Laos was threatened in 1949, the Colonial Paras saw action there as well. In June, for example, the entire 2nd BCCP jumped onto the Plain of Jars, while earlier in the year the 3rd BCCP had jumped to aid Muong partisans.

◀ Foreign Legionnaires examine the scene of a Viet Minh ambush during fighting in Indochina *(ECP)*

Buoyed by increased support from the Chinese Communists, Giap went over to the offensive against French forts along the Chinese border. Three paratroop units – 3rd BCCP, 3rd GCCP and 7th GCCP – were dropped as reinforcements and to open roads for resupply or retreat, but the forts eventually fell anyway, allowing the Viet Minh to capture enough arms and equipment for an entire division. By 1 January 1951, therefore, control north of the Red River had passed to the Viet Minh. By that point 5,700 Colonial, Legion and Metro paras were fighting heroically in Indochina, but they were not enough to hold back the Viet Minh tide.

That month, Giap attempted to follow up his successes along the Chinese border by attacking Vinh-Yen, a critical step towards threatening Hanoi itself. Attempting to turn the tide in this critical battle, de Lattre committed Mobile Group 2, which included one paratroop battalion; Vinh-Yen would eventually cost the Viet Minh over six thousand dead, but the guerrilla war continued, forcing the French to form Mobile Groups in an attempt to keep key roadways open. Each Mobile Group consisted of armoured vehicles, accompanied by truck-borne infantry (frequently tough Legionnaires or paras) and often engineers. Like characters in a *Mad Max* film, these Mobile Groups cruised the treacherous Indochina roadways, forcing passage through to beleaguered garrisons and keeping supply routes open. Their commanders were normally lieutenant-colonels or colonels, often paratroop officers, and a rather swashbuckling lot. As the war progressed, however, the Viet Minh became more sophisticated at fighting the Mobile Groups, setting larger and larger ambushes, at times virtually wiping out entire Mobile Groups.

Giap struck the defences along the Red River Delta to continue his pressure against the French. The outpost at Mao Khe was hit especially hard, but the 6th Colonial Paras broke through to reinforce the garrison and turn the tide. The 6th BPC (de Lattre had ordered GCCPs to be redesignated BPCs in March 1951) was commanded by Marcel Bigeard, perhaps the most famous French paratroop officer in Indochina. Having risen from the ranks, Bigeard would eventually become a

▲ Members of the Foreign Legion 1st Parachute Battalion, among the most hardened combat veterans in Indochina *(ECP)*

general. Under his leadership, the 6th became probably the most famous Colonial Paratroop Battalion. Bigeard himself is generally accepted to have provided the basis for the main character in the novel *The Centurions*.

Despite the success of the 6th in reinforcing Mao Khe, the Red River Delta remained threatened, especially along the Day River Line. To counter the threat, six hundred members of the 7th Colonial Paratroops jumped as reinforcements at Ninh-Binh on 30 May 1951. Meanwhile, Mobile Groups were pushing overland to reinforce the defenders, while Dinassauts lent amphibious support. By 18 June the tide had been turned, with the Viet Minh once again held at the Red River Line.

That November the French went on the offensive, two thousand paras of the 1st, 2nd and 7th BPCs seizing the city of Hao Binh, a key position along the Communist supply network. Though a blow to the Communists, who needed the road which passed through Hao Binh to bring in heavy equipment, this operation was not as devastating as it might have been, since the Communists still used coolies to transport a large percentage of their supplies. Hao Binh was also the capital of the Muong tribe, however, which made it an important symbolic objective. The objective was taken with little combat, since the wily Giap's troops had melted away, but the city was important enough that a large Viet Minh effort was launched to retake it. Before long, Hao Binh was surrounded and cut off, forcing the French to fight their way through with critical supplies, leading to a war of attrition which was soon a battle for control of the entire Black River line. Eventually, an entire airborne group (three battalions) was committed to defend this line, but the Viet Minh, in true guerrilla fashion, would fight only on their own terms. Eventually, being bled dry, the French pulled back east of the Black River. Meanwhile, the battles along Road 6 to supply Hao Binh had drawn on. An Airborne Task Force under Colonel Gilles had attempted to fight twenty-five miles to Hao Binh, but even the tough paras found the constant ambushes and sniping eroded manpower and morale. Finally, in January 1952, it was decided to evacuate Hao Binh, and this was completed by late February.

By forcing the French on to the defensive, Giap drained their reserves and left other areas vulnerable, especially the Red River Delta. Attempting to hold critical outposts, the French shifted mobile airborne combat teams under perhaps the three best paratroop colonels – Gilles, Bigeard and Langlais – from trouble spot to trouble spot, to reinforce threatened areas. These airborne combat teams often functioned as mobile groups, but the Colonial Paras were kept busy with reinforcement jumps as well. More and more they were being used reactively, rather than actively. During 1952, 2nd BPC jumped into Hao Binh on 8 January; 3rd BPC into Tranh-Huong on 4 September and then into Phat-Diem on 11 October; 6th BPC into Tu-Le on 16 October; and 6th BPC into Ban-Som, Thailand, on 27 December.

The Tu-Le jump by the 6th BPC was the beginning of one of the most heroic episodes involving the Colonial Paras in Indochina. The final battle for the T'ai Highlands began in October, with Bigeard's 6th Colonials being dropped to fight a rearguard action, while other troops evacuated their positions and pulled back. By 17 October the 6th was already in combat against heavy odds, but they held at Tu-Le until the 20th, buying time for many of the other garrisons in the Highlands to pull back. Finally beginning their own retreat, the 6th's progress was slowed by their wounded, whom they carried with them; the Paras never left their wounded, who were likely to be tortured to death due to the particular hatred the Viet Minh had for them – a well-earned hatred, since the Paras were not known for their gentle treatment of prisoners. During the retreat, the 6th was decimated by ambushes, which cost sixty per cent of the battalion, but their own toughness and Bigeard's leadership kept them together as a cohesive fighting force, as they clawed their way out.

As the situation in the T'ai Highlands worsened, Operation Lorraine was launched on 29 October in an attempt to destroy the Communists' primary supply depots, to stall their offensive. On 9 November Airborne Group No. 1, consisting of 2,350 men of the 3rd Colonial Paras and two Legion Para battalions, dropped on Phu-Doan, seizing

◀ French Foreign Legion patrol moves through the jungle in Indochina in search of the Viet Minh *(ECP)*

it against light opposition. To link up with them, a major motorized force was advancing overland. Phu-Doan proved to be a very important supply centre; among the items captured were some of the first Russian trucks and weapons supplied to the Viet Minh. Once Airborne Group No. 1 had linked up with the mobile groups advancing overland, the drive continued, but it soon became obvious that Lorraine would not stop the Viet Minh from taking the T'ai Highlands. Therefore the column was ordered to pull back, fighting its way through ambushes to return to its jump-off point by 1 December. Not unduly dependent on depots, the Viet Minh had been annoyed by Lorraine, but not stopped.

During 1953 French control of the country shrank, as did the number of airborne operations, though the year would see three major operations, including the largest jump of the war. The first of these was launched on 17 July at Langson by 2nd BPC along with Legion and Metro para units, with the mission of hitting Viet Minh supply depots again. Operation Camargue on 28 July was designed to open the 'Street Without Joy' (Highway 1) by trapping the 95th Viet Minh Regiment, which had been operating in the area and periodically cutting the road. The primary thrust combined armoured and amphibious pincers. Two para battalions were in reserve, however. Neither of the para battalions included Colonial Paras, but the operation points out the inefficiency of the French counter-guerrilla war, so it will be discussed here anyway. When the two Para battalions were finally committed, they jumped too late to close the cordon, allowing most of the Viet Minh to escape. As with much of the French effort, too little was used too late.

On 20 November that year, the French undertook their largest airborne operation of the war when 4,525 paras, including the 1st BPC, jumped to seize the airstrip at Dien Bien Phu. Though most of the paras were pulled out after seizing the base, they would soon return. On 31 January 1954, Dien Bien Phu came under Communist artillery fire, and for the next month and a half the fortress faced bombardment and probing attacks. The real offensive, however, began on 12 March. The next day more than 3,500 parachutists, including the 1st and 6th BPCs, jumped to reinforce the garrison. During the epic defence of Dien Bien Phu, Bigeard's 6th Colonial Paras added to their legend, carrying out bloody counter-attacks to regain strongpoints taken by the Communists. So critical were the paras to the defence of Dien Bien Phu that command of the defences effectively passed to the 'Paratroop Mafia', which included officers such as Langlais and Bigeard. When Dien Bien Phu fell, most of the surviving paras marched into captivity, many never to return.

Shortly before the fall of Dien Bien Phu on 8 May, the newly arrived 7th BPC was considered for dropping into the fortress, but by then the French command realized that this would probably be a waste of good men. As a result, the 7th did not get a chance to make a combat jump. Although there were one or two jumps by members of the GCMA (French Special Forces) after the fall of Dien Bien Phu, the French war in Indochina was really over. France and the Colonial Paras now had a new war to fight in Algeria.

The record of the Colonial Paras in Indochina was a heroic one, including well over fifty combat jumps; 2nd Colonial Paras made twenty-one jumps themselves, while 3rd Colonial Paras made seventeen more. Many of the Colonial Para units were virtually wiped out – the 1st at Ba-Vi, the 3rd at Na-Cham, and the 6th at Mao Khe, to name a few – yet they were reconstituted, and jumped back into action. Unlike US airborne and airmobile troops in Vietnam, the Colonial Paras couldn't count on helicopter gunships, nor even air support much of the time. A lot of the time, in fact, it was down to their M1A1 Carbines, MAT-49 SMGs and light machine guns, and not much else, to stop the Viet Minh. Veterans of the Colonial Paratroops are justly proud of their record; occasionally one will still see an old 'Colonial' in a parade, or at an old paras' tavern. On his arm is likely to be a distinctive and garish Indochinese tattoo, more often than not a dragon, along with his para brevet and brevet serial number. And, perched atop his no-longer-young head might be a worn red beret with the badge of the Colonial Paratroops. Chances are, though, no matter how wrinkled or fat the wearer, the beret will still be worn at the jaunty angle of a hard, lean Colonial Para just arrived in Tonkin. One doesn't see many Colonial Para veterans, though; most never came home from Indochina.

7 MALAYA

With the assistance of Moscow, the Malayan Communist Party (MCP) had been formed in 1927, and as with many of the guerrillas who fought against the Axis during the Second World War, the MCP had supplied a substantial percentage of the seven thousand Malayan guerrillas who were trained to fight the Japanese.

It was not until June 1948, when Chinese terrorists/guerrillas murdered three Europeans that the Malayan insurgency moved to the stage of bloodletting. Although theoretically at the end of the war the guerrillas of the Malayan People's Anti-Japanese Army, which had been trained by SOE Force 136, had disarmed and returned to civilian life, many of the Chinese Communist members had retained their arms and remained in the jungle. Malaya, still under colonial rule, seemed ripe for revolution in 1948.

MCP leader Chen Ping had five thousand trained guerrillas, supported by the Chinese Communists, when the insurgency began, most operating from established jungle bases. Using his ten guerrilla regiments as a basis, Chen Ping planned to wage a three-phase guerrilla war according to Mao's precepts. During the first phase, attacks would be launched against rubber plantations, tin mines, rural police stations or local government facilities to destabilize the government locally and erode public confidence in it. During the second phase, guerrilla bases would be established in newly 'liberated' areas from which the government had been driven in the first phase, thus allowing the guerrillas to build strength and train for the third phase, during which a full-scale assault would be launched against cities, resulting in a final takeover.

While Chen Ping had the advantage of a cohesive guerrilla force already in place, British forces in Malaya at the time were under strength and the government was unprepared to deal with an insurgency. British High Commissioner Sir Edward Gent was reluctant to resort to oppressive measures, thus allowing the Communists to operate almost with impunity at the beginning. However, Gent was soon recalled and replaced by Sir Henry Gurney. Gurney quickly declared a State of Emergency, with tough laws, including detention without trial for suspected CTs (Communist Terrorists). Still, many problems remained in dealing with the insurgency: there was no single commander to co-ordinate government, military and police so that they waged a cohesive campaign; late responses to guerrilla attacks – unavoidable since guerrillas could pick and choose targets – led to erosion of confidence in the government, and a widespread belief that the security forces were incapable of dealing with the threat; thirdly, inflexible police and army officers with pre-war colonial attitudes contributed to the problem as well, since they could not adjust to the exigencies of counter-guerrilla warfare.

In an attempt to counter the Communists' freedom of action, the counter-terror campaign was divided between police guarding populated areas, and the military controlling the jungle, where the CTs had their bases. The first step in taking the campaign to the jungle was rigorous patrolling, to prevent the CTs from becoming too well established. However, the Army, even the famous Gurkhas, had to gain experience and relearn the lessons of jungle warfare. Normally the Gurkhas have proved formidable jungle fighters, but many sent to Malaya had not been fully trained when they arrived. As the Army gained experience, they carried out sweeps, but of such large scale and so cumbersomely that they were rarely successful in making contact, since the CTs knew they were coming well in advance. The harsh jungle conditions were hard on the searchers who were unaccustomed to them. However, since eighty per cent of Malaya is jungle, with a seventy- to eighty-foot canopy and dense undergrowth, to win the war the security forces would have to learn to live and fight in the jungle.

Support for the CTs in the jungle was provided by the Min Yuen ('the masses') in the persons of Chinese squatters living on the outskirts of the jungle and providing food, manpower and other support for the CTs. Police and Army troops would sweep through these settlements, destroying food caches, but there were always more, and this technique only alienated the population even more. Far more effective were the two hundred 'Jungle Squads' formed by the police, and particularly 'Ferret Force', made up of ex-members of SOE Force 136, all highly trained

in guerrilla warfare, who would carry out deep penetration jungle patrols for weeks at a time. Ferret Force itself did not last long, but it proved the technique which the SAS and other units would use effectively later to help win the campaign.

Although on the surface the CTs seemed to be winning during 1948 and 1949, the authorities did manage to avoid the necessity of evacuating mines and rubber plantations, thus forcing the CTs into acts of violence against the local population. Since rubber and tin prices were driven up as a result of the insurgency, the government actually had more money available to fight against the guerrillas. In effect, acts by the guerrillas were giving the government the financial means to combat them! Fortuitously, Lau Yew, the most experienced guerrilla leader, was killed during a police ambush.

By 1949 the CTs had withdrawn into the jungle, venturing out to raid, killing about five hundred people in the process, but losing seven hundred of their own either killed or captured. Since the CTs needed to reach populated areas to carry out their attacks, they tended to locate within a few hours of those target areas, thus giving the security forces the opportunity to ambush them as they used the access trails. As security forces became more sophisticated, patrolling companies would often leave behind four- to five-man ambush parties along likely infiltration or exfiltration routes. Although some CTs took refuge just across the border in Thailand, this was never really a safe haven, as the Thais co-operated with the Malayan security forces, in 1949 granting the Malayan police the right to pursue CTs up to ten miles inside the Thai border.

Another problem faced by the CTs was lack of broad-based support, since the insurgency was primarily among the Chinese minority. In 1949 Chin Peng received orders from the Chinese Red Army to rename his force the 'Malayan Races Liberation Army'; however, it remained ninety per cent Chinese. When this cosmetic name change failed to attract widespread Malay support, terror was used in an attempt to recruit Malays, but this soon proved counter-productive, though at least one prominent Malay Communist leader - Abdullah - did emerge. However, he was soon countered by loyal Pahang Kampang bands led by his cousin Yeop Mahidan, who proved an astute counter-guerrilla campaigner. The government had also begun dropping pamphlets offering CTs a chance to come over. This so angered Chin Peng that he made possession of these pamphlets an offence carrying the death penalty. Obviously, he realized the loyalty of many of his followers was at best questionable.

◀ Members of the Rhodesian SAS use a raft during a patrol in Malaya

◀ *Inset*: Members of the Rhodesian SAS between operations in Malaya; note the maroon beret with the SAS cap badge

Relocation to the New Villages

Although government successes had been growing through 1949, Chinese squatters providing guerrilla support still had to be dealt with. As a result, the drastic step of resettling them was taken. The resettlement plan had the double purpose of isolating guerrillas from their support, and also of protecting the Chinese settlers. Director of Operations at this time was Lt-General Sir Harold Briggs, and it was his name which was given to this resettlement plan. Under Briggs the security forces were proving more effective, and the resettlement plan offered hopes of future success, but the CTs continued to strike and then fade into the jungle as the May 1950 total of 534 terrorist incidents illustrates. Still, during that year rubber and tin production actually rose, and by 1951 Chen Ping had to admit the bulk of the Malayan population did not support him.

In a reversion to the more classic form of guerrilla warfare as taught by Mao, Chen ordered that attacks against civilians would cease, while infiltration of labour unions would receive higher priority and the war against the police and military would continue in an attempt to erode the British long-term will to fight, through attrition.

To counter Chen Ping's strategy, when he became Director of Operations Briggs had offered a four-part plan of his own: 1. make populated areas secure; 2. destroy Communist organization within populated areas; 3. isolate CTs from their food and manpower sources; 4. force CTs to attack the security forces on ground of the police or military's choosing. Additionally, under Briggs effort was better centralized as the police and military established joint ops rooms, and integrated intelligence under a single Chief of Intelligence.

During October 1951 the High Commissioner, Sir Henry Gurney, was killed during an ambush, goading the British government into finally taking the insurgency seriously. At this point, with about ten thousand CTs facing about ninety thousand members of the security forces, a 'Supremo' with control of the civil government, police and military was named, in the person of Sir Gerald Templer, in February 1952.

By 1951 the resettlement plan, which had begun in 1949, was about halfway complete, and well on the road to being highly successful. There were two types of New Village: dormitory, for those who worked on plantations or in the mines, and agricultural, for those who were farmers. The establishment of the villages and movement of the populace into them was only part of the plan, however. In addition, the security forces would protect the populated areas, isolate the CTs from their support, and force the CTs out of their lairs and into ambushes set for them. The New Villages played a part in each of these three objectives.

Each New Village was carefully planned, with water, room for chickens or pigs, and garden plots. Each family moved to one of the villages was given title to their land – something they had never had as squatters, construction materials to build a home, and $100 in cash to live on until settled. To protect the village and keep the CTs out, each village was surrounded by perimeter barbed wire and had its own police post. As the village became established, it would also provide its own Home Guard unit. Later, as communities were declared free of terrorists, committees would be elected in the villages to govern their own affairs.

Although instituted by Briggs and called the 'Briggs Plan', the resettlement strategy had actually been developed by Gurney before his death. Another of Gurney's successful policies was the offer of rewards for CTs killed or captured. CTs who came over to the security forces and turned in their former comrades were also eligible for rewards. To isolate CTs from the population even more, Gurney instituted a national identity card system, a system which Chen Ping immediately realized could mean trouble for his fighters; hence, he took draconian action against the registration teams travelling throughout the country.

Once the New Villages had been established, a policy of starving out the CTs began, with the institution of a list of restricted goods which could not leave the New Villages. Food and medical supplies particularly were included. Everyone leaving the populated areas was searched for contraband, and in the more sympathetic areas rice was issued already cooked, since it would only keep for a couple of days before turning bad. Tinned goods sold in these areas were punctured as they were sold, to prevent them finding their way to the CTs. As the food shortages began to be felt among the guerrillas, more and more turned themselves in, proving the success of the plan. Finally, desperate CTs were forced to plant jungle gardens, the presence of which often gave away their location to reconnaissance aircraft, which would vector ground troops to destroy them or to set ambushes for CTs tending them.

General Sir Gerald Templer took office in February 1952, with authority over all aspects of the war. Templer's brief was to defeat the Communists and prepare Malaya for independence. By combining the police, military, and civil authority under his own supreme leadership, Templer could begin the task of raising the population's morale and restoring faith in the government, prior to defeating the MCP. At the suggestion of Robert Thompson, his Permanent Secretary of Defence, he also began bringing the Chinese actively into the war on the government side. Home Guards were formed to protect the New Villages, their arming illustrating government faith in their loyalty. Despite fears that the arms would be turned over to the CTs, overwhelmingly the Home Guards proved loyal.

As part of his overall strategy, Templer started the famous 'hearts and minds' campaign, predicated on the philosophy that the most important aspect of winning a guerrilla war was showing the people that the government deserved their loyalty. To unite the diverse ethnic groups and start preparing the country politically for independence, the Alliance Party was formed under Tunku Abdul Rahman, soon after Templer assumed command. Templer realized that the police would have an increasingly important role to play in countering the guerrillas, and thus had British Army officers seconded to the police to assist in training, and arranged for the police to receive scout cars, automatic weapons and other modern equipment.

Templer, who had been a Director of Military Intelligence at the War Office, knew the importance of intelligence. Therefore he built up the Police Special Branch and had them work more closely with Army Intelligence. The results were impressive as the flow of information about the CTs increased dramatically, leading to more successful operations.

Although Templer worked hard at winning over the population, in areas which proved supportive of the terrorists he was still willing to take drastic measures, such as instituting twenty-two-hour-per-day curfews. However, he offered the carrot as well as the stick in these towns, as he arranged a secret method for villagers to inform on local CTs, which would thus lift the curfew. Frequently, after such a crackdown, terrorist support was eroded and volunteers for the Home Guard from these areas increased dramatically.

So successful was Templer's combined military and civil campaign that in 1953 Chen Ping announced that, along with eighty key subordinates, he would flee across the border to Thailand and continue the fight from there. More and more starving terrorists were turning themselves in, too, as the combination of the food denial programme and the pamphlet drops showing well-nourished former CTs worked on the will to resist of the less committed guerrillas.

Although the British had fought well in the jungle during the Second World War, most of the troops fighting in Malaya had to relearn the lessons of jungle warfare, before beating the terrorists in the jungle. They learned to live in the jungle for weeks at a time, carrying out far-ranging patrols, often using Iban trackers from Borneo. Initially, the CTs were the experts at ambushes, but the security forces learned well, and by 1953 were taking their toll of the terrorists. Nevertheless, typically, it still took a soldier 1,800 man hours on patrol before he was likely to make contact with a CT. Even if they did not make contact, however, the security forces were driving the CTs deeper and deeper into the jungle.

Food remained a CT problem in the deep jungle so they forced the aborigines who dwelt there to grow food for them, presenting the security forces with a new challenge, countering the CT influence

▲ Rhodesians of the Special Air Service just prior to an operation in Malaya

over the aborigines. To some extent turned CTs, formed by Special Branch into the Special Operations Volunteer Force, helped by acting as jungle scouts to track down their former comrades. But it was the building of jungle forts in the aborigine areas to help protect them which paid the greatest benefits. These forts helped with the local 'hearts and minds' campaign, providing medical and other assistance, but also being well situated for intelligence-gathering, and offering CTs disenchanted with the war a convenient place to turn themselves in. CT intimidation of the aborigines backfired, since it led to the formation of an irregular aborigine force, called the 'Senoi Pra'ak'. Though often armed only with blowpipes, this force killed more CTs during the last two years of the war than the security forces; remembering their own treatment at the hands of the guerrillas, they enjoyed the hunt immensely.

Missions by the RAF proved useful for resupplying the deep penetration patrols, and also for intelligence-gathering, particularly by spotting jungle vegetable plots planted by guerrillas. Fixed-wing planes were used for pamphlet drops and broadcasts, while helicopters served for medical evacuation and rapid removal of captured documents to the intelligence centres. Occasionally, air strikes were called in against suspected CT

camps, but Templer felt that the risk of losing popular support through bombs going astray outweighed any advantage of such strikes, so except in direct support of patrols, offensive air power was used sparingly.

By 1952 there were forty thousand troops in the security forces – twenty-five thousand British, ten thousand Gurkhas and five thousand Commonwealth. Of the British, about half were National Servicemen. It should be noted that of the forty thousand only about ten thousand in twenty-three battalions were line combat troops. Of the combat battalions, six were British, seven Gurkha, seven Malay, two King's African's Rifles and one Fiji. Particularly beginning in 1953, the reconstituted Special Air Service was especially effective in the jungle, and by 1955 and 1956, five SAS squadrons were conducting long-range patrols in the jungle, which often forced guerrillas into ambushes set by the Gurkhas or other troops. It was a Gurkha battalion, 1/10, which eventually achieved the highest number of CT kills for the war, with approximately three hundred. Supplementing the forty thousand regulars by 1954 were two hundred thousand in the Home Guard, handling most static security duties.

As free elections approached in 1955, Templer turned military power over to Lt-General Sir Geoffrey Bourne, and civil power over to Sir Donald MacGillivray. As expected, the elections were won by Prime Minister Tunku Abdul Rahman's Triple Alliance Party. This party, representing all three races of Malaya, offered Chen Ping an amnesty, but he was unwilling to come to terms without political recognition. Another indication that the campaign against the guerrillas was being won was implementation of Templer's 'White Areas' plan, in which those portions of the country free of guerrillas had curfews, checkpoints etc. removed and were allowed to resume a normal existence. By mid-1955, half of the country had been declared 'white', allowing security forces to concentrate on the remainder of the country.

On 31 August 1957 the complete handover of authority to the elected government took place, though British security forces remained to combat the approximately two thousand CTs still at large, primarily in Jahore. So successful were they that by the end of 1958 only about 250 CTs remained in the field, and the campaign was virtually won, though the final CTs did not give up until 1960. Even at that point, about five hundred hard core remained just across the border in Thailand, and some sympathizers remained in Malaya.

During the campaign, the guerrillas suffered 6,711 killed, 1,289 captured and 2,704 surrendered. Government forces lost 1,346 police killed and 519 military killed. As is unfortunately the case in guerrilla wars, many civilians were killed as well, 3,283.

Analysis of the Campaign

Various factors combined to allow the British to fight a successful counter-insurgency campaign in Malaya. First, geopolitical conditions favoured them, as there were no bordering states sympathetic to the guerrillas to give them a haven and a supply base. Additionally, during the most critical portion of the war, Communist China, which would have been the MCP's staunchest and nearest supporter, was preoccupied with the Korean War. These two factors, combined with effective Royal Navy coastal patrols, meant the guerrillas suffered a chronic shortage of arms and, eventually, food. The CTs suffered two other real weaknesses, in that they did not appeal to the bulk of the ethnic Malay population, as they were primarily Chinese-based, and the British had already promised independence, thus removing much of the support for an anti-colonial revolution. It should be noted, too, that the MCP never managed to get world opinion on their side.

On the government side, the use of air power for resupply and medevac allowed long-range jungle patrols to harry the CTs and prevent their entrenchment in safe areas. Realistic jungle training and the re-emergence of the SAS as a deep-patrolling counter-insurgency force proved an important aspect in defeating the guerrillas, too. The Briggs Plan was a key element, since it removed the 'sea' (as Mao referred to it) in which the guerrillas could swim. By establishing the New Villages, both the opportunity and the necessity for the Chinese peasants to support the guerrillas were removed, since they had the means and incentive to become supporters of the government.

The appointment of Templer as a 'Supremo' was critical, since it ensured the co-ordination of government and security forces policy against the CTs: the mailed fist of the military and police, and the velvet glove of the hearts and minds campaign. Even when the security forces got tough, however, it was with curfews and checkpoints, and not indiscriminate firepower, which could have alienated the very peasants they were trying to woo.

Notwithstanding its eventual failure, when the insurgency started, things did not look auspicious for the government, which through lack of timely action had allowed the insurgency to become established. Though the experience of jungle fighting in the Second World War was just behind them, the British military had already geared their thinking to a nuclear confrontation or an armoured war in Europe, and thus the lessons in jungle warfare, learned under General Slim and by such specialized deep penetration units as the Chindits, had to be relearned. The importance of intelligence in a counter-insurgency campaign had to be appreciated as well; and even once it was, it took Special Branch time to develop and cultivate sources. Eventually, however, the intelligence effort paid off, helping bring about the defeat of the CTs.

Many lessons were learned in Malaya, which would be important in future counter-insurgency campaigns: small, highly-trained units of the military or police are necessary to track down small, highly-mobile guerrilla units; properly used air-power can be very effective in a counter-guerrilla campaign, but it cannot substitute for good light infantrymen; intelligence is an absolute necessity; a 'Supremo' to ensure a co-ordinated effort against the insurgency is extremely important; the population must be won over to support the government, if guerrillas are to be defeated; the lack of a cross-border refuge can severely hinder, perhaps doom from the start, an insurgency.

SPECIAL AIR SERVICE TREE JUMPING TACTICS IN MALAYA

To enable SAS patrols to be inserted deep in the Malayan jungle, the tactic of 'tree jumping' was evolved. The country's heavy jungle canopy meant that on a jump, a goodly portion of any stick would end up in the trees surrounding the clearing chosen as the drop zone. As a result, SAS troopers began jumping with a hundred feet of rope, to lower themselves to the ground from any trees. It was soon discovered that those landing in trees suffered no appreciably higher degree of injury than those landing in cleared DZs; hence, since so much of the operations area was covered by tall trees with interlocking branches, it seemed logical to turn necessity into an advantage; jumps would now be made without even clearing a DZ, thus allowing the SAS to be jumped in virtually anywhere.

Although early jumps were made with a rope as the only additional piece of equipment, SAS soldiers such as Hugh Mercer, John Cooper and Alastair MacGregor experimented to develop the safest, most effective means of making operational jumps into trees. As a result of their experiments, a tree-jumping harness was developed and produced by prisoners in Singapore to the SAS's specifications. To perfect its use, a Bailey bridge was upended in Kuala Lumpur, to practise descents from the treetops. Though quite effective, this special harness and kit took rather more preparation prior to a jump, and about forty minutes was required to ready it for action.

The tree-jumping rig consisted of canvas 'bikini' shorts, adjusted by the jumper after they were donned, and a roll of webbed tape 240 feet long with a tensile strength of 1,000 lb. The tape was carried in the weapons container and passed through a steel ring on the front of the shorts, then threaded through a canvas tube around the waist of the shorts, then through the ring again. About six feet of tape was then pulled through and secured to the parachute harness.

After making the jump, and assuming the chute had caught in a tree, which it usually did, the six-foot length of tape was tied to a strong branch, and the remainder of the tape thrown to the ground. After lowering the weapons container to the ground, the parachutist would release himself from his parachute harness, thus leaving himself hanging by the tape. As he paid the tape out through the steel ring, he would slowly lower himself to the ground, the rate of descent controlled by the friction of the tape passing through the steel ring and canvas tube. Normally. light pressure with one hand was enough to control the rate of descent.

Once on the ground, the jumper would normally bury his rig, or otherwise destroy it so that it could not be used by the CTs in any way, then proceed on his patrol. For this reason, a new rig had to be prepared prior to each jump. A positive aspect of this was that the rig continued to evolve, incorporating improvements as needed. One design was considered, using rollers on the parachutist's chest slowly to lower the jumper to the ground even if he passed out from injuries after securing the tape.

Injury, of course, made the parachutist vulnerable to falling while lowering himself, but he was also vulnerable, since while he hung from the tree, his rifle, SMG or shotgun was in his weapon container. Should a CT come along, he was unarmed. As a result, there was a big demand for pistols among SAS tree jumpers.

Although this technique did prove relatively effective in Malaya, experience soon showed there really was more likelihood than initially thought of serious injury. By the end of the Malaya campaign, therefore, the SAS had virtually abandoned the technique, though tree jumping is still practised by special forces units as an option for clandestine insertion.

▶ An SAS tree jumper prepared for a jump in Malaya *(IWM)*

THE SPECIAL AIR SERVICE IN MALAYA

After an excellent record in North Africa and Europe during the Second World War, the Special Air Service had been disbanded at the war's end. However, in an attempt to keep some behind-the-lines raiding capability, a Territorial Army regiment had been formed, drawing on many SAS veterans, in 1947. Designated 21 SAS (Artists), this reserve unit would, in wartime, assume the SAS's traditional mission.

As the Emergency in Malaya drew more attention from Far East Command in 1950, 'Mad Mike' Calvert, a war veteran of Burma and the SAS, was sent out to evaluate the situation at first hand, often going out on patrols with the security forces or carrying out one-man patrols of his own. Calvert made a number of recommendations, many of which became key elements of the Briggs Plan, but he also suggested the formation of a penetration unit to harry the CTs in the deep jungle. As a result of this recommendation, and the success of Ferret Force, in 1951 he was asked to form such a unit for Malayan service. Calvert named his new unit the Malayan Scouts (SAS) and immediately set about recruiting jungle fighters, garnering veterans of SOE, SAS, Force 136, Ferret Force, even some French Foreign Legion deserters, but also recruits who would later prove to be undesirable. These initial hundred recruits formed A Squadron of the Malayan Scouts. B Squadron was composed of members of 21 SAS sent out to Malaya, though by some accounts they had initially been intended for service in Korea. C Squadron was recruited in Rhodesia, where there were 1,200 volunteers for one hundred places. Among those selected were two who would become famous in Rhodesia's own counter-insurgency war. Commanding C Squadron was Peter Walls, later to command all of Rhodesia's security forces, and serving in the ranks was Ron Reid-Daly, later to form and command the Selous Scouts.

To prepare his unit for close combat in the jungles, Calvert carried out very realistic training, using live grenades and live ammunition. To teach stalking skills, troops donned fencing masks to protect their eyes, and stalked each other through the jungle with air rifles. The sting of a pellet drove home the lessons of ambush and silent approach far better than hours of lectures. When the troops were ready they began carrying out patrols to scout and ambush the CTs. Eventually, SAS patrols would last over a hundred days, obviously destroying the myth that British soldiers could not operate for more than two weeks in the jungle. Other missions included river patrols, missions to protect and aid the aborigines, booby-trapping CT food caches, and rigging grenades and ammunition to explode prematurely.

The new unit proved successful, and in 1951 it was renamed 22 Special Air Service Regiment. Late in that year Calvert, suffering from illnesses contracted in the jungle, was replaced by Lt-Colonel John Sloane in command of the regiment. Under Sloane, jungle food denial operations became a high priority. During 1952 Major John Woodhouse was sent to the UK to formalize the selection and training procedure for recruits being sent out to the SAS. As the CTs were driven deeper into the jungle, the SAS found itself almost constantly in pursuit from 1953 on. In 1954 they worked extensively with aborigines deep in the jungle, aiding them medically and in defending themselves. In a traditional SAS role, they also proved invaluable at gathering intelligence from their aborigine friends and through their patrols. The Iban scouts brought in from Borneo were SAS trained, and achieved formal military status as the Sarawak Rangers.

Early January 1955 saw Lt-Colonel George Lea as the new regimental commander. Under Lea there were some changes in squadrons, C Squadron returning to Rhodesia to be replaced by a New Zealand squadron. In 1956 a squadron drawn from the Parachute Regiment was sent out as well, bringing SAS strength for the final eradication campaign to five squadrons with 560 men. The final SAS commander in Malaya was Lt-Colonel Anthony Deane-Drummond, who took over in 1958.

During nine years in Malaya, the SAS would account for 108 enemy killed and would gather much important intelligence. Their contribution was much greater than statistics can show. By remaining almost constantly deep in the jungles, the SAS maintained psychological pressure on the CTs, eventually contributing to the collapse of the insurgency. The SAS removed the last terrorist haven, and proved the British

could not only pursue them into the jungle but could become more adept at using it for ambush than the CTs.

Even more important for the future of British counter-insurgency and counter-terrorist capability, 22 Special Air Service Regiment proved itself in Malaya and was added as a regular regiment in the British Army.

▲ Member of the Special Air Service with his kit laid out for inspection, prior to a patrol in Malaya *(IWM)*

PATROL TACTICS IN MALAYA

Patrolling in Malaya, as in most types of conflict, had as its aim finding, fixing and destroying. The 'fan patrol' was widely used in Malaya, patrols of three or four men moving out from their base on set compass bearings, much like the ribs of a fan. The spacing between the ribs of the fan could be varied, but ten degrees was fairly standard. Thickness of undergrowth normally determined how far out the patrol would move; in very thick jungle, one thousand yards would be about maximum, while in less dense areas, patrols might move out to two thousand yards. Since patrols normally moved carefully and quietly to avoid alerting CTs, time rather than distance often determined how far they would move out; three hours was found to be about the maximum for operating at greatest efficiency. Once a fan patrol had reached its maximum distance or time allotment, it usually moved a few degrees to the right or left to return to base.

In an area with running water, the 'stream' method of patrolling was often used. Since the CTs frequently located their bases near streams, this method of patrolling was based on the banks of streams, a three- or four-man patrol moving up one bank and back down the other. Because maps were not always accurate in showing the tracks of streams, caution had to be used so patrols did not become involved in firefights with each other.

Whichever type of patrolling was used, the unit commander would keep a reserve at the base to act as a reaction force should one of his patrols encounter the CTs. He would also maintain radio communications with his company commander so that reinforcements could be rushed in should a really large enemy concentration be encountered. Standard operational procedure if a contact was made was for one or two troops to return to the base to alert the platoon commander, while the other two men maintained a watch on the CT camp, if possible gathering intelligence on the camp layout and the number of CTs there. Once the platoon commander had been alerted, he would leave a small security force at the camp and with his reaction force quietly join the scouts watching the CTs. He would then carry out his own recce and decide whether to attack the camp or call for additional reinforcements.

Should he decide to attack he would assign an assault force of about five to eight men plus himself, while the remainder of his available troops would be positioned as 'stop' groups to cover likely escape routes. Once the stop groups were in position, the platoon leader would move his assault group into the camp quickly, taking any enemy or bashas under heavy fire, thus inflicting casualties and driving survivors into the stop groups.

8 KENYA, CYPRUS AND CUBA

While France fought a losing battle against insurgents in Indochina, and Great Britain fought a winning campaign in Malaya, three other counter-insurgencies offering important lessons were being waged, on the African continent and on two islands, one in the Mediterranean and one in the Caribbean.

THE CAMPAIGN AGAINST THE MAU MAU IN KENYA

Although the Mau Mau atrocities should certainly be viewed with abhorrence, there was one 'refreshing' aspect to the Mau Mau rebellion: it had virtually no basis in Communism. Admittedly, Jomo Kenyatta, a leader closely associated with the Mau Mau, had spent time in the Soviet Union and been influenced at least nominally by Marxism, but the Mau Mau movement was primarily a cult, tribally based on the Kikuyu.

The Kikuyu had harboured many grievances since the British arrival in their land around the turn of the century. Their bitterness over European appropriation of the best land, while ninety-seven per cent of the population of Kenya was African, was the basis of anti-colonial sentiment, though lack of African political representation was certainly another aspect. The Kikuyu were a particularly intelligent, sophisticated tribe, which made them the most likely source of recruitment for an insurgency, as resentment grew against the virtually total European control of their country. Many African ex-servicemen who had seen war service with the British Army returned to Kenya and joined the Kikuyu Central Association, a more overt political action group.

Membership in the KCA grew rapidly after the war's end, due to conditions which were almost certain to fuel an insurgency: racial separation; a dire need for land and economic reform; vast social divisions; lack of political representation; and a poor transportation and communications network. In 1947, Kenyatta became president of the Kenya African Union, a cover for the KCA, and began making inflammatory speeches. Mau Mau activities were first reported in 1948, this development resulting in the Mau Mau being termed an illegal organization by 1950.

To exacerbate an already bad situation, the governor, Sir Philip Mitchell, was an old-style colonialist who believed that there was indeed a white man's burden, and it was caring for the Africans in Kenya, whose natural inferiority meant they were incapable of ruling themselves. Though the Mau Mau began attacking government arsenals to acquire arms and ammunition, Mitchell did not order security to be substantially tightened, nor did he increase the Police Special Branch, his only real source of intelligence. Thus, the government had little real knowledge of the Mau Mau, who were allowed to recruit and propagandize virtually unhindered. The Mau Mau, on the other hand, had a fine intelligence network, based on sympathizers working for the Europeans. Recruitment at this stage went very well, as the Mau Mau based much of their appeal on land reform and independence, both just causes. Another grievance they played upon was the government-appointed chiefs, who normally lacked public support. Such chiefs would be among their first targets when they began using overt violence.

By mid-1952, having grown to about 250,000 members, the Mau Mau began burning the huts of African officials, and the fields of European settlers. Arson was not only destructive but allowed easy escape and appealed to the ritualistic nature of the Mau Mau. By 1952, too, the Mau Mau oath had been altered to include a promise to kill if so ordered, a promise some had kept against fellow Africans by that autumn.

Around this time a new governor, Sir Evelyn Baring, arrived and declared a State of Emergency. Additional troops were sent to support the three battalions of the King's African Rifles already in Kenya. Mau Mau attacks escalated, however, and about two weeks after the declaration, the first European farmer was killed. Attacks against both Africans and Europeans now increased, with mutilation often a hallmark. It should be noted, by the way, that these mutilations, at least to some extent, were the result of lack of firearms and the resultant use of the panga as the Mau Mau's primary weapon. Showing the adaptability and heartiness that had allowed them to thrive in Kenya in the first place, the white farmers proved adept at developing relatively effective local defences, often eating and sleeping with a pistol near at hand, since a favourite Mau Mau tactic was to gain admittance from an African house servant and come rushing in, slashing with their pangas.

Baring took some important steps, augmenting the police with the Army and upgrading Special Branch to increase his intelligence capability. Even more important was the formation of the Kikuyu Home Guard, which proved effective because it knew the area and knew the Mau Mau, eroding the base of Mau Mau support by drawing from the same tribe and thus turning the fight into a more personal matter.

Despite these important steps, at this point the Mau Mau were still able to thrive in natural sanctuaries such as Mt Kenya and the Aberdare Range which bordered the African Reserve, thus having easy access to food and support. To counter the growing Mau Mau bands, the Kenya Police were augmented by the Kenya Police Reserve drawn from local whites, some of whom committed atrocities of their own, and by the Tribal Police, who were Africans under the local white district officer. British troops supporting the police did not speak Swahili and were widely dispersed, initially inhibiting their effectiveness, though they did offer a counter to really large Mau Mau bands.

In a move to eliminate the Mau Mau leadership, Kenyatta and his primary subordinates were arrested and deported, but this failed to stop the violence. In fact, in one way it escalated it, by allowing lower level but more militant leaders to take over. As a result, during 1953, attacks against Europeans and loyal Africans increased, the massacre of eighty-four loyal Kikuyu at the village of Lari in March by one thousand Mau Mau being one particular atrocity. This massacre backfired on the Mau Mau, as it both hardened government resolve and alienated many former supporters of the Mau Mau.

At their peak, the Mau Mau fielded somewhere between twelve thousand and fifteen thousand fighters, supported by villagers and residents of Nairobi. As the government instituted more effective countermeasures, however, these numbers shrank. The administration of the Mau Mau oath, for example, was made a capital offence, while curfews, restrictions on movement, and an anti-Mau Mau propaganda campaign were designed to deny the insurgents support. Many forested areas – which were Mau Mau refuges – were declared free-fire zones where anyone encountered could be shot.

To co-ordinate the counter-insurgency campaign more effectively, Maj.-General W. R. N. Hinde was brought in as a military adviser to the governor, after a few weeks being made Director of Operations. Though Mau Mau attacks persisted, their brutality was turning much of the African population against them. Under General Sir George Erskine, more troops arrived, too. Hinde was named second in command to Erskine, who took the effective step of clearing a one-mile strip between the forest and the African reserve and putting police stations between the two as a buffer – what the French would have termed a *cordon sanitaire*. Initially, under Erskine, the Army tried large-scale sweeps, which were not very successful since it was so obvious to the Mau Mau when the Army was coming. As has been shown in previous chapters, small, mobile patrols are much more successful, a fact Erskine soon discerned as well. The use of light aircraft as spotters for these small patrols proved effective too.

As a result of the erosion of Mau Mau support, aggressive patrolling and improved intelligence, by late 1953 the government was gaining control of the situation. The capture early in 1954 of 'General China', a principal Mau Mau leader, disclosed crucial intelligence when he cracked under interrogation. The establishment in March 1954 of an efficient War Cabinet, consisting of the Governor, Deputy Governor, Commander in Chief and Chairman of the European Committee, was another key step in reducing the Mau Mau threat.

To remove much of the Mau Mau base of support, in the spring of 1954, thousands of suspects were put in detention camps. Most importantly, though, Nairobi was cordoned and searched, identity cards being issued to all inhabitants as part of Operation Anvil. This operation not only broke Mau Mau power in the city, but cut them off from their primary intelligence sources. Many believe, in fact, that Anvil was the campaign's turning point.

That same year the most effective counter-guerrilla tactic of the war was launched, the creation of pseudo-terrorist gangs operating in the forest. Composed of turned Mau Mau, loyal Kikuyu and a few Europeans with blacked faces and bulky clothing, these gangs not only accounted for many Mau Mau killed or captured, but undermined their confidence in each other. In the buffer zone between reserve and forest, sharp stakes and barbed wire were added to separate the Mau Mau from their supporters. The food denial programme was stepped up as well. Graphically illustrating how public opinion had changed, a large portion of the population voluntarily became involved in clearing portions of the jungle. The security forces helped make Mau Mau life even harder, mixing aggressive patrols with ambushes.

With better intelligence, sweeps grew more successful, while the pseudo gangs not only produced kills, but also many intelligence windfalls. As a result of increased government success and the increased support of the government's measures by the African population, the Mau Mau threat was almost over, though mopping up continued over the next few years. Note, however, that although the Mau Mau had been defeated, their goals of independence and land reform were nevertheless soon accomplished, and within a few years Jomo Kenyatta was President of Kenya.

Analysis

The Mau Mau suffered from many weaknesses which prevented them from ever becoming a true threat to the government. Mau Mau influence never really affected more than twenty per cent of the population, or ten per cent of Kenya's land area; therefore, the insurgency was relatively easy to contain, particularly as it had no support outside the country. Mau Mau strategy was nebulous at best, too: they never really attacked the communications or infrastructure of the country. As a result, power stations, railways, bridges and European officials were all safe. The Mau Mau lacked leadership, weapons and external support; all normally important elements for a successful insurgency. Nevertheless, they did gain substantial political power for the Kikuyu, and cost the government £55 million to combat them. During the campaign, the security forces suffered 1,169 casualties, civilians 2,846, and the Mau Mau 16,802.

In addition to the Mau Mau weaknesses, astute British use of pseudo gangs, combined with small unit patrols and denial of food and support, defeated the insurgents.

THE USE OF PSEUDO GANGS AGAINST THE MAU MAU

Particularly in the later stages of the Kenyan counter-insurgency campaign, use by Special Branch of pseudo gangs to infiltrate and then kill or capture roving bands of terrorists proved particularly effective. Initially, these pseudo gangs had been formed to gain intelligence within the Reserves but they evolved into fighting groups as well. Led by European officers in black face make-up, they were able to get close enough to the enemy to kill or capture them. Such pseudo groups were composed of loyal Kikuyu, sometimes drawn from tribal police or regular constables, white officers, and turned Mau Mau. The latter were most important for lending credibility, since they knew the latest secret signs, finger snaps, oaths, etc., with which to convince the Mau Mau of their authenticity.

Their white officers trained turned Mau Mau in the use of small arms and grenades and in close combat, and in return learned about the Mau Mau and bushcraft. When operating with the pseudos, the European officers used potassium permanganate solution to give their skin the right colour. Eventually, as the Mau Mau learned of the existence of these pseudo gangs, it was often necessary for European officers to paint their entire bodies, in case a shirt was suddenly jerked up to look for white skin. A weaker potassium permanganate solution was also used to give their eyes the proper yellow coloration. The hair was normally the most obvious giveaway for white pseudos, and though they tried using floppy hats, eventually many used wigs, often obtained from the hair of dead terrorists. So they would not give away their group, Europeans had to learn to squat, eat, take snuff, and in general act as genuine Mau Mau. To get the proper look and smell they wore captured Mau Mau clothing, and did not wash. Even so, each white in a pseudo group had a cover man or bodyguard, whose primary job was to draw attention away from him.

Like the gangs, the pseudos would call at villages at night for food, but in the process would gain information. The night hours offered the advantage of making it easier for the Europeans to escape notice, but it was also the time when the real Mau Mau came. Often the information they gained about Mau Mau gangs would be passed to tracker-combat teams consisting of three Europeans, fifteen African constables, and a Wanderobo tracker, but in some cases the pseudo gangs would follow up their own leads by merging with other gangs before arresting or ambushing them. As might be expected, the pseudo gangs had to be very careful not to get into firefights with the security forces.

The system of using turned Mau Mau in this way worked, and throughout the pseudo operations there were virtually no instances of converts going back over to the Mau Mau. Normally, pseudo gangs consisted of eight to ten, often with one or two women members, since real Mau Mau gangs had female members. In general, pseudos did not receive pay, but many shared rewards for the terrorists they had accounted for. Such pseudo operations were not new, but it was in Kenya that they were formalized into a highly successful counter-insurgent tactic. Later in Rhodesia, the Selous Scouts would perfect the technique.

CYPRUS

Due to Cyprus's important strategic position, Great Britain had no immediate plans for granting independence after the Second World War, and indeed there was no real movement on the island for independence. Instead, the Greek majority – about eighty per cent of the island's population of 520,000 – wanted union with Greece. The Turkish minority wished to remain under British control. The Greek insurgency, therefore, was a nationalist one based on ethnic background, and as in Kenya there was little basis in Communism. There had been a previous short-lived Greek insurgency in 1931, but though it had been crushed its roots had endured.

The spiritual and political leader of the Greek Cypriots was Archbishop Makarios of the Greek Orthodox Church, but to lead the fight for *Enosis*, union with Greece, he chose George Grivas, a Cypriot who had served as an officer in the Greek Army during the Greek Civil War, then later studied Communist insurgent tactics. In 1951, Makarios put Grivas in charge of the Cypriot military campaign against the British. Grivas realized early on that Cyprus, having little rough terrain and an extensive road network allowing rapid troop movement, offered little scope for guerrilla warfare. He also realized that Cyprus, as an island, could be easily isolated by a British naval blockade. He therefore concluded that a campaign based on sabotage and swaying public opinion would be his only chance of success. Thus decided, he spent the next three years in Athens gathering arms and smuggling them to Cyprus, as well as building support in Greece. Even after three years, however, he had less than a hundred guns in the country when he returned to begin training a few selected guerrillas as the basis for *Ethniki Organosis Kyprion Agoniston* (EOKA).

Grivas began the insurgency in April 1955 with widespread bombings and attacks against the police, but Britain continued to ignore the broad-based desire for Enosis among Greek Cypriots. Bombings would prove so much a part of the EOKA campaign that by the time fighting had ceased, EOKA had placed 4,758 bombs, 2,976 of which either did not explode or were discovered. Thoughout that spring, student demonstrations intermixed with acts of terrorism continued. The greatest problem the British faced was the open hostility of the population, who would not co-operate at all with the security forces. EOKA for the most part, followed Mao's precepts in dealing with the people, thus retaining their support. Under strength and not trained for dealing with widespread terrorism, the police force was initially overwhelmed.

In October 1955, Field Marshal Sir John Harding was named the new governor of the island, empowered to negotiate with Archbishop Makarios and also to use military force against EOKA. Initially, Harding took the important step of organizing the colonial administration, police and military under one security force command, as had proved successful in Malaya, then setting up a unified intelligence force. Talks with Makarios continued until February 1956, when they broke off, and the Archbishop was arrested and deported to the Seychelles Islands. Grivas became the movement's political leader by default.

That month also saw the arrival of one of Britain's most effective military units, the 16th Independent Parachute Brigade, on the island. At this point Grivas had about 275 fighters with about a hundred weapons, plus about 750 villagers who were part of OKT, Grivas's ambush team. Harding still did not realize the depth of support for EOKA, but he declared a State of Emergency, including severe edicts such as the death penalty for possession of a firearm, detention without trial, powers of banishment, and rewards for information on wanted terrorists. These measures, as well as collective punishments such as curfews, community fines, and searches during which the population was humiliated and insulted, turned the Greek population against the security forces even more. When two terrorists were executed in spring 1956, Grivas retaliated by kidnapping and executing two soldiers.

With almost three hundred hard-core terrorists based in the Troodos Mountains and towns, Grivas's power was at its peak. In June 1956 Operation Pepperpot was launched to cordon off the mountains and search them. Twenty terrorists were captured during the sweeps, Grivas himself barely evading capture. Pepperpot was successful enough to force Grivas to change his strategy from one of guerrilla warfare to one of urban terrorism. As acts of violence by EOKA increased, and as the hostility of the population grew, some British troops committed violent acts against suspected terrorists. However, the Greek policy of constantly 'crying wolf' about security forces' abuse backfired in this case, since such reports were normally discounted. Turkish members of Special Branch were also known for a willingness to use torture to obtain information from Greek Cypriot prisoners.

Overall, however, the intelligence situation was bleak. British conscript troops showed little enthusiasm for being on Cyprus, and Harding remained inflexible, using large troop concentrations against small, elusive EOKA bands. EOKA attacks against the Turks resulted in a backlash as well, as *Volkan*, a Turkish reprisal group, was formed. In 1957, Sir Hugh Foot replaced Harding. More a diplomat than a soldier, he negotiated for Cypriot independence throughout the year, with intermittent terrorist incidents highlighting the need for a solution. In 1958, Grivas switched to a 'passive resistance' strategy, theoretically based on Gandhi's successes in India.

Finally, early in 1959, Grivas agreed to a cease-fire, disbanded EOKA, and returned to Greece a hero; Archbishop Makarios returned from exile, to lead the Greek Cypriot community. However, the Cyprus situation was not really resolved, thus setting the stage for the later civil war.

Analysis

Throughout their campaign against EOKA, the British lacked clear-cut political aims and thus were fighting a holding action. Lack of intelligence allowed Grivas to remain at large with most of his fighters throughout the campaign, since checkpoints, patrols, and cordon and search operations, though of value, could not compensate for the lack of community support. EOKA suffered disadvantages in the campaign as well, since Greece was never willing to give its full support to the insurgency for fear of damaging relations with Great Britain. Grivas found, too, that the Cypriots were not particularly warlike. Grivas's strong political support was invaluable, but it also proved to be the downfall of his insurgency when Archbishop Makarios decided to accept independence, rather than the *Enosis* Grivas had campaigned for. Finally, Cyprus's small size, and the shortage of large wild areas, meant there were few places in which guerrilla forces could be concealed. On the other hand, the geography of Cyprus also made it difficult for the security forces to isolate the population from the guerrillas, as they had done in Malaya and Kenya. While the campaigns in Malaya and Kenya had ended in the defeat of the insurgents, Cyprus was at best a draw, and had shown what a relatively small number of urban guerrillas could accomplish.

CUBA

Although Fidel Castro and Che Guevara attempted to create a revolutionary folk myth about the Cuban revolution being the ultimate people's war, it was actually an insurgency heavily dependent on the middle class, rather than the peasants it later purported to have served. In fact, the myths surrounding the Cuban revolution and Fidel Castro, important elements in the attempts by Cuba to export revolution along with sugar cane over the last three decades, have come to be much more important than fact.

When Castro launched his first attempt to seize power, on 26 July 1953 against a military post in Oriente Province, he was easily defeated, although the date was to lend its name to his future movement.

At the time, the Cuban economy was heavily dependent upon sugar; the large sugar companies exercised substantial control over all aspects of Cuban life. Much industry and many utilities were owned by United States interests, offering a convenient 'anti-imperialist' rallying point. The ruling Batista government, though better than some other Latin American governments, was corrupt and had not addressed the need for land reform and education for the rural peasants. Additionally, there were many unemployed intellectuals, dissatisfied and looking for a cause. Initially, Castro's 26 July Movement (later to be called the M-26 Movement) was only one – and a minor one – of various dissident student or labour groups.

Contrary to Mao's revolutionary precepts, the Cuban revolution was not based on the rural peasants, but upon the urban middle class. Leadership throughout the revolution would be drawn from the intelligentsia; Castro himself was a lawyer, while Che Guevara was an Argentine physician. Castro had grown up in Oriente Province, and he based his revolution in this rural area, where the peasants became an important source of food, intelligence and recruits. Throughout the country, there were at least 500,000 destitute peasants, whose support Castro would seek.

Though wooing the peasants, Castro was careful not to alienate the middle class, realizing that they could be a useful source of financial support. His calls for land reform, tax reform, education for all, medical care and public works had a broad-based appeal.

Early in his revolution Castro began establishing agents throughout Latin America. His own supporters were initially trained in Mexico by Colonel Alberto Bayo, a Republican veteran of the Spanish Civil War. It was at Bayo's training camp that Castro first met Che Guevara, who was appointed medical officer for the revolutionary army.

When Castro and his forces left Mexico and landed in Cuba in 1956, he expected a mass uprising to break out in support; when this didn't materialize, he took a hard core of followers to the mountains and began a campaign of subversion, terror and propaganda. This highly successful propaganda offensive stressed that Batista had seized power illegally, consolidated it with illegal elections, had no desire to help the poor, and was encouraging vices such as prostitution and gambling. Prior to 1957, Batista's control of the news media limited widespread dissemination of pro-Castro propaganda. The broadcast of news of Castro's supposed death in 1956 discredited the media, however, and Castro was 'resurrected' as a folk hero.

Castro's machismo and public image stood him in good stead at home and abroad. Foreign correspondents, particularly from the US, were captivated by him and wrote laudatory stories, while criticizing the corruption of the Batista regime. Castro frequently lived up to or surpassed his image, too. For example, unlike the stereotypical Latin American guerrilla with a sub-machine gun, he carried a scoped Winchester Model 70 rifle which he could fire quite well, once personally disrupting an attack by killing a government radio operator with a head shot. His group's considerate treatment of captured government troops was another form of propaganda.

When Castro arrived in Oriente Province in 1957, he had eighty-three hard-core followers. However, his M-26 Movement grew in many ways. That year, for example, it merged with the Civic Resistance Movement which, though less radical, had substantial support. It was Castro, the military leader in the field, with his thirty- to forty-man platoons, often broken down to ten- or fifteen-man squads in inhospitable terrain, who captured the public imagination. Castro proved an able organizer as well, as his influence spread, even organizing collective farms and cottage industries to support his revolutionary army.

By mid-1957, Castro's guerrilla base in the Sierra Maestra was secure, allowing additional recruits to be trained there. Initially, the highly competent Colonel Berrera Perez commanded the government forces in Oriente Province; however, just as Perez's pacification campaign was showing some signs of success, he was removed from command due to jealousies within Batista's corrupt command structure. Removal of competent commanders such as Perez, as well as the excesses of Batista's *Servicio de Intelligern Militar* (SIM) soon disillusioned most of the Army, causing entire units to go over to the rebels. Though some arms were smuggled into Cuba, far more were either captured, or surrendered by defecting government troops.

When large sweeps by Batista's army failed to neutralize the threat posed by Castro and his men in the summer of 1957, the government switched to a containment policy, and cordoned off the Sierra Maestra. However, Castro, now with about 175 fighters, launched hit-and-run raids, sabotaged communication lines, attacked small garrisons, and ambushed patrols; by 1958 Batista's forces were incapable of containing him or of protecting their own communication lines. When larger operations were launched against him, Castro's forces made use of the scoped long-range rifles they had brought with them when they landed, picking off the point man. Lacking trained light, mobile counter-insurgency forces, the Cuban Army attempted unsuccessfully to use conventional tactics.

As US support for Batista waned during 1958, Castro's popularity in the US and at home grew, and by late 1958 he had about a thousand troops in the field, including a second group under his brother Raul Castro in the Sierra del Cristel. By splitting his forces in this way Castro had placed his brother in an excellent position to harass the rear of any forces sent against himself, and similarly he was able to harass any forces sent against Raul.

While Castro's strength in the field grew, his supporters in the cities staged strikes and demonstrations, and sabotaged utilities and public buildings. Sugar plantations were also burned. Tired of the fighting, many influential Cubans were asking Batista to step down, but he refused. In March 1958, Castro nearly overstepped himself with a general strike, but the Communists, always a powerful force in the unions, opposed him. Had the government acted decisively after this failure, there is some chance they could have regained much lost ground. But by the time they launched a ponderous offensive in May, Castro's prestige had already recovered. This offensive was eventually brought to an unsuccessful close by the onset of the rainy Caribbean hurricane season.

Castro did not remain passive, though, increasing his undeclared war of sabotage and terrorism and gaining a powerful ally in the summer of 1958 when the Communists committed themselves to supporting him. In frustration, Batista's security forces became brutal, progressively alienating even more of the population. Now approaching the stage of moving out of the mountains and defeating the Cuban Army in the field, the revolutionaries were augmented by increasing numbers of regular units coming over to them without a shot being fired. Finally, Batista resigned, allowing Castro's supporters to seize Havana on 1 January 1959. A week later Fidel Castro entered the capital in triumph after a victory tour of the island.

Analysis and Consequences

One of the most important lessons to be learned from the Cuban revolution is the critical importance the cult of personality can play in an insurgency. Fidel Castro played masterfully upon the Latin-American love of machismo, just as he portrayed the romantic guerrilla-leader-in-the-hills for US correspondents, always making sure that the social reform aspects of his revolution were emphasized. So skilled has Castro been at projecting a desired image, that despite the middle-class basis of his M-26 movement, his revolution has come to be viewed throughout the Third World as the classic example of a people's war.

Batista faced some extreme difficulties in combating Castro, not the least of which was that he could never match Castro's public appeal. Additionally, widespread corruption in the Army limited its effectiveness, as many high-ranking officers actually did not want to see Castro defeated, since his presence meant larger military appropriations to skim from. Foreign domination of the Cuban economy gave Castro an excellent rallying point in his appeal to the people. It was the nationalization of foreign companies, which were primarily American owned, that led to the strong anti-Castro US foreign policy, which soon drove him into the Soviet sphere, bringing the two superpowers near to war during the Cuban missile crisis in the early sixties.

Shortly after gaining power, Castro and Che

began planning to export their revolution throughout Latin America. In his book *Guerrilla Warfare*, Che hypothesized that people's war would soon erupt throughout the Southern Hemisphere, with the Andes being the base for revolution in Latin America. He emphasized three primary lessons about people's war: 1. a popular force can defeat established governments; 2. the countryside is the necessary base for guerrillas; 3. insurgents do not have to wait for the perfect moment to act, but can seize the initiative and make their own opportunity. Despite its wide appeal among American student radicals of the 1960s, there is nothing particularly profound in Che's work: it certainly is not as important as Mao's writings on the same subject. Nevertheless, it did offer a ready treatise in Spanish on insurgency, and played its part in developing the tactics used by the urban and rural guerrillas which have plagued Latin America for the last three decades.

After falling out with Castro, partly over his mishandling of his position as Minister of Industry, Che was sent to various countries as a sort of ambassador of revolution. In a preview of future Cuban activities in Angola and Mozambique, Che led the first export of Cubans to Africa when he took 125 'volunteers' to the Congo in 1965. The next year, in November, he took twenty more Cubans to Bolivia, where he attempted to foment revolution. Considering his status as the supposed guru of guerrilla warfare in Latin America, however, he proved remarkably unsuccessful. The local Indians were especially suspicious of outsiders, particularly this Argentine/Cuban, and offered him little support. On the contrary, they staunchly supported the government forces, which were basically a peasant Army, once again illustrating the usefulness of having an Army which reflects the population it protects. In October 1967, Bolivian Rangers, trained by the US Army Special Forces, hunted down Che and killed him.

Though Castro's posturing and attempts to export his revolution have made him a bogeyman to the US government for more than a quarter of a century, his very love of playing to the press proved unwise, since his declaration of a master plan to spread revolution served to alert the United States and Latin American governments, which then prepared to counter him. The development of the US counter-insurgency capability, in fact, received a substantial impetus from Castro's bellicose pronouncements.

9 ALGERIA

Even before the fall of Dien Bien Phu, events in Algeria were transpiring which would lead France into another counter-insurgency campaign.

Circumstances in Algeria had certain similarities to those in Kenya, in that the roots of insurrection could be traced to a minority of European colons who, along with a very small minority of Muslims, dominated the colonial government and land ownership. Of all the major French possessions in North Africa, Algeria was the one most closely related to France, even being considered a part of metropolitan France. As a result, though Morocco and Tunisia would receive independence in 1956, Algeria did not. The Algerian insurrection certainly did not spring into existence without precedent either. The French Foreign Legion had made a career of counter-guerrilla warfare in Algeria and Morocco, and various nationalist and Communist movements had existed in Algeria throughout the twentieth century.

The PPA (*Parti du Peuple Algerien*) was one of the more militant of these movements and on VE Day, 8 May 1945, instigated riots that caused the deaths of up to a hundred Europeans. In retaliation, European 'militias' attacked Muslim settlements, killing between twenty-five and forty-five thousand. Two nationalist parties – UDMA (*Union Democratique du Manifeste Algerian*) and MTLD (*Movement pour le Triomphe des Libertés Democratiques*), attempted a political solution in the later 1940s. The MTLD, it should be noted, was linked to the PPA.

The French government offered some reforms, but they contained little of real substance, and the European and Muslim élite retained power over the vast Muslim majority. The fall of France in the Second World War, however, had shown French weakness, and many returning veterans who had fought for France in Algerian regiments expected to find reforms. One of these ex-soldiers, Ben Bella, formed a militant group known as OS (*Organisation Secrete*), which split from the MTLD in 1947. Bella proved an astute student of guerrilla warfare, drawing on Mao, Sinn Fein, and Tito's partisans for inspiration, fielding five hundred trained guerrillas by early 1950. Bella also allied with other guerrillas under Belkacem Krim operating in Kabylie.

The OS started its overt operations in 1949 by robbing the Oran post office of over three million francs. As a result of a crackdown in the wake of this operation, however, Ben Bella and others were arrested and imprisoned. Some of Bella's main followers escaped to Cairo, though, where he joined them in 1952 after escaping from prison.

Early in 1954 the OS was reformed as the CRUA (*Comité Revolutionnaire pour l'Unité et l'Action*). Ben Bella and a few others remained in Cairo to organize support, while the remainder of the leadership returned to Algeria to organize active guerrilla groups. Initially, they divided the country into six *wilayas*, each under a Bella lieutenant. In October that year, no doubt partly influenced by French failure in Indochina, these leaders decided to resort to force.

Conditions for a popular rebellion were ripe, too. Ninety per cent of the country's wealth was owned by only ten per cent of the population; about one million Muslims were unemployed, while most others worked for starvation wages; eighty per cent of Muslims received no education at all. When any reforms were attempted, they were sabotaged by the colons, who wanted to retain the status quo and, hence, their position. The unstable post-war governments in France certainly didn't help either as they constantly lacked the power to take decisive action. Finally, the colons were so contemptuous of the Muslims that they didn't really take the nationalist movements seriously.

On 1 November 1954, thousands of guerrillas struck at over thirty targets, primarily gendarmerie posts in eastern Algeria. Simultaneously, they distributed fliers for the FLN (*Forces de Libération Nationale*), the latest incarnation of the OS. Surprisingly for a militant organization, the fliers were quite reasonable, asking for independence, while guaranteeing that colons would retain their land and France would retain a special relationship with Algeria. The fliers were ignored, however, and the French sent

◀ Members of the 2nd REP practising reaction shooting with the MAT-49 SMG. A good close quarters weapon for counter-insurgency usage, the MAT-49 has seen wide service in French counter-guerrilla operations throughout Africa (*J. Hon*)

6e REGIM
MAC
D'INF
ÊTRE ET

NT DE PARACHUTIST
CROIRE
NTERIE DE
ne COMPAGNIE

armoured columns towards the Aures Mountains to eliminate the rebels, while three parachute battalions were rushed from France as reinforcements. The police over-reacted, arresting Muslims indiscriminately; often these were moderates, who changed to militants while in custody. The armoured thrusts, as might be expected, proved futile against irregular bands unwilling to stand and fight. Now committed, the FLN launched a campaign of terror against Muslim moderates, forcing many to join their cause.

The rebellion spread and by April 1955 Governor-General Jacques Soustelle had declared a limited emergency. Still hampered by the colons in attempts at reform, he did manage to establish *Sections Administratives Spécialisées* (SAS), which sent French officers to remote areas as administrators. Use of the SAS initials was probably not accidental, since the French Special Air Service in the Second World War had established a proud reputation within France. When a new wave of FLN terrorism erupted in August 1955, Soustelle slid from moderation towards a harder line. France had hoped to avoid internationalization of the Algerian issue, but African and Asian countries brought the situation up in the UN, and moderate Algerians published a manifesto which affected public opinion within France. Meanwhile, FLN was receiving active support and arms from the Arab League.

Already well on their way to creating a public relations disaster, the Army and police handled things ineptly, with indiscriminate arrests, destruction of villages, and brutal use of torture during interrogations. Such tactics, of course, made the Army and police the best recruiters for FLN, which continued to gain support. Even as French troop commitments grew, garrisoning towns left insufficient manpower for sweeps or cordons. Recalcitrance on the part of the colons, and the unwillingness of the French government to offend them, made a negotiated solution ever less likely. Colon arrogance increased even more when they won a victory over the French government in 1956, over the appointment of General Georges Catroux as the new governor-general. So violently did the colons oppose his appointment that the French government gave in, and named the more palatable Robert Lacoste as governor-general; however, this capitulation by the French government caused many moderate Muslims to give up hope of a negotiated solution and turn to the FLN. The French Premier, Guy Mollet, compounded the problem by remaining ignorant of the issues behind the Algerian revolt.

In the wake of their defeat in Indochina, the French Army had developed a counter-revolutionary method based on a 'dynamic strategy' of indoctrinating soldiers and populace with counter-revolutionary beliefs. Unfortunately, with typical French ethnocentricism, this approach ignored the fact that virtually all Muslims in Algeria had a strong desire for independence. It should be noted as well that this doctrine took on Fascist end-justifies-the-means overtones when put into practice.

When the Army executed two terrorists in March 1956, the FLN responded by killing Europeans. Other events that year combined to help the FLN cause as well. Morocco and Tunisia on Algeria's borders, now independent, offered sanctuaries and sources of arms, while the Suez campaign in the summer drew away French troops, and in the aftermath eroded French prestige even more. Even the arrest of Ben Bella later in the year backfired, as it took place while he was under the protection of the Sultan of Morocco and thus offended this influential leader. By the end of 1956 the FLN had about eighty-five thousand guerrillas in the field, supported by over twenty thousand auxiliaries. To oppose them, the French Army had about four hundred thousand troops, mostly tied to static garrison duty.

Everything certainly wasn't going all the FLN's way, as there were divisions within the movement as well as among other nationalist groups. Additionally, communication with the leadership in Cairo was taking up to three months, and tribal rivalries still took precedence over FLN aims, particularly in more isolated areas. As a result of this lack of cohesion, the French Army inflicted heavy losses on isolated groups, killing fourteen thousand guerrillas during 1956.

In August 1956, Ramdane Abbane, a dynamic young leader, began challenging for control of the FLN at a conference of rebel leaders. Once he had gained control, he established a new internal leadership in the *Conseil National de la Revolution Algérienne* (CNRA). Even more militant than the previous leadership, Abbane began pushing for an all-out urban terrorist campaign.

As a result of this campaign, Lacoste was forced to turn the pacification of Algeria over to Maj-General Jacques Massu, the tough commander of the 10th Parachute Division. In January 1957 the Battle of Algiers began. Living in the warrens of the Casbah and extorting funds from native merchants, the insurgents felt relatively safe in Algiers, particularly since there were only about one thousand police to control twelve hundred hard-core insurgents, plus another 4,500 supporters. The native quarter was particularly infamous as the home of many terrorist bombers. With a blazing hatred of Communism and all insurgents, Massu's Para colonels were willing to use drastic methods to root out the terrorists.

Massu used the *Detachements Operationnels de Protection* (DOP) to provide information, much of it gained from informers. Additionally, Muslim militias were used, but perhaps most effective was the 'ilot' system of making one person responsible

◀ French MAC 50 which saw wide usage in France's counter-insurgency war in Algeria

for each family, another for each building, then one for each block, etc. As a result, virtually any Muslim could be located within Algiers without delay. Use was also made of agents provocateurs, to expose terrorists. Feeling that captured terrorists did not merit quite the same treatment as soldiers, Massu's Paras frequently used torture, particularly field telephones attached to the genitals. Erosion of morality within the French Army was best illustrated not by isolated use of torture, which happens in any war, and particularly in counter-insurgency campaigns, but by the fact that such torture became a military matter of policy.

Massu's methods were harsh, but they were also successful. By October 1957 the FLN infrastructure in Algiers was virtually destroyed. To follow up this success a massive pacification campaign was launched in the countryside. However, the large numbers of innocents who had been detained or killed in Algiers and the countryside by the Army had driven much of the population over to the FLN, in what was now viewed by most Muslims as a fight to the death.

In accordance with Mao's doctrines for basing an insurgency on the countryside, the FLN organized rural villages under OPA, the arm of the FLN which handled propaganda, taxation and recruiting. Under FLN organization, the wilayas were broken into zones and subzones. Each zone theoretically supported a battalion of about 350–75 moujahidine, full-time, paid guerrillas, augmented by part-time moussebilines and fidayine. With Morocco as their western base and Tunisia as their eastern base, the insurgents had a ready supply of arms.

To counter FLN influence, the French tried their traditional North African *tache d'huile* tactics, while to separate guerrillas from the population they relied on their quadrillage system of garrisons to pacify areas. By late 1957 or early 1958, however, quadrillage was tying down at least three hundred thousand troops. While up to ninety per cent of available strength was thus in static positions, the Foreign Legion, Commandos-Marine and Paras formed a mobile reserve for search and destroy operations, known as ratissage. Early pioneers of air mobility in counter-insurgency operations, these troops were often delivered via helicopter. As in Indochina, however, the use of so many static garrisons in effect abandoned much of the countryside to the guerrillas, while the increasing use of conscripts eroded the Army's effectiveness even more, and caused increasing civilian dissatisfaction in France with the war. Public support in France waned even more as examples of Army brutality, such as using children ahead of patrols as mine detectors received publicity.

French intelligence found the Byzantine technique of promoting dissension among various guerrilla groups worked sometimes. The French Navy also had limited success in running a naval blockade, but arms still arrived in great numbers across the borders from Morocco and Tunisia; despite heavy diplomatic pressure, these countries continued to support the insurgents. The Army, frustrated by the presence of these cross-border havens, built a fortified barrier consisting of electrified fence, radar, patrols, searchlights, pre-zeroed artillery and mines. Known as the 'Morice Line', this barrier had a free-fire zone on either side. Though expensive, the Morice Line did interdict infiltration rather effectively. However, cross-border pursuits and air raids into Tunisia proved diplomatic disasters which provoked the UN and resulted in diplomatic pressure against France, even from staunch allies.

Attempting the population relocation which had proved so successful in Malaya, the French created one of their worst public relations disasters, through inept handling of the situation. Thousands of Muslims died in poorly run relocation camps, forcing many former non-combatants to fight on the side of the FLN rather than be relocated to what they now viewed as death camps. After such disasters, attempts at civic action faced a long uphill struggle. The distrust most of the population now felt for the French Army can be blamed for part of the failure, but the primary cause was that the French were not addressing the needs and desires of the people, while the FLN were.

Dissatisfied with the lack of progress against the FLN, in spring 1958 European 'Ultras', the most radical of the colons, staged an uprising in Algiers, resulting in Charles de Gaulle becoming Premier once again. Although both military and colons expected de Gaulle to be a hardliner, he surprised them by proposing widespread reforms, taking strong control of the military, and cracking down on the vigilante-like 'Committees of Public Safety' which were operating in Algeria. After putting a civilian administrator in control of the Army in Algeria, he made overtures to the FLN and other nationalists about a negotiated settlement. In October 1958, de Gaulle kept his promise of reforms when he announced his Constantine Plan to raise wages, improve housing, implement land reform, and improve education for Algerian Muslims. Additionally, he offered the rebels an amnesty.

The FLN refused to negotiate, and the colons bitterly opposed even the offer of negotiations and amnesty. The rebels, overestimating their strength, attempted to move into the 'third phase' of guerrilla warfare by openly engaging the French Army. As a result, French security forces, now numbering 550,000, were killing thousands of rebels each month. Much of this success can be attributed to the development of specialized light counter-insurgency forces by General Salan, and his successor General Challe. Known as *Commandos de Chasse*, these sixty- to a hundred-man units operated in rebel country for weeks at a time, carrying out raids, ambushes, intelligence-gathering missions, and calling in artillery or air strikes. Challe enhanced mobility with extensive use of helicopters.

All these factors combined to defeat the FLN push to seize Algeria by force, but de Gaulle realized that France could not afford the economic cost of continuing the war indefinitely and viewed the military primarily as a tool to force the FLN to negotiate. In September 1959, de Gaulle made a speech offering self-determination to Algeria. Challe and Massu, as well as virtually all of the colons, opposed the idea, and by January 1960 Massu was openly criticizing de Gaulle. European militias in Algeria expressed their displeasure more openly, setting up barricades and not dispersing until French soldiers eventually fired upon them. In January 1961 de Gaulle held a referendum which approved his self-determination policy, then approached the FLN secretly for talks.

French military officers opposing de Gaulle's policies were relieved and recalled to France, the most prominent being Raoul Salan, who along with other officers and the most hard-line colons had formed the *Organisation de l'Armée Secrete* (OAS), which early in 1960 had begun a campaign of terror against the de Gaulle government inside France. Enough members of the Army were convinced of OAS's aims and its slogan, 'French Algeria or Death', that in April 1961 Army units led by the famous 1st Foreign Legion Parachute Regiment rebelled openly. The rebellion failed, however, as the bulk of the Army remained loyal to de Gaulle, particularly the conscripts.

The FLN, now realizing their aims would be realized through negotiations, reduced their guerrilla activities, although the OAS continued their wave of terror. By spring 1962, OAS had been defeated, though many members remained underground and would continue to plot for years. Algerian independence was now agreed upon. During the Algerian campaign, the French Army had lost approximately twelve thousand troops, while Muslim auxiliaries had lost another 2,500. Losses among European civilians were about three thousand. Depending on whose figures one believes, losses among Muslims were between 150,000 and 600,000.

Analysis

The FLN enjoyed several very real advantages in their guerrilla campaign. Most importantly, they were fighting a popular war, supported by most of the population and pursuing what were perceived as just goals. Additionally, they had the Islamic religion as a strong unifying force, both internally and externally with their allies in the Arab League, and particularly in Morocco and Tunisia. Morocco and Tunisia, both former French colonies, offered the FLN moral and material support just across the borders of Algeria, thus keeping the insurgency from being isolated. The FLN also had many trained soldiers, veterans of the Second World War, with a sound knowledge of French weapons and tactics to draw upon during the early years of their insurgency. Finally, by not being so overtly Communist as the Viet Minh or the Communist terrorists in Malaya, the FLN did not become quite the bogeymen to France's NATO allies that they might have been. Tactically, though the FLN could not fight on equal terms with the massive French Army deployed

against them, by remaining a force in being they could cause such an economic and political drain that France would eventually be forced to sue for peace.

Theoretically, the French should have had an Army skilled in counter-insurgency after the years in Indochina, but many of the lessons had not been learned. For example, they still tied too large a proportion of their troops to static duties, and gave up too much of the countryside to the insurgents. The excesses of the colons infected the Army and turned large portions of the population against the Army, thus depriving the security forces of most friendly sources of intelligence, and forcing an even greater reliance on torture and on informants of dubious reliability.

▼ French paras being inserted via a Sikorsky H-55 in Algeria *(ECP)*

It must be remembered, too, that the French Army, coming away from defeats in the Second World War and in Indochina, had something to prove, which often coloured its operations in Algeria. These losses had illustrated French vulnerability, as well, and given the Algerians confidence to begin their fight for independence, a fight joined by many veterans of Indochina who had been captured and indoctrinated by the Viet Minh. Attempts at normally workable counter-insurgency tactics, such as population relocation, often failed through ignorance, obstruction by the colons or poor administration, eroding any base of support the French might have retained.

Although the Morice Line has often been criticized as another manifestation of the Maginot Line mentality, it actually proved relatively effective against infiltration. Its problem was not that it didn't work, but its maintenance cost. Formations of Commandos de Chasse were nothing new, such mobile hunter groups having proved effective throughout the history of counter-insurgency warfare. Their success reaffirmed the importance of using the right type of troops on counter-insurgency operations. The French operational use of the helicopter was important, too, as a preview of future counter-insurgency campaigns in Vietnam, Rhodesia, Afghanistan and elsewhere.

The most important, and most obvious, lesson to be gained from the Algerian insurgency, however, remains that a successful counter-guerrilla war cannot be fought if the political and social needs of the people are not addressed in conjunction with military counter-guerrilla operations. Guerrillas must be separated from the people, both physically and psychologically, in order to defeat an insurgency. Particularly in view of later wars in Vietnam, Rhodesia and Afghanistan, the Algerian campaign illustrates that guerrillas do not really have to *win* a war; they just have to remain in existence long enough for the war to become economically or politically untenable for the other side.

FRENCH FOREIGN LEGION PARAS

Among the French troops which distinguished themselves in far-away colonial campaigns, none holds the special place of the *Légion Étrangère* – the French Foreign Legion. And, among the élite ranks of the French Foreign Legion, the Legion Paras have during the last four decades carved a

▶ Jeep patrol of the 2nd REP; note the regimental crest on the jeep's radiator. Such jeep patrols offer a very economical counter-insurgency weapon when used by highly trained troops such as the 2nd REP *(J. Hon/AMI)*

▼ Tough Foreign Legion paras on patrol in Africa. The man in the middle is armed with the semi-automatic M49/56 rifle, while the man at the left has a MAT-49 SMG *(ECP)*

1655 0394

bloody niche for themselves as France's ultimate counter-insurgency weapon.

The genesis of the Legion Paras can be traced to the need in Indochina for an airborne reaction force, to be inserted wherever the Viet Minh threat was greatest. As a result, it had been decided by spring 1948 to form two Legion paratroop battalions. In April of that year, a platoon each from the 2nd and 3rd REI (*Régiment Étrangère d'Infanterie*) and from the 13th DBLE were put through a jump course at Hanoi, and formed into the *Compagnie Parachutistes du 3e Régiment Étrangère d'Infanterie*. By 9 June the company had made its first combat jump at Cao-Bang.

To bring the Legion Paras up to their authorized two battalions, a parachute cadre had been established at the Legion's home base, Sidi bel Abbes in North Africa, in May 1948. Based on this cadre, the *1er Bataillon Étrangère des Parachutistes* (1st BEP) was formed on 1 July 1948. Once its training was complete, 1st BEP prepared to depart for Indochina, while 2nd BEP was formed and began training on 1 October 1948, sailing for Indochina the following January. Both units contained a number of Second World War parachute veterans, particularly former German *Fallschirmjäger*.

During the next five years in Indochina, the two Legion Para battalions were normally in the thick of the fighting, making more than two dozen operational jumps between March 1949 and March 1954. Operation Bayarad, on 18 March 1949, saw the first operational jump by 1st BEP, followed by another in October to reinforce the Loung Phai outpost. In October 1950, 1st BEP jumped to support garrisons retreating from the Cao-Bang Ridgeline. During its heroic fighting retreat, the 1st BEP took such heavy casualties that on 31 December 1950 it was disbanded, the 2nd BEP absorbing its survivors. The 1st BEP's demise was short, however: it was reconstituted with replacements from 3rd BEP, which had formed in Algeria in 1949 to supply replacements for the 1st and 2nd in Indochina. After carrying out security operations for the next few months, 1st BEP jumped at Hao Binh on 10 November 1951 during Operation Tulipe. Almost a year later on 9 November 1952, the 1st took part in another major combat jump as part of Operation Marion.

During early 1953, 1st BEP operated around Kontum, An Khe, and Ban Me Thuot, prior to deploying to Laos that autumn for operations on the Plain of Jars. Back into parachute harness, the 1st jumped to secure Dien Bien Phu on 21 November along with four other Para battalions, as part of Operation Castor. Soon, the other Para battalions were replaced by 'leg' infantry units, but the 1st remained as part of Dien Bien Phu's garrison. Their primary mission was to mount aggressive patrols around the fortress and to assault and retake any strongpoints lost to the Viet Minh. The 1st and later, after it jumped as reinforcements, the 2nd BEP performed heroically, but by the time Dien Bien Phu fell a total of only 160 men of both Legion Para battalions remained in action. Even after the unit's virtual destruction, it rose once again, reforming in August 1954 from wounded veterans, replacements and rear area cadre.

◀ French Foreign Legionnaires go into action from a Piasecki H-21 helicopter in Algeria (*ECP*)

The 2nd BEP, after arriving in Indochina in January 1949, was initially used as a reaction unit, and had made seven combat jumps by September 1950. On 4 October 1951, 2nd BEP jumped again at Gia Loi in the T'ai Highlands, seeing some of the heaviest combat of the war. The battalion followed this encounter with more heavy fighting along the Black River between December 1951 and January 1952, as they attempted to hold portions of the river line.

On 9 November 1952, the 2nd BEP jumped along with the 1st BEP and a Colonial Para battalion to attack key Viet Minh supply depots during Operation Marion, then preceded the 1st BEP onto the Plain of Jars between April and July 1953. That July, 2nd BEP jumped once again against Communist supply areas in Operation Hirondelle. Early in 1954, 2nd BEP next took part in an amphibious landing at Tuy Hoa as part of Operation Arethuse. For the next couple of months, the 2nd operated in the Central Highlands, but as the situation at Dien Bien Phu became critical parachuted into the fortress on the nights of 9 and 10 April. After being annihilated during Dien Bien Phu's fall, the 2nd was reconstituted late in May 1954, primarily from members of the newly arrived 3rd BEP.

Following the French withdrawal from Indochina, the Legion Paras found themselves slated for another counter-insurgency campaign in Algeria. The need for even more paras as mobile reaction and strike units in Algeria resulted in conversion of the 1st and 3rd BEPs to full regiments on 1 September 1955, and the 2nd BEP on 1 December that year. It was soon realized, though, that there was insufficient trained manpower for three full Legion Para regiments, so the 3rd was disbanded to provide manpower for the 1st and 2nd REPs.

In Algeria, the REPs were used primarily as élite light infantry, committed to ratissage operations or as airmobile infantry in the reaction role. Legion Paras were involved in six operational jumps between April 1956 and April 1958, but none involved an entire regiment. Most, in fact, were raids using between 150 and 250 paras.

Traditionally, the Legion has drawn the toughest combat assignments and in Algeria – a traditional Legion operational area – this was even more the case. Tough Legion Paras played an important role during the winter of 1956–7 in clearing the Casbah, then the next winter acted as a reaction force along the Morice Line. For the remainder of the Algerian war, the two REPs were used on patrols, clearing operations and sweeps – the usual counter-insurgency tasks. They were also used as an airmobile reaction force which

▲ At left, the pocket crest of the 1st REP, and at right the crest of the 2nd REP

was heli-lifted into action upon contact being made with the FLN.

While serving in Algeria, the two REPs suffered over 1,500 casualties; however, they inflicted up to ten times this number on the enemy. Legion Paras were especially admired by local colons for their hardline stance against the FLN, and many married into local families. As might be expected, this affinity with the colons influenced many Legionnaires to support the 22 April 1961 *putsch* against the de Gaulle government. The 1st REP, often considered the best unit in the French Army, led the revolt, but though many members of 2nd REP sympathized with the goal of keeping Algeria French, they did not revolt. As a result of their participation in the failed revolt, the 1st REP was disbanded on 30 April 1961. Despite this dishonour, veterans of the 1st REP are normally proud of participation in the revolt, many still retaining 1st REP unit crests with the date 22 April 1961 engraved on the back. Some 1st veterans joined OAS and continued to fight as terrorists, while others became mercenaries in other parts of the world.

There has always been a certain fear of the Legion within the French government, and in the aftermath of the revolt it appeared as if the only remaining Legion Para regiment, the 2nd, might be disbanded as well. In March 1962 the regiment was moved to Telergma, and then to Mers-el-kebir in September. In June 1963, however, with the appointment of Colonel Caillaud as its new regimental commander, 2nd REP's future was assured. Caillaud realized that France would need an élite, highly mobile counter-insurgency/intervention unit which could be committed without worry about adverse publicity at home. Since only its officers are French, the remainder of the Legion's members being foreigners, 2nd REP could fill this slot admirably. Therefore Caillaud converted 2nd REP to a para-commando regiment trained for amphibious, mountain, HALO (High Altitude, Low Opening), recon, and other special operations.

In June 1967 the rejuvenated 2nd REP moved

2

2
1e CIE

3eCie/2eREP
TFAI

DESTRUCTEURS
SNIPERS

into its current home at Camp Raffali on Corsica. Now part of 11th DP (*11e Division Parachutiste*), 2nd REP trains intensively for its intervention/counter-insurgency mission. Recently, in fact, the anti-terrorist mission has been added as well. Life in the 2nd REP is not all training, however; the regiment has been involved frequently on active service.

In April 1969 the 1st and 2nd Companies deployed to Chad, followed by the 3rd and Recce Companies in September. Their primary mission was patrolling along the Libyan border to interdict infiltration. All four companies had returned to Corsica by December 1970, but Legion Paras redeployed to Chad in 1978 and 1984 to counter Libyan and internal threats. 2nd REP training teams have also worked closely with the armed forces of Chad. Members of the 2nd REP have also served in Djibouti, supporting GIGN, the French anti-terrorist unit, during the 1976 rescue of kidnapped French schoolchildren.

The 2nd REP made a combat jump on 19 May 1978 at Kolwezi, Zaïre, to rescue western civilians held hostage by FNLC rebels. After an appeal by President Mobutu of Zaïre for assistance, France committed the 2nd REP to Operation Leopard. As should be expected of France's principal intervention unit, within twenty-four hours of being alerted, the 2nd REP were deployed to Kinshasa. Twelve hours later, they were chuted up in unfamiliar T-10 parachutes, ready to jump over the dropzones at 1515 local time. Soon after landing, paras of the HQ, 1st, 2nd and 3rd Companies had secured the dropzones and moved out to rescue the hostages. By nightfall, the hostages had been rescued, the FNLC driven into hasty retreat, and a perimeter secured. At dawn on 20 May, the 4th Company and remaining elements of the regiment jumped in to help evacuate the hostages and drive the FNLC across the border, killing approximately 250 in the process, while suffering only five 2nd REP killed. An interesting point in reference to this operation is that the US 82nd Airborne Division and the Belgian Para-Commando Regiment were alerted as well for the operation, but while those two countries dithered, France committed the 2nd REP, saving numerous innocent lives in the process.

The 2nd REP has remained an important tool of French foreign policy, being deployed to aid former colonies or protect French interests around the world. The 1,275 2nd REP Paras are the élite of the already élite Foreign Legion, and receive pay one-third higher than other Legionnaires. The 2nd REP retains a highly flexible organization, allowing rapid deployment and making the regiment particularly well suited for counter-insurgency operations. Six companies make up the current 2nd REP as follows:

HQ Company – includes administrative, signals, maintenance, medical and supply personnel.

Recce and Support Company – includes an HQ Platoon, Motorized Recon Platoon, CRAP Platoon (*Commandos de Renseignement et d'Action dans le Profondeur*) – this HALO-trained unit is the LRRP/pathfinder unit for the 2nd REP and has recently received specialist hostage rescue assault training as well, two anti-tank platoons (equipped with a total of sixteen MILAN anti-tank missile launchers), an AA Platoon (equipped with four 20mm twin AA guns) and a mortar platoon (with eight 81mm mortars and four 120mm mortars).

1st Parachute Infantry Company – specializes in night, anti-tank, urban warfare, airmobile operation.

2nd Parachute Infantry Company – specializes in mountain/ski operations.

3rd Parachute Infantry Company – specializes in amphibious operations and combat swimming.

4th Parachute Infantry Company – specializes in sniping and demolitions.

Each parachute infantry company consists of an HQ platoon and three combat platoons. Each platoon comprises one officer, four NCOs and thirty Legionnaires. Enough vehicles are available so that the entire regiment can operate motorized, though on a combat jump normally they have to operate as leg infantry until the transport can be brought in.

The Legion Paras continue a proud tradition from Indochina to Algeria to Zaïre to the next trouble spot their skills are needed. The 2nd REP are not just professional soldiers, but professional fighting men. Normally at any given time, at least one company of the 2nd REP is deployed overseas, generally somewhere with a strong likelihood of action.

◀ Pocket crests for companies within the 2nd REP: at top left the 2nd Company, reflecting its specialization in mountain warfare; at top right, the 1st Company, reflecting the specialization in night operations; at bottom left, the 3rd Company; at bottom right, the 4th Company, reflecting the specialization in demolitions

10 BORNEO AND ADEN

After the counter-insurgency wars of the fifties in Malaya, Kenya and Cyprus, British forces were the most experienced counter-guerrilla fighters in the world. During the 1960s, they would gain even more experience in Borneo and Aden.

BRUNEI

In the early 1960s, President Sukarno of Indonesia was flexing his muscles with expansionist plans to create a Pacific superpower. In 1962, he took West Irian from the Dutch without a fight, but the planned formation of Malaysia had placed a roadblock in Sukarno's way. His alliance in 1963 with the Indonesian Communist Party, the PKI, gave him a potential third column among Communists throughout the future components of Malaysia; but Sukarno's chance for action came not from within Malaysia, but from the small, oil-rich Sultanate of Brunei, which was wavering about joining the Malaysian Federation.

Under pressure from the British and Malayan governments, the Sultan held elections, during which the People's Party won all sixteen seats. Sultan Sir Omar Ali Saifuddin then nominated seventeen of his own supporters, however, nullifying these gains. As a result, the TNKU, the militant wing of the People's Party, began recruiting guerrillas under Yassin Affendi, the TNKU military leader, who soon had eight thousand poorly trained and virtually unarmed guerrillas in jungle camps.

The rebels did, however, have clear-cut objectives: to seize the Sultan and use him as their figurehead leader, seize police stations as a source of weapons, and seize the oilfields and take Europeans working there hostage. The rebellion began early on 8 December 1962 with attacks on the Sultan's palace, police stations, the Prime Minister's residence and power stations. Some police and power stations were taken, but other police posts held out, and the Sultan escaped being captured.

In response, two companies of Gurkhas were flown in from Singapore. Major Lloyd Williams, in command of the Gurkhas, decided first to secure Brunei Town, then the threatened oilfields. The rebels were advancing on the police station protecting the oilfields, using captured Europeans as shields. As the initial contingent of Gurkhas began fighting through to the oilfields, reinforcements arrived, and soon the entire 1/2 Gurkhas were available for action, followed on 10 December by the Queen's Own Highlanders.

It was decided an air assault on the oilfields was necessary, so a hundred men were airlanded nearby, capturing the airfield. Over the next two days, the town and oilfields were retaken and the hostages freed. It still remained to retake Limbang from the TNKU, however. This mission was assigned to 42 Commando, Royal Marines, which had arrived on 11 December. Using landing craft, they assaulted the Limbang area from the river on 13 December, retaking the town and rescuing the British Resident, who was to have been hanged by the rebels that afternoon. By the time mopping up had been completed, the rebels had lost forty killed and 3,400 captured, while the remainder had fled into the jungle with their leader Yassin Affendi.

Many TNKU attempting to escape to Indonesia were hunted down by Kelabit irregulars, who would later provide a very useful source of intelligence during the Emergency. Indonesia had supported TNKU and now continued to work against the Malaysian Federation.

In response to the rebellion and the growing militancy of Indonesia, Maj-General Walker took command of British forces in Borneo on 19 December. A Malaya veteran, he listed the following requirements for success in countering guerrillas, soon after he took command: co-operation of all branches of the armed forces and police; sound intelligence; speed, flexibility, and mobility of security forces; secure bases; domination of the jungle; winning the hearts and minds of the people.

With the Commando assault ship HMS *Albion* available, Walker had ready helicopter support as throughout the spring the remaining TNKU rebels were hunted down. In May 1964 the Gurkhas captured Yassin Affendi, virtually ending the revolt. Walker had proved a particularly apt

◀ Members of the Parachute Regiment, being highly trained and highly mobile, make excellent counter-insurgency troops *(MoD)*

commander, drawing on his experience in Malaya to carry out the correct military response without losing the support of the local population.

BORNEO

Sukarno's strategy for undermining the fledgling Malaysian Federation was to use guerrilla warfare to separate Sarawak and North Borneo from the remainder of the Federation. To implement this strategy he would rely heavily on his defence minister, General Abdul Nasution, who had written a book on guerrilla warfare based heavily on Mao's tenets. As events would later show, however, the Indonesians had failed really to grasp the principles of popular war.

From the Indonesian point of view, conditions favoured them. They could base guerrillas just across the border in Kalimantan and could count on the regular Indonesian Army for a decisive strike when conditions were right. Their confrontation would take place in Sarawak and Sabah, the 1,000-mile land border and 1,500-mile coast of which allowed easy infiltration. Not only that, but a potential third column existed, in West Sarawak's Clandestine Communist Organization (CCO).

On 12 April 1963, thirty Indonesian Border Terrorists (IBTs) crossed into Sarawak to attack a police post, looting the bazaar and retreating across the border. In the process, they left fake documents linking the raid to TNKU, thus attempting to make it seem a popular extension of the Brunei revolt. These guerrillas had been pulled from a heterogeneous mixture of races and trained by Indonesian special forces units.

Realizing from his Malayan experiences the necessity for quick reaction against guerrillas, Walker immediately brought in reinforcements. During the next few weeks the police and the army cracked down on the CCO, seizing over eight thousand shotguns in surprise raids. To inhibit infiltration, curfews were established along the border and forts were built as patrol bases. Nevertheless, another crossing took place on 17 May 1963 when IBTs crossed and attacked civilian targets. The Indonesians set up guerrilla bases all along the border as well, in preparation for a rash of cross-border raids.

When elections showed that the population of North Borneo, despite CCO and Indonesian attempts at intimidation, favoured the Malaysian Federation, Sukarno ordered the incursions from these guerrilla bases to be stepped up. He also invited the CCO into Kalimantan to give them a safe haven for operations into North Borneo.

Despite Sukarno's opposition, the official creation of Malaysia took place in September 1963, thus making the counter-insurgency

◀ Members of the Royal Australian Regiment became experienced counter-insurgency jungle fighters in Borneo and Vietnam *(Australian War Memorial)*

campaign a Commonwealth matter. As a result, the upper levels of command changed, but General Walker remained Director of Operations. As of late 1963, forces under his command faced about 1,500 IBTs supported by Indonesian special forces. To oppose them, Walker had five infantry battalions as a mobile defence force. Although the helicopter had already shown its value as a counter-insurgency weapon, at this point he had only about a dozen, as well as some fixed-wing aircraft.

To provide intelligence/early warning, Walker was fortunate in having an SAS squadron and the Gurkha Independent Parachute Company deployed as a border screen. The Border Scouts were also raised from local tribesmen as an intelligence net. Some raiders still made it through the thinly deployed defenders, however, one group hitting Long Jawi in Sarawak. Quick reaction by the Gurkhas resulted in thirty-three of this force being killed as Gurkha cut-off parties were dropped by helicopter ahead of fleeing IBTs. This raid proved, too, that IBTs really did not understand Mao's precepts concerning the population, as their wanton slaughter turned the population of North Borneo even more firmly against them.

By December 1963 Sukarno was resorting to the more open use of Indonesian regulars as thirty-five Indonesian Marines and 138 'volunteers' infiltrated and attempted to attack a Malay troop barracks, no doubt intending to discourage the inexperienced Malay troops. 1/10 Gurkhas quickly responded, however, and over the next month hunted down and captured or killed all but six of the raiders. In the aftermath, Indonesia claimed that the Marines involved had resigned and joined the guerrillas out of idealistic opposition to Malaysia.

Although the UN arranged a ceasefire to begin on 23 January 1964, the Indonesians continued their incursions, while posturing at the conference table in Bangkok. Throughout the negotiations, Indonesian military aircraft buzzed towns in Sarawak, and on 4 March 1964 full-scale incursions began again. More and more, however, it was Indonesian regulars crossing the border. Commonwealth security forces were particularly frustrated in combating infiltrators due to their ability to retreat across the border to safety. As a result, General Walker asked for a 'hot pursuit' option, but this was denied. In June 1964 Sukarno used negotiations as a ploy once again, but his unwillingness really to negotiate soon led to their breakdown.

Throughout the confrontation, eight Gurkha battalions were being rotated into North Borneo on six-month tours, and along with the SAS and 40 Commando, proved most effective in the jungle. Other British troops improved dramatically, though, after attending the Jungle Warfare School in Malaya and becoming acclimatized.

To help counter the infiltration problem, in the most heavily threatened areas well-defended border forts were set up at six-mile intervals, with companies carrying out rigorous interdiction patrols from these bases. Due to their vulnerable forward locations, such forts were defended by claymore mines, punji spikes, tripwires and minefields. Often a fort would have a single 105mm howitzer, its fields of fire interlocking with those at other border forts. Mortars and machine guns offered more close-range protection. Another technique used in Borneo, later to be widely used in Vietnam, was the artillery 'raid' in which a 105mm howitzer would be lifted into action against the enemy by helicopter. From the forts, sections of ten to twelve men would move forward to operate along the border in four-man teams. If enemy infiltrators were encountered, two men would

▼ The M-16 rifle has proved a particularly useful weapon for counter-insurgency forces, particularly with troops such as these, capable of good fieldcraft

trail them, while the other two linked up with the rest of the section and contacted company HQ.

During these jungle operations, the FN rifle proved too heavy and unwieldy, so Walker requisitioned the Armalite rifle for use by those troops operating along the border. It soon became obvious that lightweight radios and other equipment were necessary as well.

In August, large-scale raids by Indonesian paratroopers and Marines occurred, even against the Malayan mainland. Though these raiders were normally quickly mopped up, the threat did finally gain for Walker approval to carry out cross-border operations into Kalimantan for up to five thousand yards within Indonesian territory. It should be admitted that the SAS had already been operating across the border for some time, but approval allowed them not only to gather intelligence in Kalimantan but also to ambush infiltrators and carry out acts of sabotage. The Royal Marines Special Boat Squadron also raided along the Kalimantan coast.

Pre-emptive infantry raids across the border, known as 'Claret Operations', were also authorized, though they remained classified top secret. Initial authorization for penetrations to five thousand yards was raised to ten thousand yards and finally to twenty thousand yards. As a result, the Indonesians were driven back from the border. Ironically, since Sukarno had vowed to crush Malaysia by 1 January 1965, pride meant that he could not publicly admit these crossings, which his forces were powerless to stop. Hence, he could not complain as long as raids were neither too protracted nor too obvious. Though Claret raids came under rigid controls, they were quite successful. Normally, air support was out of the question, but artillery support was just across the border, often heli-lifted in just prior to the raid.

While pre-emptive raids, ambushes, etc kept the Indonesians off balance, the border defences were strengthened, using a three-zone defence in depth. To protect the flanks, the Royal Navy interdicted infiltration from the sea, while the RAF flew

URBAN CLOSE COMBAT AND THE FN BROWNING HI-POWER

To counter urban assassins in Aden, the SAS developed what they called 'Keeni-Meeni' squads, which took their name from a Swahili term describing the movement of a snake in the grass, and which had become SAS jargon for undercover operations. Men of the regiment who resembled Arabs were chosen for the twenty or so members of these undercover squads. Normally, they would operate at night in twos or threes, often using a British officer in uniform as a stalking horse to lure assassins under their guns. Although they killed and captured some terrorists, the most important aspect of Keeni-Meeni

operations was that other British units learned the technique and employed it effectively; also, for the SAS it was the basis for their later counter-terrorism specialization, and for later operations in Northern Ireland.

The weapon chosen for such operations was the FN Browning Hi-Power 9mm pistol, the standard sidearm of the British Army. Although at eight inches in overall length, and thirty-two ounces in weight, the FN automatic was not the easiest pistol to conceal, it was accurate, reliable and had a large magazine capacity of thirteen rounds. More importantly, it was in the Army supply system. The FN Hi-Power remains one of the world's best combat pistols, more than half a century after its invention.

To teach them to employ the FN pistol as quickly and effectively as possible, those selected for the Keeni-Meeni teams, already above average shots with the pistol, were put through a special Close Quarters Battle (CQB) course. This course was based on the techniques of a Colonel Grant Taylor, who reportedly had worked with the American FBI. The Taylor philosophy was that achieving tactical surprise was critical to winning a gunfight; hence, its particular applicability to Keeni-Meeni operations. Training was designed to give the soldier complete confidence in his weapon, to teach him to concentrate on making the kill, to react quickly, and most of all to have an attacking attitude based on the understanding that in an armed encounter it was the soldier's life or the enemy's; it should be the enemy's which was forfeit. This same basic philosophy is still followed today in training the SAS's excellent VIP protection and counter-terrorist teams.

The Taylor system of firearms training relied heavily on teaching what was usually known in SAS as the 'Law of the Gun'. To be most effective with the weapon, the members of the Keeni-Meeni squads had to be able to shoot instinctively. Hence, CQB training included instinctive pointing of the weapon from a 'battle crouch'. Proper grip, trigger squeeze and pointing technique were practised 'dry' (without ammunition) and 'live' (with ammunition), until the members of the Keeni-Meeni squads were extremely deadly men, able to draw their pistols rapidly from beneath Arab garb and engage and stop any armed opponent.

◀ The FN Browning Hi-Power which the SAS used so effectively on undercover operations in Aden

aerial surveillance missions. By 1966 aerial spotters were working very closely with mobile patrols, quickly locating and tracking down infiltrators.

In March 1965 General Walker had been succeeded by Maj-General George Lea, another experienced counter-guerrilla fighter, who had commanded the SAS in Malaya. By the second half of 1965, the insufficient logistics support of the Indonesian front-line troops was telling on morale and combat potential among the infiltrators. World opinion was now obviously against Indonesia as well. On 30 September 1965, six senior generals were killed during a coup attempt, resulting in General Suharto cracking down on Communists in Indonesia and starting secret talks with Malaysia about ending the confrontation.

Over the next few months, Sukarno was slowly removed from power, the Borneo Confrontation finally ending on 11 August 1966. During the fighting, 114 Commonwealth troops had been killed and 181 had been wounded. Showing how well the Army had performed its mission, only thirty-six civilians had been killed, and fifty-three wounded Indonesian and CCO casualties on the other hand amounted to over 1,500 killed, wounded or captured. One very real residual benefit of the excellent performance of Commonwealth troops was that Malaysia retained the British military bases, and actively sought continued British military ties.

Analysis

The counter-insurgency campaign in Borneo offers ample reasons why the British won and the TNKU/CCO/Indonesians lost. First, and perhaps most importantly, the insurgents never really had popular support. The Indonesian threat to North Borneo was, in fact, really an external threat, an invasion, but one fought along guerrilla lines. Good intelligence from the locals, the Border Scouts and the Special Air Service, combined with excellent communications using radio rebroadcast stations on the high ground, allowed security forces to be used most effectively to contain and eliminate threats. Though helicopters were not present in optimum numbers, those that were available were used to the utmost to provide mobility, allowing rapid response to incursions. The recent Malayan experience of both Directors of Operations provided leadership familiar with counter-guerrilla warfare; thus lessons did not have to be relearned. Availability of Gurkhas and the Special Air Service, already possessing effective jungle skills, was another asset, particularly since many of the Indonesian infiltrators were themselves well-trained jungle fighters. Nevertheless, the SAS and Gurkhas managed to beat them in the jungle. The Jungle Warfare School in Malaya proved invaluable for preparing other troops to fight in the jungle environment as well.

Among the other factors contributing to British/Malaysian success was the effective use of a joint HQ to control the military and police, and the presence of a major logistical support centre nearby, at Singapore. Once again it should be stressed that the support of the local population is the key element in a counter-insurgency, and the security forces managed to pursue their campaign with little real effect on the life of the population. The security forces retained extremely high morale throughout the campaign, as well.

On the Indonesian side, there were certain advantages; most obviously the long border with North Borneo. Once Commonwealth forces were given permission to operate across the border, however, this became a rather dubious advantage, as Indonesian troops and CCOs had to face the threat of ambush miles inside their previously safe area. The use of Indonesian Special Forces in the guerrilla role provided infiltrators with a higher level of training, but they also lacked local support in their area of operations. Despite General Nasution's book on guerrilla warfare, the importance of a guerrilla being able to 'swim in the sea of the people', as Mao described it, was lost on the Indonesians. Atrocities committed by infiltrators worked to ensure that large segments of the population would support Commonwealth forces. In simple terms, the Brunei revolt and Borneo Confrontation offered a counter-insurgency campaign in which counter-guerrilla forces did most things right and guerrilla forces did most things wrong; the results were then a foregone conclusion.

ADEN

In February 1959 the Federation of South Arabia was formed from six territories bordering the British Protectorate of Aden. Over the next four years Aden and ten other territories joined. Initially it was assumed that the FSA would remain a member of the Commonwealth, retaining a strong British presence; however, Arab nationalists wanted the British removed as soon as possible. By 1962, after a coup by left-wing Army officers deposed the traditional ruler, the Imam, Yemen gave active support to the nationalists in the FSA, particularly the pro-Yemeni ones. At the same time, the deposed Imam, with Saudi support, was waging a guerrilla war against Yemen's new rulers, a war aided by many mercenaries, including SAS veterans.

Within FSA, two main nationalist groups had emerged – the National Liberation Front (NLF) and the Front for the Liberation of South Yemen (FLOSY). The NLF was in the strongest position, having received backing by Egypt. Nationalist feeling had been building up, with tribes in the Radfan even more rebellious than usual, and an Emergency was finally declared in December 1963, after a grenade attack on the High Commissioner. Even so, the British underestimated the depth of support for the nationalists. To subdue the rebellious tribes in the rugged Radfan, a punitive expedition of FSA troops and supporting British troops was sent in. Having fought for hundreds of years in an area perfectly suited to guerrilla warfare, the tribal fighters simply faded away, returning after the Army had left. All the expedition really accomplished was the fanning of an already simmering rebellion.

The nationalists wanted to discredit the pro-British FSA and intimidate the population, particularly the police. This was accomplished primarily by assassins who would stalk their targets within urban areas, often using a woman as a 'mule' to carry the assassination pistol until needed. To demoralize the British, grenade attacks against officers' messes, schoolchildren, or any other likely target were used, as were booby traps and letter bombs. Mined roads and snipers also accounted for members of the police and military. Popular demonstrations were used to attract attention, and occasionally to lure the security forces into an ambush when responding.

One of the greatest political problems in the FSA was the divided loyalties among various former sheikhdoms and sultanates. Additionally, much of the population, including many members of the FSA government, supported the nationalists. Intelligence was inadequate due to lack of sympathy for the security forces, and the fact that as many as ten different intelligence agencies were operating, prior to a 1965 amalgamation. Even those who might normally have been willing to supply information were intimidated. Additionally, key Special Branch officers were primary assassination targets.

As a result, lacking good sources of intelligence, the security forces had to resort to patrols, checkpoints, and observation posts. Some of the latter – run covertly – proved quite effective, as observers could vector police or military to unsuspecting urban terrorists. The open spaces of Aden also allowed the use of observation aircraft as well as Hawker Hunter ground-support aircraft. Armour was also used, though not particularly effectively, as it was normally easily avoided. The Special Air Service did its usual professional job, providing reconnaissance for other ground forces and calling artillery and air strikes on to insurgent positions. There were never really enough troops available, however, to control the countryside effectively, nor enough intelligence really to control the city, particularly since the British were not willing to resort to the harsh methods used by the French in Algiers.

When a British White Paper in 1966 announced the British intention to pull out, any residual popular support remaining was lost. A population which knew it would soon be on its own with the NLF and FLOSY was not likely to support the British. Finally, in November 1967, as the British were pulling out, the NLF and FLOSY began fighting each other; when the FSA Army gave its support to the NLF, the fate of the country was decided. The NLF would rule the new country of South Yemen.

Analysis

The British started the Aden campaign with most of the population already sympathetic to the nationalist cause, and the British government not really having the will to fight to maintain control in southern Arabia. As a result, all the security forces could do was buy time. The rough FSA terrain was particularly well suited to guerrilla warfare, and the area of operations was too large to control with the troops available. Finally, punitive operations were not only ineffective, but actively helped rebels gain public support. The presence of a military supporter just across the border in Yemen meant as well that the NLF had access to arms and a safe training area.

As usual, the Special Air Service performed well in Aden, particularly in the reconnaissance role. Aircraft were also used effectively. British infantry performed well, too, though were rarely deployed for the types of action they had been trained for. The real problem was that the security forces had no clear-cut objectives, once the British government announced its plans to pull out of southern Arabia. Political will is often more critical in counter-insurgency warfare than military might; it was certainly lacking in Aden.

11 VIETNAM

By now the Vietnam War probably ranks as the most intensively analysed guerrilla war in history, yet even so, many of the issues involved remain misunderstood and misinterpreted. Vietnam veterans know that, in battle, they virtually always defeated the Viet Cong and the North Vietnamese Army. However, while winning the military battle, the United States and the Republic of Vietnam were losing the political battle – not just in Vietnam, but in Laos, Cambodia and within the United States. Therein lies the most important lesson that must be learned from Vietnam. Ho Chi Minh and Vo Nguyen Giap understood the political nature of guerrilla warfare; John Kennedy, Lyndon Johnson, Richard Nixon, Nguyen Cao Ky, William Westmoreland, and most of the rest of the American and Vietnamese political and military establishments did not.

When the Viet Minh and French negotiated an end to the Indochina War, the Communists actually believed that when elections were held in the South, the populace would vote to unify under Ho Chi Minh. The Republic of Vietnam was founded in 1955 with Ngo Dinh Diem as President. Although the Geneva Accord had called for elections to settle the issue of reunification, Diem refused to hold them in 1956. When the 17th Parallel division had been accepted by both sides – gleefully on the part of the Viet Minh and Soviets, it should be noted, since it exceeded their greatest expectations – the Communists had expected the South to fall on its own, or to be voted out of existence. However, as South Vietnam prospered, the Politburo in Hanoi decided to raise insurgency once again in the South, using those Viet Minh who had remained in place, as well as others who had moved north at the end of the French Indochina conflict. When renewed guerrilla fighting began in 1959, there were about five thousand Viet Cong (as the Viet Minh were now known), supported by about 100,000 sympathizers.

At this point, many factors made South Vietnam particularly fertile ground for guerrilla operations. The jungle-covered highlands allowed the establishment of secure guerrilla bases in areas difficult for security forces to penetrate, while the concentration of the population along the coasts, as well as the road and rail networks, made the country particularly vulnerable to sabotage against communications. In addition to the highlands, the Mekong Delta was another suitable guerrilla base. Add the long sea coast and 600-mile jungle frontier with Laos and Cambodia, and guerrilla infiltration and supply, particularly along the Ho Chi Minh Trail, became virtually impossible to interdict. The ARVN (Army of the Republic of Vietnam) was organized and trained for conventional rather than guerrilla war. Very few of the light, highly-mobile counter-guerrilla forces necessary to deny areas to guerrillas existed within the ARVN.

On the other hand, the National Liberation Front (NLF) had long experience of waging guerrilla war, and with its leadership underground in South Vietnam or across the border in Cambodia, controlled a military structure based on village irregular militias, regional militias and regular VC guerrillas.

Most of the combat burden did not fall on the ARVN, but on lightly equipped regional and provincial forces. Often, in fact, the best ARVN units were retained in Saigon as counter-coup forces, rather than being committed against the VC.

President John F. Kennedy was especially interested in countering the spread of Communism, and took the threat of the VC very seriously. After General Maxwell Taylor's 1961 visit, Kennedy approved increased military aid, though Charles de Gaulle advised him strongly against heavy American involvement in Vietnam; however, America was launched on a path of military support for the Diem regime. Initially, the aim was just to support the Vietnamese and help them prepare for their own defence, but basic impatience, a strong American characteristic, would soon lead to increasingly direct American involvement in the war.

Partly as a threat to North Vietnam, and as a force in place to move against infiltration routes through Laos and Cambodia, a US Marine Brigade was sent to Thailand in 1961. As a counter-

◀ Australian advisers and troops such as this one from the Royal Australian Regiment proved particularly effective at small unit patrolling in Vietnam *(Australian War Memorial)*

insurgency tactic, this was less productive than had been the deployment of teams from the 77th Special Forces Group (Airborne) to Laos in 1959, to train the Royal Laotian Army in counter-insurgency. Success in training Kha and Meo tribesmen as counter-guerrillas, though, was a good example of proper counter-insurgency methodology, as it pitted those with local knowledge and commitment against the guerrillas. Conventional military minds, however, normally prefer deploying large forces of infantry, armour, artillery and aircraft, which allows generals more scope for involvement; effective mobile counter-guerrilla forces are normally commanded by junior officers or NCOs.

Most Special Forces personnel in Laos were removed in 1962, when by agreement the country was supposedly declared a zone free of foreign military personnel. As usual, the North Vietnamese and other Communist forces used such agreements for their own ends, removing few troops, while the Americans removed their military advisers. This agreement, in fact, set the stage for increased use of the Ho Chi Minh Trail to supply guerrillas in South Vietnam, with little fear of US action. Despite his many failings, South Vietnamese President Diem realized the North Vietnamese would ignore such an agreement and initially refused to ratify the agreement, doing so only grudgingly, after strong US pressure.

Within Vietnam, by 1962 the Strategic Hamlet Programme had been implemented, as an attempt to use the techniques which had been successful in Malaya to pacify the countryside, but with only limited success. US Special Forces advisers had begun working with village defence forces late in 1961, too, beginning the Civilian Irregular Defence Group (CIDG) programme, which would prove to be one of the most successful strategies of the Vietnam conflict. Under this programme, village defence forces received very basic weapons and tactics training so they could protect their own villages from attack while continuing to function as farmers. To supplement this militia, full-time 'strike forces' were maintained at central locations to respond to calls for help from any village under attack. Other US military advisers were assigned to ARVN forces, while US logistics and helicopter units provided direct support.

During this period, the VC carried out political action on three fronts: consolidating the 'liberated' areas under their control to build their economic, military and political strength; organizing the countryside; and proselytizing the ARVN and civil service to gain converts. Simultaneously, to undermine faith in the government, kidnappings, acts of sabotage and assassinations were carried out. In areas where they had moved into the more aggressive stages of guerrilla war, the VC openly ambushed ARVN patrols or attacked police stations.

The Diem government never really achieved widespread support among the people. For most peasants, the ARVN 'protectors' were actually viewed as a scourge visited upon them, since the underpaid and underfed soldiers normally resorted to looting. It was not by accident that the Vietnamese word for soldier was derived from the word for bandit. Such a view of the Army could only work in the favour of the VC. VC irregulars, on the other hand, were drawn from the peasantry themselves. Exacerbating the situation, officers willing actively to pursue the campaign against the Communists were often shunted aside in favour of inept political appointees, thus eroding the morale of the Army from within, while losses to the VC eroded it from without. Finally, as Buddhist opposition grew to Diem's regime, which was based heavily on the Catholic autocracy, Diem ordered raids on Buddhist temples by government forces, thus alienating much of the population on religious grounds.

Realizing that they were backing a loser in Diem, the US tacitly gave approval to the coup which removed Diem and replaced him with General Duong Van Minh. Rather than bringing about stable government, however, this led to a series of coups, until finally General Nguyen Van Thieu and Air Vice-Marshal Nguyen Cao Ky took power in June 1965. While much of South Vietnam's military leadership had been involved in these months of political in-fighting, the Viet Cong had taken advantage of the turmoil to consolidate and expand its control of the countryside. By 1964, in fact, the VC were moving towards the classic third phase of guerrilla warfare, as they prepared actively to engage battalion or larger-sized ARVN units. Engagements normally resulted in VC victories as well, making conversion of members of the armed forces that much easier for the VC.

As the likelihood increased of South Vietnam falling, attacks on American ships in the Gulf of Tonkin set the stage for increasing US involvement. Finally, as the Communists were about to cut South Vietnam in two in 1965, the United States actively entered the ground war by deploying US Marines and then the 173rd Airborne Brigade.

Since the Second World War, the United States has been a great believer in air power, and in Vietnam an attempt was made to destroy the North Vietnamese capability to pursue a war by striking at the economic infrastructure. Roads, railways, fuel installations, etc. were struck repeatedly; however, the need to strike only at military targets forced US airmen to enter and leave the North over very tight corridors, along which the North Vietnamese would eventually concentrate their air defences. Though heavy losses were indeed inflicted on the North, the flow of war materials and manpower to the South never really faltered. It is questionable whether an all-out bombing offensive against civilian as well as military targets would have made any difference, and although fear of world condemnation of an unlimited bombing offensive militated against broadening the scope of allowable targets, it is doubtful that most of the war's critics could have been much more vocal than they were anyway. As with much of the Vietnam War, self-imposed limitations on air strikes in the North amounted to no more than an attempt to fight a war without actually fighting a war.

As the US troop build-up continued through 1966 and 1967, and US infantry became involved in combat, it quickly became obvious that conventional US troops were too ponderous to catch the VC. The Communists fought only when they chose, forcing the US military into a reactive mode. Using booby traps and snipers, the VC could eliminate one or two members of a US patrol, and demoralize many others. The systems of tunnels used by the VC also added to the level of surprise they could enjoy, frequently allowing VC to hide quite literally beneath US troops, one massive tunnel complex being found directly beneath a US divisional base.

Though certain Special Forces reconnaissance and ambush units, Navy SEALs, Army Long-Range Recon Patrols (LRRPs) and a few other highly-trained mobile units took a heavy toll on the VC, for the most part the US pursued a quantitative rather than qualitative approach. Numbers soon came to obsess Military Assistance Command Vietnam (MACV), as they worried more and more about body count and weapons captured than about whether the VC/NVA threat was increasing or decreasing. One important tactical development, however, was the use of helicopters rapidly to insert infantrymen to follow up contacts. In Algeria and Borneo, especially, such tactics had been used previously, but in Vietnam air mobility truly came of age.

By 1968 as troop commitment peaked, the US was fighting a war of attrition. This was a bankrupt strategy, however, since politically the US Congress and electorate were unwilling to accept the losses commensurate with this strategy, defending a country that was of little real strategic US importance. Even when the US was inflicting extremely heavy casualties on the VC, the Communists could still increase their numbers through recruitment.

The irregulars trained by the Special Forces proved quite effective at countering the VC in their own areas, but as the war progressed these units underwent a change from local irregulars fighting to defend their ancestral lands, to United States mercenaries, often fighting along the borders with Cambodia and Laos in Special Forces 'fighting camps', located to interdict infiltration. Though more effective than most ARVN regular units, these Special Forces-trained irregulars had lost popular support for their effort, and frequently the land in the highlands they had defended as local militias had reverted to VC control.

In an attempt to substitute technology for manpower, the McNamara Line, consisting of sensors which would detect infiltrators, was suggested as a means of sealing the South to infiltrators. Huge sums were eventually spent on this and other interdiction schemes, including the construction of the largest building in South-East Asia, the 'Igloo White' computer complex at Nakhon Phanom, Thailand, to monitor the sensors which were eventually planted along the Ho Chi Minh Trail. Even so, political realities were being ignored. The situation in the countryside was being made worse by the ineffective handling of land reform by corrupt administrators siphoning off money intended to give peasants their own land. In this, as in many other aspects of the war, the corrupt South Vietnamese government was its own worst enemy.

By late 1967 and early 1968, 540,000 Americans were in the country, suffering casualties of hundreds per week. Keeping them there was costing the American taxpayers $30 billion per year. Despite this massive investment of resources, between 1965 and 1968 the Americans had for the most part been kept occupied by the North Vietnamese Army (NVA), while the VC had increased their control of the countryside. Discontent with the conduct of the war was growing in the United States, and victory seemed further away than it had in 1965. Though winning every major battle, the US was losing the will to fight, and, as troop frustration grew with not being able to tell who the enemy really was, events such as the Mai Lai massacre and other atrocities took place.

To deal with the most complex war it had ever fought, the US fielded the youngest army it had ever sent to war - an army, it should be noted, which the sons of the middle and upper classes found ways to avoid serving, thus leaving the least well-educated pool of manpower to draw troops from. Such young troops tend to be action- not thought-oriented, and being forced to cope with an enemy which dressed and looked just like the peasants they were theoretically defending understandably became confusing, particularly when sudden life-or-death decisions had to be made. Such decisions are difficult for highly experienced professional soldiers; for inexperienced conscripts in Vietnam, pulling the trigger was often the easiest solution.

The 1968 Tet Offensive was a premature attempt by the VC - at the direction of General Giap - to move to the third stage of Mao's guerrilla warfare. The VC were not received by a population which rose in sympathy. Instead, after some initial successes, they were resoundingly defeated, suffering at least 30,000 casualties. Press coverage of the events in Saigon, however, particularly the assault on the US Embassy, shocked the American public and eroded even more the national will to continue the fight. As an adjunct to the Tet Offensive, the American Marine Base at Khe Sanh was invested by NVA and VC. Arguments persist to this day about the

LRRP

significance of Khe Sanh. Some hold that it was Giap's attempt to bring about an American Dien Bien Phu, but others feel that the Americans used it as an anvil against which they crushed substantial numbers of Communist troops with their airpower and artillery. Others believe that Giap planned the Khe Sanh operation to tie down US troops, thus allowing the NVA and VC freedom of action in other parts of the country. The truth is probably somewhere between these two views.

It is true that after Tet, the Viet Cong went into decline and from that point on the war was fought primarily against the NVA. Some even believe that Giap deliberately intended the VC to be broken during the Tet Offensive, so that when the war was won they would not present an obstacle to control of the South from Hanoi. In any case, after 1968, though still fought to some extent along guerrilla lines, the war was primarily against NVA regulars; in 1968 alone, for example, at least 100,000 came down the Ho Chi Minh Trail.

Under President Nixon the new policy was Vietnamization, more and more responsibility for fighting the war being turned over to the South Vietnamese, often too soon. Although this policy would probably have been the best one to pursue in 1964, before the US troop build-up, the fact that the US had borne much of the combat burden for four years made the relatively rapid withdrawal very hard for the ARVNs to absorb. Nevertheless, some ARVN units, particularly the 1st Division, the Airborne Division, and the Rangers, showed excellent combat potential. Over the next three years hundreds of thousands of US troops were pulled out, while those who remained were used less on combat operations. In the Mekong Delta, particularly, but in other parts of the country as well, the Phoenix Program had destroyed much of the VC infrastructure, thus allowing pacification programmes to proceed. Had the VC been the only enemy, the war would have been won.

Though it led to massive protests by the anti-war movement in the United States, the 1970 invasion of Cambodia was nevertheless a masterful stroke, as it hit directly at previously immune Communist base areas. As a result, the NVA build-up was seriously impeded, setting back their schedule for the invasion of the South by as much as a year. When this offensive was launched, on 30 March 1972, it was finally repelled with the aid of massive US airpower, more readily deployed now against an invading army equipped with tanks and other vehicles.

Once again using negotiations as its fourth combat arm along with infantry, armour and artillery, the North Vietnamese left large concentrations of NVA troops behind in South Vietnam following cease-fire negotiations. During the Easter Invasion which followed, it should be pointed out, the VC contributed virtually nothing, often even refusing to supply guides to the NVA, whom they now viewed as invaders.

After the US bombing of the North, and the mining of Haiphong Harbour in the spring of 1972, Hanoi was in dire straits. The US was not interested in defeating the North Vietnamese at this point, however, but merely in extracting itself from an economic and political quagmire. It is doubtful if Henry Kissinger was really naïve enough to believe the North Vietnamese would abide by their peace agreements. In reality, the tacit understanding was that the North would wait until the United States had completed its pull-out.

After 1972, the new name for the Viet Cong was the People's Revolutionary Government (PRG). Now that South Vietnam had become an embarrassment, the government of the Republic of Vietnam still proving incapable of implementing effective reforms to improve the lot of the rural peasants, the US began to cut back on military aid.

The fall of Saigon in 1975 was perhaps a decade later than it might otherwise have been without US involvement. The city was taken, not by a guerrilla force, however, but by a well-equipped modern army. Hanoi's grand strategy had proved successful, the VC having eaten away at the Republic of Vietnam internally and brought about US disenchantment with the war. As adjuncts to the conflict, Laos and Cambodia also fell, to indigenous guerrillas supported by North Vietnam.

Analysis

The guerrilla warfare strategy in Vietnam represented a perceptive modification of Mao's precepts to fit the particular situation in Vietnam. The key element of its success was the constant wearing away of the American and South Vietnamese will to fight. The assumption was that if a combination of the following conditions were met, the North could win:

1 the loss of American will;
2 the loss of South Vietnamese will;
3 the failure of America and South Vietnam to devise a viable counter-strategy;
4 the failure of the South Vietnamese to develop a viable government.

All four conditions were met to a greater or lesser extent.

In order to win, the North Vietnamese were willing to make extreme sacrifices and did not baulk at decisions such as sacrificing the VC during the Tet Offensive. The North Vietnamese suffered more than one million casualties, yet retained their will to fight, while the United States found less than 47,000 deaths unacceptable. This

◀ When used properly to insert small saturation patrols, or rapidly to reinforce troops in contact with the enemy, the helicopter can be a very effective counter-insurgency tool *(US Army)*

◀ Since local intelligence is an absolute necessity in counter-guerrilla operations, LRRPs (Long Range Reconnaissance Patrols) such as this troop were invaluable in Vietnam *(US Army)*

▲ Among the best counter-insurgency troops in the Army of the Republic of Vietnam were the ARVN Rangers, here being trained by a US Army Ranger adviser *(US Army)*

disparity is even more pronounced when one considers the populations of the two countries. Not bound by western traditions of 'fair play', the Communists used negotiations as a distraction while either regrouping or continuing to fight. In the context of counter-guerrilla warfare, this should be considered more an example of American naïvety than North Vietnamese duplicity.

Another advantage the North Vietnamese had was a relatively homogeneous population, united by Communism, though admittedly there were dissatisfied minorities in the Black Hills. In the South, on the other hand, factionalism between Buddhists and Catholics and the disaffected Chinese and Montagnard minorities eroded the ability of the central government to function. Additionally, the Ho Chi Minh Trail running through Cambodia and Laos gave a ready source of support first to the VC, then to the NVA operating within South Vietnam.

So important was the Ho Chi Minh Trail that many astute strategists believe that, had the United States and South Vietnam taken action to sever it in 1965, the situation in the South would have been stabilized and the Communist threat within the country eliminated. The North also was willing to make use of opposition in the United States to the war, even inviting Jane Fonda to Hanoi.

There is little doubt that the American press contributed at least passively to the erosion of the American will to fight in Vietnam, as the TV showed soldiers dying on each evening's news.

To win a guerrilla war it has been shown again and again that those attempting to counter the guerrilla need clear-cut political goals; apart from the nebulous 'domino theory' and a zeal to stop Communist expansion, the United States vacillated in its political aims in Vietnam. The continued support of corrupt government officials and military leaders, many of whom had little desire to see the war end, as they were growing rich on the black market, was particularly destructive. Certain tactical concepts proved to be particularly poor in the counter-guerrilla context. 'Search and destroy', for example, frequently lived up to its name all too well, as US infantrymen moved ponderously through the countryside destroying crops or villages, together with support for the US-sponsored government.

Some US programmes were effective. The CIDG programme initially worked very well,

▲ Members of the LRRPs, SEALs, and Special Forces became adept at ambushes, turning the guerrilla's most effective weapon against him in Vietnam *(Larry Dring)*

giving rural hamlets the ability to defend themselves against the VC, while also helping them with civil works to improve their life under the South Vietnamese government. Offering less scope for corruption, however, this programme was opposed by most South Vietnamese officials. The Phoenix Program, though vilified in the press as purely an assassination programme, was highly successful at identifying and eliminating the VC infrastructure within South Vietnam. It was also a good example of the ability of South Vietnamese officials to corrupt such programmes, as they often targeted their own political enemies for the Phoenix Program, rather than real members of the VC. As in virtually every counter-guerrilla campaign in history, small, highly trained mobile forces such as the Special Forces Delta, Sigma, Omega or MACV/SOG teams, the Navy's SEALs or the Army's LRRPs, proved cost effective and selective. Once again, pseudo-guerrillas proved effective, the United States sponsoring 'Road Runner' teams dressed as VC, which operated

along infiltration networks to disrupt and ambush infiltrators.

Even had the United States not attempted to throw technology and money at the problem – more Road Runners and fewer B-52s would have served better – without a viable central government for South Vietnam supported by a population willing to fight, the South was doomed, once the United States finally decided the economic, political and human costs were unacceptable. Stoicism has often been lauded as an Oriental philosophical virtue; for the North Vietnamese it proved a military virtue as well.

US ARMY SPECIAL FORCES

The Special Forces (SF) were formed in 1952 with the primary mission in wartime of organizing Eastern European resistance against the Soviets. During the next decade, however, its mission expanded to include training friendly airborne/commando units in counter-insurgency, as well as acting as the principal US unconventional warfare force. John F. Kennedy, particularly, was a Special Forces advocate and won for them the right to wear the distinctive green beret.

In South-East Asia, a Special Forces team had trained Royal Thai Rangers as early as 1954, but it was during the later fifties that Special Forces first deployed to Vietnam, to help form and train the Joint Observation Battalion, which would evolve into the LLDB, the Vietnamese Special Forces. Twelve Field Training Teams from 77th SFG (Abn) were deployed to Laos in spring 1959, under the legendary SF officer 'Bull' Simons to train the Royal Laotian Army in counter-guerrilla tactics and to raise irregular counter-guerrilla forces.

In order to carry out their training and support of irregulars – whether guerrilla or counter-guerrilla – Special Forces were organized into basic units known as A-Detachments, or A-Teams, consisting of twelve members as follows: Team Commander (captain), Team Executive Officer (first lieutenant), Operations Sergeant, Heavy Weapons Leader, Intelligence Sergeant, Light Weapons Leader, Medical Specialist, Radio Operator Supervisor, Engineer Sergeant, Assistant Medical Specialist, Assistant Intelligence Sergeant, Radio Operator.

Note the presence of the two medical specialists, who were highly trained, even to the level of performing field surgery. Part of their mission was to win local support with medical care. In addition to being team demolitions expert, the engineer sergeant could also help with local public works projects. The two intelligence specialists set up local agent nets for either guerrilla or counter-guerrilla operations, and the two weapons leaders were specialists in training irregulars in the use of small arms and weapons up through mortars or heavy machine guns.

In an attempt to counter the growing VC influence in the central highlands of Vietnam, the Rhade Montagnard village of Buon Enao was selected late in 1961 as the pilot for the Civilian Irregular Defence Group (CIDG) Program. Under this programme, SF along with LLDB trained local defence forces to protect their villages, while also assisting them with public works projects. By April 1962, twenty villages were protected under this programme, and by August two hundred villages in Darlac Province were protected by CIDG irregulars. So successful ws the programme that the entire province was considered secure by the year's end. During the same year, Special Forces had also established their first Border Surveil-

▲ To interdict enemy infiltration, sensors were sown along the Ho Chi Minh Trail *(USAF)*

▶ One of the many sensors sown, to detect VC/NVA infiltration into South Vietnam. Note its appearance, which is intended to camouflage it as a plant *(USAF)*

lance camps to watch the borders with Laos, Cambodia and North Vietnam for infiltrators. Once again, Montagnard hill tribesmen were widely used.

The CIDG Program expanded to the point that by the end of 1963 there were 43,000 hamlet militia members, supported by 18,000 full-time strike force members. At least another 12,000 local irregulars were assigned to various special interdiction missions. Already by late 1963, however, the CIDG Program was moving away from its original local defence mission, as border interdiction increasingly became its primary goal. By 1964, area development aspects of the programme were being neglected in favour of establishing fighting camps in position to interdict the borders. The CIDG were being converted from agrarian militia to mercenary border guards. The Montagnards, though they worked well with Special Forces, had always been considered a second-class minority in Vietnam, and their hatred of the Vietnamese surfaced with a revolt in September 1964. Though Special Forces advisers managed to bring the Montagnards under control, the simmering dissatisfaction would remain throughout the war, particularly after the CIDG Program was turned over to the Vietnamese.

Another very effective Special Forces operation in Vietnam was the Greek letter projects. Organized to carry out reconnaissance missions within Vietnam, Projects Delta, Sigma and Omega were based on teams of two or three members of Special Forces and four to eight indigenous troops, sometimes members of the LLDB. Missions carried out included intelligence-gathering, hunter/killer raids, snatches of key VC personnel, rescues, psychological operations, photographic reconnaissance, calling in airstrikes and tapping VC communications. If large enemy concentrations were encountered, a reaction force, often drawn from the MIKE Forces, would be called in.

The MIKE Force, or Mobile Strike Force, had developed by summer 1965 as a special reaction force for the CIDG Programme, based on three light infantry companies plus an HQ and totalling about six hundred men. Such forces fell directly under Special Forces control, rather than indirectly through 'advising', and thus could be employed more effectively. Also formed as an offshoot of the MIKE Forces were the Mobile Guerrilla Forces, which consisted of a Special Forces

▼ US Army LRRPs such as this one were used to gather tactical intelligence and to carry out ambushes or raids against VC guerrillas *(US Army)*

A-Detachment, a MIKE Force Company and a thirty-four-man Combat Recon Platoon. These forces were designed to operate independently for thirty to sixty days in remote parts of Vietnam, carrying out missions to destroy or sabotage VC storage areas, ambushing the VC, and calling in air strikes. The Mobile Guerrilla Forces were exceptionally effective.

Once US conventional forces arrived in some numbers, SF irregulars often acted as stalking horses to draw VC attack, so that US airmobile troops could fix and destroy the enemy. The most important contribution, however, was the intelligence-gathering carried out by the Greek letter units. Another real contribution to the counter-guerrilla campaign made by the Special Forces as a result of the Greek letter units was the formation of the MACV Recondo School at Nha Trang. This school, which taught a three-week recon/commando course, trained many of the LRRPs who proved such effective local intelligence sources, as well as training the indigenous troops assigned to Delta, Sigma and Omega.

As the Special Forces fighting camps became more important to the interdiction effort, they were designed so they could be built from prefabricated components within thirty to forty-five days. Planned with interlocking fields of fire, extensive barriers of mines, tripwires, barbed wire and phougas (field expedient napalm), the camps functioned as centres from which aggressive patrolling could take place, while as little as a quarter of the camp strength was needed to defend them. Since the VC had owned the night for much of the war, patrols from fighting camps made it a point to set ambushes at night to inflict casualties and to erode VC confidence. The success of these fighting camps often helped win over the local population. But, as a result, by 1967 they were coming under heavy VC attack. To counter this threat, MIKE Force strength was increased for reinforcing threatened camps.

During the Tet Offensive, Special Forces irregulars helped defend many towns under attack; more importantly, they harried the VC as they retreated, increasing their casualty level still fur-

◀ The helicopter was both a great advantage and a great disadvantage in Vietnam, as its mobility helped fix and destroy an elusive enemy, but its noise frequently gave warning of operations *(US Army)*

▲ In an attempt to deny the VC the support of the population, sympathizing villages were often destroyed, as with this flamethrower. This policy, of course, often alienated large portions of the population *(US Army)*

◀ *Inset:* To allow air transport to supply isolated bases such as Special Forces fighting camps, USAF Combat Control Teams could even guide in C-130 transports *(USAF)*

ther. However, in the months following Tet, as the Vietnamization of the war took place, fighting camps were turned over to Vietnamese control, the CIDG troops often becoming Vietnamese Rangers.

While the Greek letter projects carried out special missions within Vietnam, MACV/SOG (Military Assistance Command Vietnam/Special Operations Group) carried out such missions into Laos, Cambodia and North Vietnam. Many of these cross-border missions were for intelligence purposes, but others were more direct action to ambush or assassinate NVA/VC or to call in airstrikes. Various 'black' operations included the planting of munitions designed to detonate in the weapon in Communist arms supplies, to erode confidence in their weapons. POW rescue missions, and assistance of downed aviators, were among the other SOG tasks, all of which were performed effectively. SOG reconnaissance teams were normally composed of a combination of SF and indigenous personnel. However, Road Runner teams carrying out pseudo-guerrilla operations were normally composed entirely of indigenous personnel.

Although Special Forces were often misused in Vietnam, overall they provided highly effective counter-insurgency training and leadership. Had the CIDG Program continued as originally intended, it is possible that large portions of the countryside would have been pacified, allowing the South Vietnamese Army to be prepared to counter the threat from North Vietnam. The value of troops such as the Special Forces as force multipliers was proved in the counter-guerrilla as well as the guerrilla role for which they were formed. For their indigenous counter-guerrillas to be most effective, however, the South Vietnamese government needed to implement massive reforms making CIDG troops true citizens, so they could then be citizen soldiers.

▼ Special Forces fighting camps such as this one were sited to interdict infiltration routes, but were also very prone to attack; hence, their design for all-round defence with mortar pits, interlocking fields of fire by machine guns, minefields, etc

◀ US airpower proved a valuable counter-insurgency tool, but as a result US air bases became targets of VC and NVA infiltration. The combination of barbed wire and security police with dogs helped inhibit such infiltration *(USAF)*

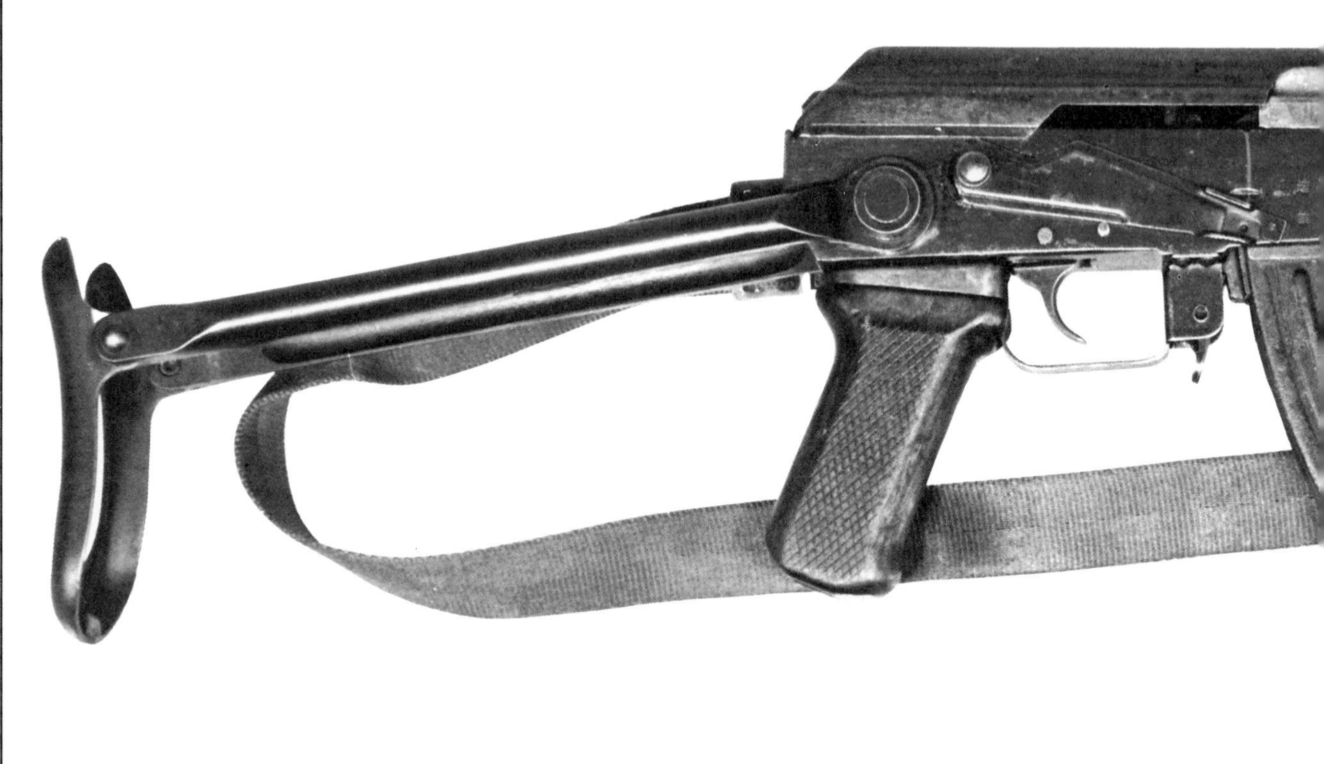

THE AK-47

The AK-47 Assault Rifle is the world's most widely used small arm, being the standard infantry weapon in the Soviet Union, the rest of the Warsaw Pact, China and various Third World countries. Because of Soviet, Chinese and Cuban support of insurgencies during the last three decades, too, the AK-47 has become the principal arm in the hands of guerrillas all over the world.

The AK-47 chambers the M43 7.62 × 39mm round developed during the Second World War, probably based on information about the German intermediate assault rifle round. Although keeping the standard Russian 7.62 bore diameter, the M43 round is rimless and substantially shorter, an advantage for an assault rifle, since it allows for a more compact weapon, and easier-to-carry ammunition. These are particularly important considerations for guerrillas, since their weapons often have to be carried for long distances in jungles or over mountains.

The AK was designed by Michael T. Kalashnikov, a Tank Corps senior sergeant, who won a Stalin Prize and was made Hero of Soviet Labour for his invention. Basically a composite design, drawing on previous Western and Soviet weapons, the AK is gas operated with a piston and rotating bolt. Its greatest appeal, both in the Soviet and Chinese armies and with guerrillas, is that it is easy to produce, easy to maintain (it will continue to operate for long periods even without maintenance in many cases) and is reasonably accurate. The chrome-plated bore survives even jungle climates

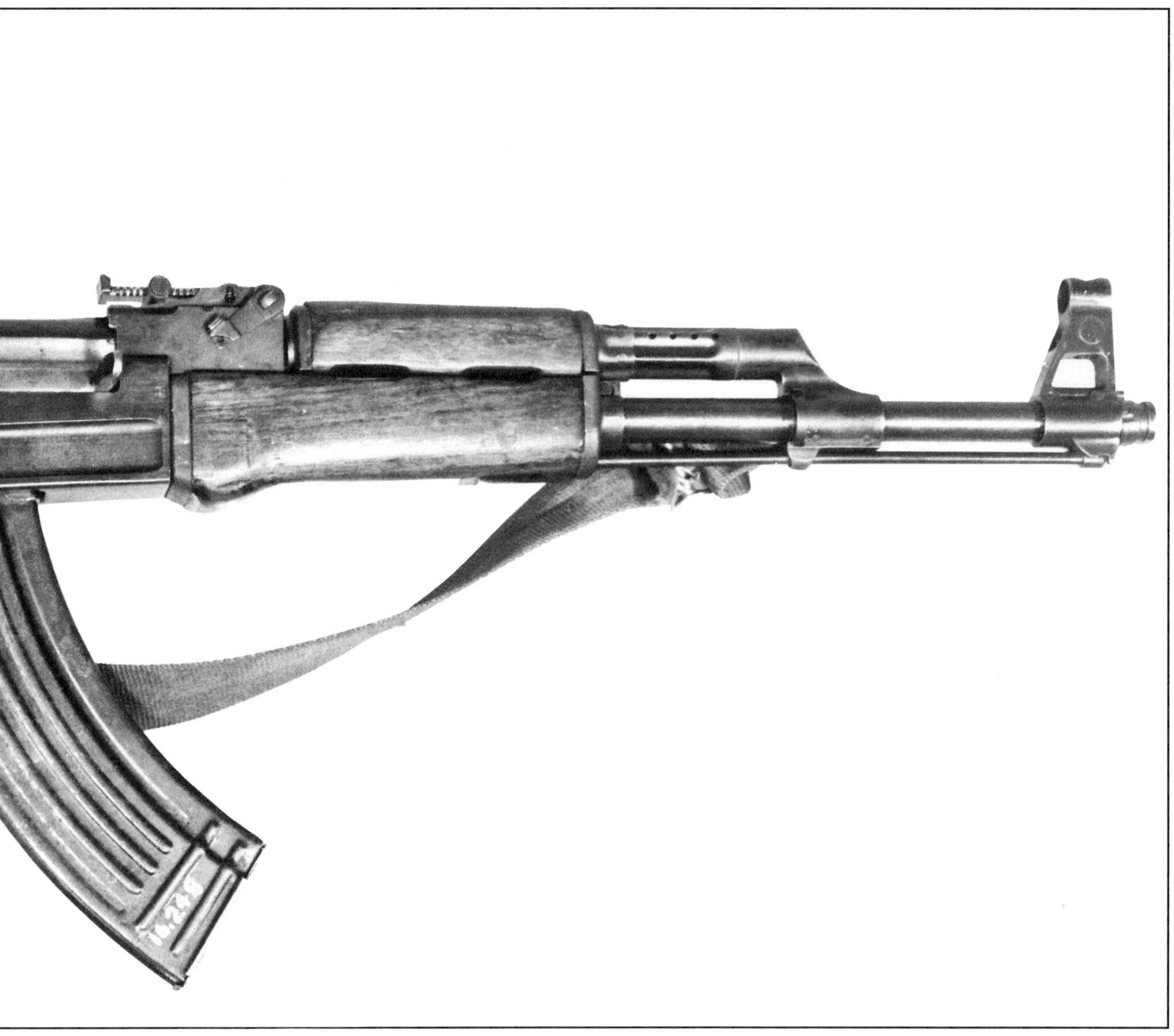

relatively well. Another real advantage for its use by poorly trained troops is that the weapon is extremely easy to operate. The safety lever, for example, has three positions: safe in the up position, full automatic fire in the middle position and semi-automatic fire in the bottom position.

The AK-47 takes its designation from the fact it was standardized in the Soviet Army in 1947. Since then it has been produced in various versions, including the AKM, a modernized version using more stampings and designed to be lighter; the RPK, a light machine gun version; the SVD, a sniper rifle using a strengthened action to handle the 7.62mm M1908 cartridge for sniping; and the AK-74, a compact version, chambered for the 5.45mm cartridge. The standard AKM is 35.65 inches in overall length, weighs 9 lb 7 oz unloaded, and has a magazine capacity of thirty rounds.

▲ For the last twenty-five years the Soviet AK-47 has been the weapon of choice for insurgents supported by the Communist bloc, due to its ease of maintenance and use *(West Point Museum)*

The AK is widely produced and even more widely distributed, and is the most likely weapon to be encountered in the hands of guerrillas.

TAP MK2 NO14 K

12 OMAN

Throughout the 1950s and 1960s, Oman remained a backward land, kept in isolation from the twentieth century by its Sultan. There had been a revolt against the Sultan during 1958–9, which was finally broken with the assistance of the Special Air Service, two squadrons of which scaled the Jebel Akhdar at night for a surprise attack.

Old Sultan Sa'id bin Taimur had done little to bring his country into the twentieth century, preferring to rely on Oman's isolation, keeping out of the public eye. Some Omanis, however, particularly among those resident in Dhofar Province, had left and had seen something of the outside world. As a result, they realized how backward educationally, technically, medically and politically their medieval sultanate really was. Other problems came in the form of Iraqi-trained guerrillas on the Musandam Peninsula, who were fomenting trouble among tribesmen there. Members of 22nd SAS were sent to this peninsula in Gemini rubber boats and by HALO parachute jump in 1969 to counter this threat. The main threat, however, was in Dhofar.

To understand the guerrilla campaign which was mounted by some of the discontented Dhofaris, Oman's geography must first be understood. The country is divided into two parts: to the north it is inhabited by about 500,000 tribal Omanis; to the south, four hundred miles across a barren desert, is Dhofar Province, with a population of about 50,000 and many millions of barrels of oil beneath the ground. From June to September Dhofar has a monsoon which, for Arabia, creates a surprisingly fertile area near the coast. Above the coast is a high jebel with a plateau leading to the border with the People's Democratic Republic of Yemen (formerly the Federation of South Arabia). Dhofar is inhabited by mixed groups, including nomadic cattle and camel breeders on the jebel. The Dhofaris tend to be more Ethiopian than Arabic in appearance.

That Britain would come readily to the aid of Oman was the consequence of many considerations. First, the Sultanate had had a treaty with Great Britain since 1798. Additionally, the oil reserves in Dhofar are among the largest in the world, and Oman occupies a critical strategic position on the Straits of Hormuz, so much in the news during the Iran/Iraq War. British officers, in fact, have traditionally served on contract with the Sultan's Armed Forces (SAF).

When initial guerrilla warfare broke out on the jebel during the mid-1960s, the SAF carried out punitive expeditions, often striking against innocents and alienating even members of the jebel population loyal to the Sultan. As a result, the Dhofar Liberation Front (DLF) grew in support. However, the DLF was soon challenged and submerged by the Communist People's Front for the Liberation of Oman (PFLO), which was based in the PDRY. Among other acts, the guerrillas (known as *adoos*) constantly descended from the jebel to mine the road connecting the port of Raysut to Mirbat. The adoos had also driven the Sultan's Armed Forces from the jebel and, armed with AK-47 and SKS rifles, as well as Soviet and Chinese machine guns, mortars and recoilless rifles, did not appear an easy target to dislodge.

As with many guerrilla armies, the adoos were organized into hard-core fighters and part-time militiamen. In addition to harassing traffic on the roads, they could infiltrate down from the jebel at night to lob mortar rounds at the town of Salahah, or the airbase there. Meanwhile, throughout the latter part of the sixties, the PFLO had consolidated its power on the jebel through a campaign of terror and propaganda, while preparing for the future by sending children to the PDRY for indoctrination. Lack of understanding of the Dhofaris on the part of the SAF, combined with the old Sultan's unwillingness to reform his country, made the PFLO appear to be the best hope for liberation the Dhofaris had.

The first positive step towards countering the guerrilla threat occurred in July 1970, when the Sultan's son Qaboos deposed his father in a coup, assisted by the British at least tacitly. Almost immediately, Qaboos instituted reforms and a civil development campaign to win back the people. The PFLO had become arrogant, alienating the Dhofaris by their use of torture to compel them to deny Allah, or by demanding sexual access to their daughters. Now

◀ Among the many options for inserting members of the SAS into an area of operations is the HALO jump, for which this trooper is equipped

disillusioned, many former DLF members came down from the jebel and surrendered to the Sultan. It was apparent that with a sincere plan for civic development on the jebel, the people could be won back, but first the jebel would have to be secured militarily. To accomplish this, the SAF needed to be upgunned and better trained. Just as importantly, their fear of operating on the jebel had to be overcome. Although occasionally the SAF had penetrated on to the jebel for a few days as a show of force, the belief was widespread that operations there during the monsoon were absolutely impossible.

The problem, then, was that to win the campaign, the SAF had to establish control of the jebel, so that civic action could begin. The Dhofaris, with some justification, did not view the SAF as their army. The officers were British, and the other ranks were mainly Baluchis or Northern Omanis. To assist the SAF in their mission, the Special Air Service was brought in from Great Britain. Their three primary missions would be provision of intelligence, provision of trained medics for the first phase of the civic action programme, and raising indigenous Dhofari *firqats* to fight for the Sultan.

One of the SAS's first steps was the establishment of two four-man civic action teams at Taqa and Mirbat, each of which set up a clinic. Ex-DLF members were recruited for intelligence, while the medics gained additional intelligence from patients. Since the Dhofaris were especially concerned about their animals, a vet was brought in as well, to help improve the livestock's health. As they became established, the SAS began carrying out propaganda exercises. One real masterpiece was the slogan, 'Islam is our Way, Freedom is our Aim.' This slogan was intended to nurture the growing resentment of the PFLO for its atheism and its attempts to subjugate the tribal units on the jebel. So that information could be broadcast to the jebel from Radio Dhofar, initially, transistor radios were either given away or sold very cheaply to the jebelis when they came down to the bazaar. The godlessness of the Communists became a particularly telling point against them.

Any jebelis who came down and surrendered were treated well, too. Drawing upon the ranks of disillusioned former guerrillas, the SAS began forming counter-guerrilla irregulars into firqats. The fact that many members of the SAS spoke Arabic obviously proved a real advantage during this stage.

Additionally, the SAS carried out operations with the SAF and worked with them on improving their patrolling skills. The Sultan's Air Force proved valuable, too, since the open ground on the jebel was well suited to air operations, though the adoos could easily take refuge in caves. Often, the new firqat leaders would fly with British pilots of the Sultan's Air Force, identifying adoo supply dumps for bombing.

As the SAS trained the firqats, they found that there was no lack of fighting spirit, though there was much of the bickering which often infects irregulars. Long years of working with irregulars, however, had taught the SAS how to deal with such problems. For example, members of the firqats initially wanted to be armed with AK-47s rather than FN rifles, since the AKs were lighter and easier to carry. Realizing that many of the jebelis were experienced riflemen, however, the SAS set up targets and asked them to shoot both rifles, convincing them in this way of the FN's superior accuracy. Once firqats went into action,

▲ In each Special Air Service squadron, one troop, known as mobility troop, was specially trained for desert operations, using the famous SAS 'Pink Panther' Land Rovers

it was soon discovered that adoos were much more willing to surrender to their former comrades, the firqats, than to the SAF.

By March 1971 it was time to re-establish a position on the jebel, to prove that the adoos did not really control it. The SAS and some firqats moved into position at the Eagle's Nest, and though they had problems with the lack of water, took a toll on the adoos over the next few days before pulling back. It was decided as a result of this expedition to establish a permanent base after the monsoon. The distrust between the jebelis and the SAF still had to be overcome, so firqats were used to act as scouts for the SAF, thus increasing both understanding and efficiency.

Although they were being beaten, both militarily and in the campaign for the support of the people, the adoos were certainly not out of the fight. In fact, during 1971 they received some highly trained assistance from former regular soldiers in various Gulf armies, including the Trucial Oman Scouts, who had deserted, then been trained in China and the Soviet Union. These 'pros', however, proved less of an asset than expected, since they considered most of the adoos rank amateurs and disdained carrying out operations with them. Nevertheless, some of them were particularly well-trained mortarmen who continued the harassment of the SAS, firqat and SAF positions at night. Adoo support was definitely eroding, though, particularly as those deserting and joining one of the Sultan's firqats received quite good pay. As a result, the adoos had to post at least three men at outposts to watch each other and prevent desertion. This proved a marked drain on available manpower. The PFLO also attempted to regain some lost support among the people by being more tolerant of Islam, but they found it hard to make up lost ground. Relying on only one supply route from the PDRY, adoos were particularly vulnerable to supply problems. When the government instituted a food denial programme, including restriction on movement of food, this had a telling effect on adoo health and morale. Once the SAF and the firqats moved on to the jebel in force, the problem of finding food would become even greater for the adoos.

The long-awaited move took place in October 1971, when a permanent base was seized atop the jebel by two SAS squadrons, two SAF companies, five firqats, and supporting engineers. The former SAF base at Lympne was the point of initial seizure, but this was soon expanded as bases were established at Jibjat and White City. Now back on the jebel, civic action had to begin there as well, so the SAS medic teams moved up, while members of SAS helped the jebelis get their cattle down to market. To gain jebeli confidence and show his own confidence in them, Qaboos visited the jebel as well.

Now definitely on the defensive as the SAF expanded its control on the jebel and the civic action teams moved into the resecured areas, the PFLO attacked Mirbat in July 1972, to prove they were still a force to be reckoned with. Two hundred and fifty adoos, supported by mortars and recoilless rifles, carried out the assault, timed to hit while the firqats were away. The limited number of SAS and SAF defenders, however, held and broke the attack, thus eroding the credibility and confidence of the PFLO even more.

That year also saw the establishment of the Hornbeam Line running north on the jebel for area control, to allow civic action to take place with less fear of attack from guerrillas. Over the next two years more and more helicopters became available, too, including Hueys from Vietnam by 1973–4. As a result, it was easier to lift troops and civic action teams on to or off the jebel. Beginning in 1973, large numbers of Iranian Special Forces were deployed to the jebel to assist with the campaign. Though they did not, for the most part, speak Arabic, they did prove useful for manning the Hornbeam Line and later 'lines' established for area control.

By 1973, as well, a fairly established pattern had emerged for the development of the firqats. Initially, they were organized and trained; then they were used on operations against the adoos; finally they were used for clearing and controlling their tribal area, and to assist with civic action programmes. To enable civic action to include larger projects, such as well-drilling, thus alleviating many endemic problems with water shortage on the jebel, a civilian agency was established to operate on the jebel and in other parts of Dhofar. By 1975 when the Jordanian Special Forces arrived to assist with final pacification of the country, most remaining adoos were in the west. However, their backs were now to the border with the PDRY, as the SAF, firqats, SAS, and supporting allies such as the Iranians and Jordanians tightened the cordon around them. In a desperate attempt to support the remaining PFLO, artillery from within the PDRY fired on SAF, so the Sultan ordered air strikes into the PDRY to silence this support, prior to driving remaining Communist guerrillas across the border into the PDRY.

A few scattered adoos remained at large on the jebel, but by September 1976, when the SAS was pulled out, the country was secure.

Analysis

The campaign in Oman was won for a few very simple, yet highly critical reasons. The coup which brought Qaboos to power was an absolute necessity, and he proved a strong, decisive leader, able to exert total military and civil control. With Qaboos in charge, the simple plan of securing areas militarily so that civil development could take place was implemented. Another extremely important factor was that the huge oil revenues meant the Sultan could afford the military and civil costs of carrying the campaign through to its conclusion. Willingness to bring in the SAS and make effective use of their special talents also proved a critical aspect of the campaign, as SAS medics were the initial wedge to open the hearts of the Dhofaris to civic action programmes. Equally important was the SAS's ability to work with indigenous counter-guerrillas and the firqats, to turn them into an effective fighting and intelligence source. Availability of airpower, particularly helicopters, gave the Sultan's forces another important edge.

Although initially the PFLO had many advantages, particularly the intransigence of the old Sultan and the support of the PDRY, their ardent Communism carried the seed of their own downfall, its concomitant atheism eventually alienating the Dhofari Muslims. Although they had learned certain lessons of guerrilla warfare, they had not learned Mao's precepts about the importance of retaining the support of the people. Next to Islam, the jebelis felt most strongly about their tribal unit, and the PFLO alienated them further by trying to eliminate this entity. Once they began losing the support of the people, another basic weakness of the PFLO became apparent, since they were highly dependent upon a single supply line from the PDRY.

In simple terms, as long as supporting the PFLO appeared to be in the interests of the Dhofaris, they did so, but once the new Sultan proved that he would be better able to help them, time was against the PFLO and in favour of the Sultan's forces.

13 RHODESIA

Rhodesia's situation was quite similar to that of Kenya, in that during the first part of the twentieth century there had been a policy of racial separation, in particular concerning land ownership. The native Africans lived primarily in Tribal Trust Lands, often located in the least fertile areas, while European farmers controlled the most productive land.

By the 1960s, Great Britain was pressuring for land and political reforms in Rhodesia. However, a combination of reaction against the Mau Mau Rebellion in Kenya, particularly in view of the murder of Europeans which had been part of it, along with opposition to the British Labour government, led to UDI, the unilateral declaration of independence of Rhodesia from Great Britain, on 11 November 1965, establishing an independent state under the leadership of Ian Smith.

The Zimbabwe African People's Union (ZAPU) had been formed in 1961, and the Zimbabwe African National Union in 1963, in opposition to White rule. ZAPU, led by Joshua Nkomo, drew its support mainly from the Matabeles, who made up about nineteen per cent of Rhodesia's African population. ZANU, led by Robert Mugabe, drew its support from the Shonas, who made up about seventy per cent of Rhodesia's Blacks. In September 1963, ZANU had sent five men to the People's Republic of China for guerrilla warfare training, to form the nucleus of ZANU's armed wing, ZANLA, the Zimbabwe African National Liberation Army. There was dissension between these two nationalist groups, and as it grew, ZAPU formed its own armed wing, known as ZIPRA, the Zimbabwe People's Revolutionary Army.

Initially, the guerrilla strategy pursued by these two groups was based on the assumption that they could frighten the Europeans into making massive concessions, and bring about British intervention. By 1966, when this had not materialized, a campaign to destabilize the White government and gain African support began. At first, Black Rhodesians living outside Rhodesia, in Zambia and Tanzania, were recruited, and on 28 April 1966 the first clash between ZANLA and the Rhodesian security forces marked the beginning of the guerrilla war. On 16 May, part of the same ZANLA group murdered a European couple. Eventually, of fourteen guerrillas who had

▼ The Rhodesians made very wide use of their parachute troops to cut off escaping guerrillas, particularly through the use of RLI Fireforce members

infiltrated with this group, thirteen were killed or captured.

By August 1967, ninety ZIPRA guerrillas had infiltrated in one group, but they found little support among local Black Africans, who reported them, resulting in forty-seven guerrillas being killed and twenty captured during the next three weeks. Undaunted, early in 1968, 123 ZIPRA guerrillas crossed the Zambesi River and set up six base camps within Rhodesia. Once again, however, the security forces acted quickly, within a couple of months destroying all the bases and killing sixty insurgents. While other large incursions from Zambia continued, their very size allowed the security forces to use track-and-kill tactics rather effectively. By 1969, guerrilla losses had been so great that both groups halted infiltration. ZIPRA, having suffered most heavily, became most conservative, not taking military action again for some years.

These relatively easy early victories gave the Rhodesian government a false sense of security; neither political reform nor increased military expenditure seemed justified. The lull was short-lived as far as ZANLA was concerned, however, as they emerged as the primary fighters in the 'struggle for liberation'. ZANLA, the more Chinese-oriented of the two guerrilla movements, maintained an emphasis on Mao's precepts, working primarily on the political education of labourers and peasants. The more Soviet-oriented ZIPRA still theoretically emphasized military action, particularly the use of land mines.

At this time, both groups were based in Zambia. However, ZANLA also enjoyed free use of bases in Mozambique, courtesy of FRELIMO, which was fighting the Portuguese in that colony. FRELIMO supported ZANLA to some extent philosophically, but primarily because destabilizing Rhodesia would support their aims for the conquest of Mozambique. An additional advantage accruing to ZANLA from this arrangement was that the mountains in north-eastern Rhodesia, being less populous than other areas, were more suitable as a guerrilla base. Since ZANLA was still working on the first stage of their guerrilla war, having this relatively safe base area within Rhodesia itself suited their goals quite well.

In December 1972 ZANLA began attacking White farmers again. Though Rhodesia at this stage had four intelligence agencies – Army, British South Africa Police (BSAP), Special Branch and Internal Affairs – the lack of good sources in Tribal Trust Lands, and particularly in north-eastern Rhodesia, had prevented their discovering that ZANLA was moving freely back and forth across the border and had established a base in Rhodesia. More importantly, in the long term, they were building strong support among the local population. Ironically, while ZANLA guerrillas were infiltrating into Rhodesia from Mozambique, Rhodesia had its two best units, the Rhodesian Light Infantry (RLI) and the Special Air Service (SAS), operating in Mozambique in support of the Portuguese.

The situation continued to worsen in north-eastern Rhodesia, as local Africans now refused to turn in ZANLA guerrillas. As a result, the very positive step was taken of establishing a Joint Operations Centre, known as 'Hurricane', to co-ordinate counter-insurgency operations in the area. Initial strategy was based on a combination of population control and border closure. Tactics to implement this strategy included a cordon sanitaire (which actually wasn't all that sanitaire), patrolling, a twenty-kilometre no-go area along the border, detection devices along the border, control of food and population movement through Protected Villages, and eventually martial law. The plan was to remove the population – which was done against their will in most cases, it should be noted – then after 'sterilizing' the area, to channel guerrillas into that area, which would become a killing zone where the security forces would eliminate them. In a further attempt to stop infiltration, in 1973 the border with Zambia was closed.

Unfortunately, the Rhodesian government did not react as effectively on the political front. By allowing local commissioners to enforce collective punishment on villages found to have been assisting guerrillas, many Africans were simply goaded into further support for the guerrillas. In one case during 1974, two hundred people were forcibly resettled in this way.

In July 1973, the guerrillas had begun abducting schoolchildren, seizing 292 at St Albert's Mission, in one instance. Although the security forces rescued all but eight of the children, such abductions could only erode the government's credibility as a defender of the people. Moving the population to 'Protected Villages', where they were frequently worse off than before, certainly didn't improve their degree of patriotism. Eventually over 750,000 were moved, to over two hundred such villages.

As the available White manpower began to reach its limits, national service was extended from nine to twelve months by the end of 1973. During 1974, national service call-ups were doubled in an attempt to put more manpower in the field. Various military and police powers were increased, including the right of detention without trial for up to sixty days, the right to order residents to build defensive works, and rewards for information leading to the apprehension of guerrillas.

◀ Rhodesian soldiers sweeping into a guerrilla camp after an airstrike *(David Scott-Donelan)*

◀ *Inset, top:* Turned terrorists on the selection course for the Selous Scouts *(David Scott-Donelan)*

◀ *Inset, bottom:* Selous Scouts undergoing counter-ambush training *(David Scott-Donelan)*

▲ A member of the Rhodesian Army prepares for a combat jump during the counter-insurgency war in Rhodesia. Note the SAS wings on his right shoulder

Morale within Rhodesia suffered a blow in July 1974, when the new Portuguese government announced that as of June 1975 FRELIMO would govern Mozambique. Thus, by 1975, guerillas in Rhodesia would have the Mozambique government's full support. Logistically, the Rhodesian government would now be dependent upon South Africa as a lifeline to the sea. Perhaps most importantly, FRELIMO's victory in Mozambique showed Black Rhodesians that a White colonial government could be defeated.

Continuing to view the threat as primarily external, rather than a popular nationalist revolution – which to a great extent it was – the Rhodesian government had begun mining the border with Mozambique in May 1974. Hitting at the Rhodesian economy as well as morale, guerrillas concentrated on attacking isolated White farmers during 1974, forcing the government to offer grants for building protected compounds for labourers. Increasing numbers of Africans continued to be moved to Protected Villages as well.

Militarily, the Rhodesian armed forces and BSAP were enjoying substantial success. The kill ratio was running at about ten to one in the security forces' favour, and early pseudo operations by Special Branch were so successful that the Selous Scouts were brought into existence to continue them on a grander scale. The 'Fire Force' concept played a particularly important role in inflicting guerrilla casualties. 'Fire Force' tactics depended on a combination of 'G-Cars', which were machine-gun-armed helicopters carrying four troopers; 'K-Cars', 20mm cannon-armed helicopters used for fire support; and RLI teams as a stop force, often parachuted in ahead of retreating guerrillas.

Within ZANLA itself, and certainly between ZANLA and ZIPRA, there was marked dissension which impeded guerrilla concentration on the insurgency, though the African National Congress helped moderate some of the internal strife. Late in 1974, in fact, the ANC and the Rhodesian government carried on talks leading to the release of many African political leaders who had been detained. South Africa, upon which country Rhodesia had grown increasingly dependent, had dictated this attempt at conciliation, which accomplished little. The release of the detainees was viewed by most Blacks as a victory for the insurgents.

Throughout 1975 the security forces continued to win militarily, while losing politically. By 1976, relations between Mozambique and Rhodesia had deteriorated to the point that the two countries were almost at war. Some FRELIMO troops had crossed the border into Rhodesia, while guerrilla incursions were increasing. It was estimated at this point that about a thousand guerrillas were inside Rhodesia, while another fifteen thousand were at various stages of training in Mozambique.

The European civilian workforce was being disrupted more and more for security duties, thus eroding the country's ability to support the war economically while fighting it militarily. Stretching the security forces even further, ZANLA began expanding operations southward. Despite limited European manpower, the government resisted increasing the numbers of African troops, making it extremely difficult to cope with this expanding conflict.

ZANLA's expanded area of operations now threatened Rhodesia's rail link with the outside world, too, theoretically putting the guerrillas in a position to interdict outside supply. In addition to expanding its war against the Rhodesian government, ZANLA had moved into the traditional ZAPU/ZIPRA power base in Matabeleland. The deteriorating situation resulted in erosion of civil liberties for Europeans as well. Journalists, for example, were heavily censored to avoid any negative effects on morale, while taxes were raised as the government tried to cope with the increasing expense of the war, although a good portion of this expense was being met by South Africa. National service increased once more, to eighteen months. Most worrying of all, though, was the substantial number of Europeans who were leaving the country each month. The three primary guerrilla goals at this point were to

▲ Members of a Selous Scouts selection course aboard a Rhodesian Army truck *(David Scott-Donelan)*

destroy European morale, over-extend the security forces, and cripple the Rhodesian economy by continuing to attack isolated farms. In all three areas, the guerrillas were showing marked success.

The circumstances seemed to indicate the need to strike across Rhodesia's borders at terrorist camps. Not only would such operations hit at ZIPRA and ZANLA in previously safe areas but they would also help raise sagging European morale. But though such operations were impressive, inflicting heavy casualties in some cases, they still failed to address the need to gain the support of the African population within Rhodesia, if the counter-insurgency campaign was to be successful. Cross-border operations caused tension with South Africa, too, which opposed them and removed economic support in retaliation.

By late 1976 stricter internal control measures had been put into effect in Rhodesia. October of that year had also seen the beginning of the Geneva Conference under Henry Kissinger's auspices to seek a solution to the war in Rhodesia. The Zimbabwe Patriotic Front, an alliance of ZANLA and ZIPRA, represented the guerrillas. The election in America of Jimmy Carter in November 1976 boded ill for the Rhodesians, as Carter was strongly committed to Black majority rule. In any case, during the Geneva negotiations, infiltration had continued. All the surrounding Black African states had declared their support for the Patriotic Front. The Geneva negotiations were rejected by the Smith government in January 1977, although a few reforms were finally made in March 1977, some land which previously had been available only for purchase by Europeans being made available for Black purchase. Of course, the number of White farmers selling out and leaving was such that Black purchasers may well have been all that remained.

After its long period of hibernation as a military force, in 1977 ZIPRA returned to activity, though it still did not match ZANLA as a threat. Now seeing victory as a real possibility, ZIPRA needed to show more aggression to gain political support. As of 1977, ZIPRA divided into a small guerrilla force operating within Rhodesia, while a large conventional army trained in Zambia in preparation for the third phase of the guerrilla war, when it could launch an invasion and defeat the Rhodesian Army in the field. By 1978 this army was receiving training from Cubans as well as a few Soviets.

Now facing a full-scale insurgency, the security forces formed a Combined Operations HQ in March 1977. By the following month it was estimated that 2,500 insurgents were in the country, with the number growing each month. The Combined Operations HQ was commanded by Lt-General Peter Walls, an SAS veteran of Malaya and no stranger to counter-guerrilla operations. A Psychological Operations unit was also formed, but most of its efforts failed since it was geared towards convincing Blacks to support a government really offering them little in concrete reforms.

Finally, and reluctantly, in November 1977 Ian Smith admitted under American and British pressure that majority rule was necessary before the insurgency could be overcome. External operations, which had initially shown distinct successes, by early 1978 were facing guerrillas who had adjusted to the possibility of being hit. Within Rhodesia, schools had to close because of the dangers of abduction, and urban terrorism was on the rise. Insurgent strength in the country had increased once again by the end of 1977, to over five thousand. European manpower was reaching the point where it could be stretched no further, virtually all White males between eighteen and sixty serving in some capacity with the security forces.

Forced by necessity to search for a solution, by late 1977 the Smith government was talking internally with moderate Black leaders. On 15 February 1978 an agreement was reached that would lead to a majority rule government. On 31 March a transitional government was formed to govern until majority rule, which was scheduled for 31 December 1978. Militant members of ZANLA and ZIPRA, however, continued the violence, including the shooting down on 4 September of an Air Rhodesia plane with an SA-7 missile, then murdering the survivors. This act so horrified the European population that on 12 September martial law was declared. Secret talks between Ian Smith and Joshua Nkomo also ended.

In fact, the target date was not met for majority rule, but one very positive step – one that should have been taken much earlier – was the formation of some Black militias to protect villages. Obviously, though, many White Rhodesians had given up the fight, 13,700 having emigrated in 1978. On 11 December 1978, guerrillas blew up an important oil depot in Salisbury (now Harare), showing their ability to hit critical economic targets virtually at will. By this point, stated guerrilla strategy was to disrupt internal administration of the country, intimidate the population, and make the counter-insurgency effort too costly. They were succeeding in all three. By 1979, only about twenty per cent of conscript Africans were actually inducted into the Army, while national service for Europeans had been extended to forty-two days per year for those aged between fifty and fifty-nine.

With over 11,000 insurgents in the country by the beginning of 1979, the war was obviously not being won; then in February 1979 another blow was struck against morale, when another Air Rhodesia plane was shot down, killing all on board. Though the country needed to be fully mobilized in its counter-insurgency effort by 1979, there remained serious personality conflicts and infighting among key members of the security forces. On 13 April 1979 the Rhodesian SAS launched an unsuccessful cross-border raid to kill Joshua Nkomo, in Lusaka. In another external operation, the ferry between Botswana and Zambia was sunk. Countries supporting the guerrillas were punished economically, but these strikes were not winning the internal war.

In elections held late in April, Bishop Muzorewa's United African Council won. However, he inherited a country in deep economic trouble, as so many of the Europeans, upon whom the economy depended, were serving in the security forces. To attempt to pump life into the economy, many were rapidly demobilized. This, however, took much of the pressure off the guerrillas, removing the incentive to take advantage of the amnesty which had been announced.

▲ A turned terrorist being trained to operate as a Selous Scouts pseudo learns to dismantle the AK-47 blindfolded *(David Scott-Donelan)*

On 1 June 1979 Zimbabwe-Rhodesia came into existence, though internal strife was prevalent among Black politicians. Incidents often centred around ZANLA guerrillas trying to intimidate supporters of Bishop Muzorewa. While Bishop Muzorewa attempted to rule, new negotiations were taking place under Lord Carrington, who represented the British government. The ensuing agreement resulted in Robert Mugabe being elected Prime Minister, thus bringing a Marxist former guerrilla leader to power and giving the final victory to ZANU/ZANLA.

Analysis

To some extent the counter-insurgency campaign in Rhodesia offered an excellent example of the same problem which existed in Vietnam: the military campaign was won, but the political campaign was lost. In fact, this is actually truer of Rhodesia than Vietnam, since it was technically a foreign invasion, rather than an insurgency, which defeated Vietnam. The Rhodesian Army by 1977 or 1978 was one of the best counter-insurgency forces in the world, yet their strategy of seeking out and destroying the enemy and carrying out cross-border raids gave them only pyrrhic victories. By pursuing the war as if they were dealing with an external threat, and refusing to come to grips with the problems connected with racial separation in their own country, they were – to use a cliché – treating the symptoms rather than the cause of the insurgency.

Many of the tactics which would normally have been effective in a counter-guerrilla campaign were ignored, or were implemented in a faulty manner. The Protected Villages are a perfect example of this. For a resettlement programme to be effective it should, as in the Malayan Emergency, offer those being uprooted an incentive to adapt to the new environment. Their lives should be improved, rather than destroyed. In Rhodesia, many of the Protected Villages were viewed as akin to concentration camps, and thus lost, rather than gained supporters for the government. For such settlements to work, an effective local indigenous militia to defend them is a necessity, but only during the latter stages of the war was the government willing to arm Black militiamen. Had the same egalitarian attitudes present in the Selous Scouts been more widespread, perhaps a Black militia programme could have been instituted for area control, freeing the highly mobile and effective Rhodesian 'teeth' units to hunt down guerrillas, without sacrificing large parts of the country by default. By going for kills rather than really pacifying areas, the security forces did not establish a secure base from which to expand government control. By limiting much of the war effort to the diminishing pool of Europeans, the government's choice of what was, in effect, a war of attrition, forced the surrender of large portions of the Tribal Trust Lands. The shortage of troops forced a strategy of seeking out guerrilla concentrations and hitting them hard. The RLI, Rhodesian African Rifles, SAS and Selous Scouts all became extremely adept at such operations; that is incontestable. Once again, however, it must be emphasized that while pursuing a military solution, the political realities were ignored.

The independence of Mozambique and Angola in 1974 were of extreme importance as well. Not only did these two countries grant asylum and support to the guerrillas, but they also stood as nearby examples of African countries which had overthrown their White colonial regimes. Rhodesia became more and more isolated, as neither Great Britain nor the United States would support the minority regime, while even South Africa, the logical base of support, at times pressured the Rhodesian government into making counter-productive concessions. Now, of course, South Africa finds itself standing alone as the last bastion of White minority rule in Africa.

UNCONVENTIONAL WARFARE LESSONS FROM THE SELOUS SCOUTS

To understand the Selous Scouts' methods, one must first understand the Selous Scouts' mission. The Scouts evolved to varying extents from the Tracker Combat Unit of the Rhodesian Army, the CIO (Central Intelligence Organization), and the Special Branch of the BSAP (British South Africa Police). When Major Ron Reid Daly was given the mission of forming the Scouts, Rhodesia's borders were becoming less and less secure, as ZANLA and ZIPRA terrorists infiltrated in greater and greater numbers. Though the cover mission for the Selous Scouts remained the tracking of terrorists, in reality the unit was a pseudo-terrorist unit, using turned terrorists and Black soldiers from the Rhodesian African Rifles, as well as White soldiers in black face make-up from the Rhodesian SAS, Rhodesian Light Infantry and other units. These pseudo groups would infiltrate terrorist areas of operation, passing themselves off as terrorists and attempting to subvert the terrorist infrastructure.

In many ways, the Selous Scouts learned from US counter-insurgency successes in Vietnam, drawing on the examples of the Phoenix Program, the Kit Carson Scouts and the Road Runner Teams. Even more did they resemble the successful pseudo teams which had been active earlier in Kenya. Constantly adding turned terrorists, the Scouts kept abreast of current terrorist terminology, identification procedures, and operations; often they were better informed about terrorist procedures than the terrorists themselves.

As the Selous Scouts evolved, they undertook other missions such as cross-border raids, assassinations, snatches, raids on terrorist HQs in Botswana or elsewhere, long-range reconnaissance, and various other types of special operations. One early raid typical of this kind of Scouts' mission was the snatch of a key ZIPRA official from Francistown, Botswana, in March 1974. These direct action operations resembled in many ways the MACV/SOG operations in Vietnam. The number of Vietnam veterans in the Rhodesian security forces, in fact, had a substantial influence on the conduct of the war and on slang that was used. Terrorists, for example, were often called 'gooks'.

The Scouts lured terrorists into ambushes, from which few terrorists normally walked away; captured terrorists and then turned them to serve in one of the Scout pseudo groups; or turned them over to the BSAP for interrogation. The Scouts were very successful in gathering intelligence, at least in part from captured diaries and letters. This is an important element of counter-insurgency operations. Due to the fragmented nature of their operations, guerrillas rarely have ready access to communications equipment. As a result, they may rely on written communication, leaving much open to capture. Few guerrillas are sophisticated enough to use ciphers, either, so often captured communications are 'in the clear'. Many politically inspired guerrillas are actually encouraged to keep diaries documenting their political development, and these also frequently include valuable intelligence information. Third World insurgents are generally much less security conscious than organized military forces about documents; hence, captured written material can be an excellent intelligence source, especially for order of battle data.

The Selous Scouts' training and operational doctrine inculcated audacity. At various times, for example, White Selous Scouts posed as the 'prisoners' of Black Selous Scout 'terrorists', and were escorted into terrorist strongholds, where White prisoners were highly prized. At the appropriate moment, the Selous Scouts turned their weapons on the terrorists, wreaking havoc from within. The classic example of audacity was the Selous Scouts raid on the large ZANLA terrorist camp at Nyadzonya Pungwe in August 1976. Using Unimogs and Ferrets painted in FRELIMO camouflage, eighty-four Selous Scouts penetrated Mozambique and drove directly into a large terrorist camp. Thousands of terrorists were in camp preparing for morning formations, when the Scouts opened up with 20mm cannons, .50 MGs, 12.7mm MGs, 7.62mm MGs and rifles. Estimates of the number of terrorists killed run as high as 1,000, all for five slightly wounded Selous Scouts. As the Scouts retreated to Rhodesia they blew up the Pungwe Bridge behind them, frustrating pursuit.

Audacity does not, of course, mean foolhardiness, but the importance of audacious small unit offensives has been proved again and again in counter-insurgency operations – by the SAS in Malaya, Borneo and Oman; by Special Forces in Vietnam; and by Selous Scouts in Rhodesia. Reportedly, some of the Soviets' best successes against Afghan guerrillas were achieved by small Spetsnaz units carrying out similar operations. Because guerrillas tend to think of themselves as the aggressors who take the war to the capitalist fat cats, they are often themselves extremely complacent in their 'safe' areas. By showing the terrorists that they were never safe from the 'Skuz'apo' (as the terrorists called the Selous Scouts) the Scouts had a psychologically debilitating effect quite out of proportion to their numbers. It was not uncommon, for example, for two groups of terrorists to begin shooting at each other out of fear that the other group was the Selous Scouts.

▲ A Selous Scout armed with a Soviet PK machine gun prepares for a mission *(David Scott-Donelan)*

Various lessons can be learned from this aspect of Selous Scouts operations. First, calculated audacity will often allow a small counter-insurgency force to inflict casualties quite out of proportion to the numbers of men involved. Secondly, terrorists, who rely heavily on fear as a weapon, can themselves be rendered psychologically impotent through fear when *they* become the prey of an enemy who appears, hits hard, and then vanishes; who, in effect, turns their own weapons against them.

Selous Scouts relied heavily on unconventional selection and training procedures. Unconventional, but they worked and turned out some of the finest counter-insurgency warriors of all time. Selous Scouts couldn't count on ready resupply, for example, so early on the fledgling Selous Scout had to learn to take his food how and when it came. During initial selection the Selous Scout was given one ration pack, but not told what to do with it. As the next days passed, that transpired to be the only food that would be provided. Some Scouts foraged around the training area to supplement that initial ration. Before long, an instructor shot a monkey and hung it in the middle of camp, where during the next few days of training it became riper and riper, its smell soon pervading the camp. Finally, after days of rigorous training the now ravenous trainee Selous Scouts were treated to the sight of the maggot-infested carcass being cooked to provide their first meal in days. Most managed to get it down, in the process learning that if one is hungry enough, protein can be provided from tainted meat, or even maggots. They also learned that even tainted meat is edible if thoroughly boiled, though it should not be reheated a second time. The obvious lesson here is that those being trained to survive under harsh conditions must be trained harshly.

Selous Scouts weapons training was intense and practical. Because they operated as terrorists, the Scouts were normally armed with Eastern Bloc weapons. The AK-47, RPD light machine gun and SVD sniper's rifle were all widely used. Since the Scouts often concealed pistols about their persons, a substantial amount of handgun training was included. CZ75s and Beretta 951s were popular, as were Makarovs due to their Warsaw Pact origins.

Among the very practical training techniques used to make the Scouts proficient with their weapons was an extremely effective counter-ambush drill. Scouts were trained, when under fire from ambush, immediately to direct short bursts of fire at all likely places of

concealment for ambushers within their arc of fire. The effectiveness of this manoeuvre could only be appreciated after seeing a well-drilled stick of Selous Scouts quickly sterilize 360 degrees of an ambush site. Fire discipline was important in this drill, but the Scouts had it. One Selous Scouts training officer also developed the technique of using mannequin targets dressed in terrorist attire and – for 'no shoots' – security forces uniforms. These mannequins incorporated a system of balloons (for head and torso), arranged so that a critical hit would cause the target to fall, while a non-critical hit had to be followed up to drop the target. The lesson to be remembered here is that military personnel likely to use their weapons in quick reaction ambush/anti-ambush

▲ Members of a Selous Scouts selection course pause for a moment *(David Scott-Donelan)*

situations must be trained to shoot in such circumstances. Obvious? Not to high-ranking officers in a lot of armies.

Many Selous Scouts operations were actually what might be called 'sting' operations. The use of European Selous Scouts 'kidnapped' by Black Selous Scouts 'terrorists' to infiltrate terrorist camps has already been mentioned. The Scouts carried out other classic stings, such as snatching high-ranking ZIPRA officers in Botswana by posing as Botswana Defence Force soldiers there to arrest them. To be accepted by terrorist groups the Scouts often staged fake attacks on farms, or fake hits on Special Branch informers to establish their credentials. So convincing were they that some Selous Scouts pseudo groups became legendary among the terrorists for their ferocity against Rhodesia. On the individual level, Selous Scouts were not above running cons such as convincing a terrorist that a command-detonated claymore mine was a radio, and sending him into a nest of terrorists to radio a message. Only pieces got through!

Some of the really classic Selous Scouts' cons must remain shrouded in secrecy, but even after Robert Mugabe assumed power and after the Selous Scouts were supposedly disbanded, a secret Scouts base continued to operate, from which much equipment and many weapons were evacuated to South Africa. Once again, the lesson to be learned from the Selous

Scouts' sting operations is that sometimes audacity is both more deadly to the enemy, and safer for the operators, than caution in unconventional warfare.

Under Chris Shollenberg, a former Rhodesian SAS officer, a reconnaissance troop was formed as part of the Selous Scouts. This recon unit proved what has been the case in virtually every war in history: small, highly-skilled recon units are among the most efficient and cost-effective intelligence tools in existence. After lying hidden near large terrorist camps for days, the Selous Scouts recon troops operated ahead of Selous Scouts raiding columns, or called in airstrikes. The lesson here is simple: no matter how effective electronic intelligence devices become, LRRPs remain an extremely important element in modern warfare, especially counter-insurgency warfare.

Another important element of the Selous Scouts experience which is less obvious is the necessity for a degree of egalitarianism in small élite units. Despite the underlying racism of Rhodesia at that time, the Scouts were a racially mixed unit, each member of which had to rely on the others, and were aggressively non-racist. Black Scouts were naturally aware of their differences in colour and culture, as were White Scouts, but neither was treated as superior or inferior. Because of the nature of Scouts operations, all members of the units had to trust each other implicitly, especially when the added element of turned terrorists amongst the Scouts was added. Therefore there could be no hints of racism within the Scouts. Anyone displaying such an attitude did not become or did not stay a Selous Scout.

One method of achieving the closeness and egalitarianism necessary for the Selous Scouts to function was requiring every aspirant Scout to learn the regimental songs during the final portion of the selection course. Sung *a cappella*, these functioned in lieu of a Selous Scouts band, but also, since the songs were traditional African songs – often terrorist songs at that, the words altered to fit the Selous Scouts – they formed a bond between Black and White.

The Selous Scouts system worked. The closeness of the members of the unit – even the tamed terrorists – was tested many times but rarely found wanting. In April 1975 a turned terrorist betrayed a pseudo group, resulting in the deaths of seven of them. This event is most noteworthy because it was so unusual. The closeness of the Selous Scouts continued even after the end of the war, when the White Scouts realized the danger their Black comrades in arms would face in Zimbabwe. When the White Selous Scouts went to South Africa they took many of the Black Scouts and their families along with them, and fought to have them incorporated into No. 5 Recce Commando by their sides.

The lesson to be learned here is one that successful special operations units find obvious, but conventional military commanders can never grasp. Small, close-knit élite units function best when run in an egalitarian manner. David Stirling made this a precept of the SAS when he formed it, and it remains a key element in SAS successes today. There is a chain of command in good special operations units, but no one works hard at wielding power. Nevertheless, things get done and done right. That's why the selection course is so important.

Another important lesson to be learned from the Selous Scouts experience can be applied to police or military covert operations. So successfully did the Selous Scouts pass themselves off as terrorists that they were frequently in more danger from Rhodesian security forces than from real terrorists. As a result, when a Selous Scouts pseudo team was working an area it was 'frozen' and declared off limits to any other security forces operations. This same lesson can be applied to police undercover operations or military covert, false flag, 'sheep dip' or deception missions.

Unfortunately, the greatest lesson to be learned from the Selous Scouts is that no matter how competent and effective a military unit is, political considerations can render it impotent. As Rhodesia became Zimbabwe, the Selous Scouts, though never defeated on the battlefield, were defeated at the bargaining table. The con men of the Selous Scouts were, in fact, conned out of existence by the British, the Americans, the UN and Robert Mugabe. Of course, throughout the history of counter-insurgency warfare, the failure to establish political goals has rendered military operations ineffective.

14 GUERRILLAS VERSUS MARXISM

Throughout much of the post-war era, Marxist guerrillas have carried out insurgent warfare against the West, which has found itself in the position of attempting to retain the status quo, whether it be colonial government, pro-Western democracy, oligarchy or a kingdom. During that period, Marxist guerrilla movements have until recently had the cachet of representing change. During the 1980s, however, there was a shift as recently established Marxist regimes in Africa, Asia and Latin America faced 'counter-revolutionary' guerrilla movements. Warsaw Pact and Cuban advisers, traditionally orientated towards assisting national liberation movements, have instead found themselves training national retention units.

AFGHANISTAN

Traditionally, the Afghans have been resistant to any centralized authority, even their own king or representative government. Outside authority has met even stronger resistance. With a long tradition of individual and group irregular warfare, there is no word in the Pushtuwali language for submission. These rugged individualists and their mountainous land of few roads are well suited to guerrilla warfare. The only real unifying force among the Afghans has been Islam, a religion, it should be noted, which does not encourage turning the other cheek. On the contrary, death suffered while fighting infidels offers a direct route to paradise.

The stage for the Soviet invasion of Afghanistan had actually been set a century before, when the Czars began coveting Afghanistan. Throughout the post-revolutionary era in the Soviet Union, Afghanistan had seemed a desirable target for expansion, thus substantial effort was devoted to the development of a viable Afghan Communist party. This effort appeared to have paid off in April 1978, when the Communist People's Democratic Party of Afghanistan (PDPA) seized control of the government. Nur Mohammed Taraki of the Khalq faction was named president, and by December a Treaty of Friendship and Good Neighbourliness had been signed with the Soviet Union. The Khalq regime then began repressing the Afghans to create a Stalinist state. Most of the population, viewing any form of government with suspicion, were particularly incensed by what they viewed as an anti-Islamic government. Attempts to collectivize farming were also particularly unpopular. In typical Afghan fashion, disapproval was often expressed by hacking to pieces party activists sent out to organize villages. Already by summer 1978 many parts of the country were in open revolt against the regime. The revolt was uniquely Afghan, however, having no central organization; yet by early 1979 twenty-five of the twenty-eight provinces were showing armed resistance.

Fighters were known as Mujahideen (fighters for the faith of Islam), and their fight was viewed as a jihad, or holy war. Afghan government forces found little success countering the burgeoning guerrilla problem. In fact, a substantial number of government troops deserted to join the Mujahideen. Then, on 21 March 1979, dozens of Soviet advisers were killed at Herot during anti-PDPA demonstrations. In retaliation, the Kabul regime sent in troops and airstrikes, some flown by Soviet pilots, resulting in at least five thousand killed. Mujahideen, conditioned throughout centuries of tribal warfare to the blood feud, now had the first of many to avenge. Taraki discredited, his Deputy Prime Minister Hafizullah Amin became Prime Minister on 27 March. Taking a tough stance, Amin sent the military in against the Mujahideen, though primarily they massacred innocent civilians.

The Mujahideen did not stand by impotently; in July they ambushed and destroyed a government mechanized column. The situation deteriorated, and Soviet pilots were already flying helicopter missions and a battalion of Soviet paratroopers was defending Bagram Airbase. In an attempt to crush possible resistance organizers, members of the intelligentsia and religious leaders were murdered by the Kabul regime. In reaction against these atrocities, and against the centralized government in general, several more Army units mutinied, while others were being defeated in combat. Amin meanwhile had consolidated his power, finally killing Taraki in October 1979.

By now, the Soviets were beginning to have serious doubts about Amin's ability to retain control, and were worried about losing their

▲ ▲ Afghan guerrillas became expert at scavenging amongst abandoned Soviet equipment *(Soldier of Fortune)*

▲ Often the only way of transporting captured Soviet weapons across the rough Afghan terrain was on the backs of the guerrillas *(Soldier of Fortune)*

▶ Portable rocket launching weapons such as this recoilless rifle allowed Afghan freedom fighters to harass Afghan government outposts, then fade away into the mountains *(Soldier of Fortune)*

▶ ▶ Afghan guerrilla armed with the AK-47 rifle, a popular weapon since ammunition could be captured from the Soviets and Communist Afghan forces *(Soldier of Fortune)*

newest satellite. By December 1979 they had mobile units in place on the Afghan border and had flown large numbers of airborne troops in to provide 'security' at Kabul Airport. In preparation for a Russian invasion, Soviet advisers had immobilized Afghan tanks and were using co-operative officers to tie down Afghan units, to prevent the possibility of resistance. On 27 December, motorized rifle divisions crossed the border into Afghanistan, while paratroopers moved from the airfield to seize the capital. Spetsnaz special forces seized key communications targets and helped capture and execute Amin, making way for Babrak Karmal to fly in from exile in the Soviet Union for installation as Prime Minister. With Karmal as their figurehead, the Soviets were ready to exert more thorough control over the Kabul regime.

The Soviets were astute enough to order Karmal to cease overt anti-Islamic activity, though after the Soviet invasion the desertion rate in the Army grew even higher. In some cases, Kabul troops openly fought against the Soviets. As a result, more Soviet troops had to be brought in to counter guerrilla activity, due to the unreliability of Afghan government troops. Soviet troops soon learned, too, that they were only safe in large groups, the Afghans making use of their traditional skill with the knife to erode Soviet morale. On 21 February 1980 there was an anti-Soviet uprising in Kabul – the 'Night of Allah Akbar' – which the Soviets put down with substantial bloodshed. Use of Soviet troops against Afghan civilians in this and other uprisings soon led to even more mutinies and desertions by Afghan government troops.

Soviet counter-guerrilla activity at this point was based primarily on the use of large-scale mechanized sweeps, which were somewhat successful in destroying agriculture, if not many guerrillas. PFM-1 'Butterfly' mines were seeded all over the countryside as well, in an attempt to inhibit guerrilla movement. Even when operating in relatively large contingents, some Soviet troops were cut off and hacked to pieces. The Soviet campaign against agriculture, and resettlement, resulted in a flow of refugees into Pakistan, thus offering a visible rallying point for world opinion against the Soviet invasion. With so many Afghans concentrated in refugee camps, too, Resistance groups quickly came into being, receiving some Western aid.

Having suffered heavily in 1980, by 1981 the Soviets were relying more on airpower. Although Afghanistan's open spaces lent themselves better to aerial counter-guerrilla activity than did the Vietnam jungles, this was still not a sound counter-insurgency strategy. At least, however, aircraft – both fixed-wing and rotor – could operate relatively securely, since the Afghans lacked any really effective anti-aircraft capability. Despite massive commitment of airpower, though, when ground offensives were undertaken, normally by Kabul regime troops supported by Soviet troops, and normally in an attempt to secure the approaches to Kabul and other cities, the guerrillas generally won, or at least forced a stalemate.

▲ Soviet airborne and airmobile troops carried much of the combat burden during their counter-insurgency war in Afghanistan

Moving in heavy columns along roads, the Soviets often resorted to reconnaissance by fire, a euphemism for shooting at random in the hope of killing guerrillas lying in ambush. The greatest tactical error at this point was that the Soviets did not normally secure the high ground above their routes, thus allowing the Mujahideen to ambush them from above. Sometimes this tactic was varied, as the columns would leapfrog between fire bases, which fired preparatory barrages along the route first. The key point, though, was that the Resistance had the initiative, though they were too lightly armed to fight decisive actions except under the most favourable conditions.

The Soviets learned from their mistakes in 1981, and by 1982 were having more success with large-scale sweeps, and particularly with airmobile operations against guerrilla strongholds. Though harsh, their depopulation strategy worked well in areas seen as likely to support a build-up for attacks on Kabul. The Resistance continued,

however, to harass the Soviets and the Kabul regime with traditional guerrilla tactics, often cutting the power lines leading into Kabul. Though certainly not ready to move into the full-scale military confrontation stage of guerrilla warfare, the Resistance was successfully building support both within and outside Afghanistan. By late 1983, in fact, the guerrillas had become so aggressive that Kabul regime troops and, to a great extent, Soviet troops had been driven into garrisons. Guerrilla organization and fighting ability had improved, partly through natural selection as many of the least competent had been killed or had fled to Pakistan, and partly through training, as mobile training teams and some training camps had been set up to teach the basics of small unit tactics.

During 1984 the Soviets had some marked successes with their combined arms/airmobile operations. During the major Panjshir VII offensive in April 1984, for example, a large number of highly trained airborne troops were used in support of Kabul regime troops. The tactic of inserting airmobile 'stop' groups ahead of the advance proved relatively effective, as did landing airmobile troops to secure the high ground along the route of advance. The guerrillas, however, did what good guerrillas do best and faded away, rather than engaging in combat. Instead, they launched ambushes when feasible. Other guerrilla groups attacked Kabul and Jalalabad, while the Soviets and Afghan Army were heavily committed elsewhere. Then in May, guerrillas hit Bagram Airfield, destroying several MiG-21s. Once the offensive ended, the guerrillas infiltrated back into the Panjshir Valley and re-exerted control much as before.

Meanwhile, guerrilla action around Kabul continued, with power cuts, rocket attacks and ambushes against fuel convoys. Increasingly on the defensive, in 1985 the Soviets began establishing defences in depth around Kabul, to prevent rocket attack and infiltration. These moves absorbed huge resources and continued to leave the guerrillas with freedom of action throughout most of the country. Another Soviet strategy was aimed unsuccessfully at sealing the border with Pakistan, to prevent infiltration. Many American observers secretly enjoyed watching the futility of Soviet efforts, as they remembered the flow of Soviet supplies coming down the Ho Chi Minh Trail a decade before. More and more, too, during the Reagan administration, US clandestine military aid was making its way across the Pakistan border, as was aid from China and Saudi Arabia, amongst others.

Quite often throughout 1985, Kabul regime garrisons were isolated and cut off by guerrillas. Soviet offensives, with substantial losses, would reach these garrisons, but then the garrisons would either be pulled out or left to be surrounded again. The Soviet version of food and population control (ie destroying both if possible) had forced a substantial portion of the population into refugee camps in Pakistan, hardening the already stubborn Afghans' will to resist.

Frustrated at the inability to seal the border with Pakistan, the Soviets began 'black' operations within that country, including an attempt to foment a Pathan rebellion. Offensives were launched near the border in 1985–6 in an attempt to intimidate Pakistan and to hit at Afghan supply routes. Not reliant on motorized transport, however, the Mujahideen continued to bring in enough weapons and supplies to continue their war. The Soviets were learning that interdiction tactics designed to deprive a mechanized army of supplies were not particularly effective against a guerrilla army which mostly used human and animal transport.

While the Soviets attempted to implement an interdiction policy, the most influential Resistance leader, Ahmad Shah Massoud, had begun a serious long-term campaign to drive the Soviets from Afghanistan. Deploying 120-man full-time, paid guerrilla units, Massoud sent his forces to hit Bagram Airfield, the Salang Pass Highway and the garrison at Fakhar, the last of which was defeated. Though Soviet special forces had been effective as hunter-killer light infantry against the Mujahideen during the period 1984–6, by late 1986 the Mujahideen was even taking its toll among the Spetsnaz and other élite troops.

The ineffectiveness of the Kabul regime resulted in Karmal's replacement in late 1986 as well, by Afghan secret police chief Najibullah. That year also saw Mikhail Gorbachev begin seriously talking about leaving Afghanistan. The arrival of US Stinger missiles in some quantity certainly contributed to growing Soviet discontent with the war as the Stingers took a heavy toll on Hind and other helicopters, as well as fixed-wing aircraft.

The Battle of Arghandab in 1987 demonstrated clearly that the Kabul regime could not succeed against the guerrillas. In addition to suffering hundreds of casualties, the Kabul regime lost twelve hundred troops who deserted, as well as at least thirty armoured vehicles and numerous aircraft. The heavier toll in armoured vehicles was due at least partly to the use in larger quantities of anti-tank mines by the Mujahideen.

Moving towards a military disengagement of Soviet troops, Najibullah, under Soviet prodding, began a concerted political campaign. A new constitution was framed and the name of the country was changed to the Republic of Afghanistan. Theoretically, non-Communist parties were to be allowed, although only 'approved' ones actually took part in government. New elections were held, which the Najibullah regime won. Most Mujahideen were still voting with their rifles. Backing these internal political moves, the Soviets made a series of diplomatic moves to remove Iranian and Pakistani support for the Mujahideen. Such moves consisted of a combination of incentives and threats.

Militarily, the Soviets were at the stage where they would have to commit substantial assets just to maintain the status quo in Afghanistan. The Stinger was proving such a devastating weapon in the hands of the Mujahideen that isolated Soviet garrisons were being withdrawn, since helicopter support could no longer be counted upon in the face of the Stinger's effectiveness. The success rate of the Stinger was an impressive sixty per cent, somewhere between 150 and 200 aircraft being accounted for in 1987 by Stinger and other types of anti-aircraft weapons. By 1987, too, the guerrillas had grown much more sophisticated about planning their operations. No longer did guerrillas just haphazardly head for the sound of battle. Operations were now often planned involving guerrilla groups converging from all points of the compass, and supported by mortars, artillery and rockets, while Stingers and Blowpipes swept the skies for Soviet or Kabul ground support aircraft. The guerrillas were even carrying out cross-border attacks into the Soviet Union by 1987, necessitating an increased KGB Border Guard presence.

Late in 1987 the Soviets launched what was destined to be one of their last major operations in Afghanistan as they attempted to relieve Khost, which had been besieged for months. Making use of effective flanking tactics through the mountains with specially trained mountain infantry, and using support helicopters flying below the Stinger threat area, the Soviets showed they had learned a great deal during their time in Afghanistan. Airmobile troops seized the high ground above the advance, then leap-frogged on to other hilltops. In combination the tactics were successful; Khost was relieved, but at the loss of twice the casualties inflicted on the Mujahideen during the operation. It now appears entirely possible that the Khost operation was mounted primarily for press coverage in the Soviet Union, so that the Red Army could begin its pull-out with a successful 'offensive', to show that they were not being run out of Afghanistan. Nevertheless, by spring 1988 the Soviets were pulling back to their main bases and beginning to withdraw. This withdrawal continued through to 15 February 1989, when it was completed, though Soviet advisers remained.

During a decade of fighting in Afghanistan, the Soviet Union had suffered over fifty thousand casualties and lost over one thousand aircraft; the Kabul regime had suffered far heavier casualties. Like the US Army in Vietnam, too, the Red Army had suffered some less obvious losses. Many returning veterans felt the same disillusionment with their country and army that US veterans had felt upon returning from Vietnam. The frustrations of fighting an unsuccessful guerrilla war cross ethnic and political boundaries: it is entirely likely that the Soviet experience in Afghanistan played an important part in the psychological preparation of the Politburo and the population at large for Mikhail Gorbachev's reforms.

As this is written the Soviet Union is still committed to supporting the Kabul regime. It would appear doubtful, however, that the Mujahideen, raised on a long tradition of blood feuds, will forget the large numbers of women, children and fighters who have died or been maimed in the conflict. The Soviets continue overt and covert pressure against Iran, China and Pakistan to inhibit their support for the Mujahideen resistance. There is also some possibility that the Soviets foresee the establishment of a partitioned Afghanistan, much like Korea, the area along their border forming a Communist buffer state. The lack of political cohesion among the guerrillas could help the Kabul regime survive for a while, though Mujahideen ability to isolate population centres could in the end force a capitulation.

By the autumn of 1988 the Mujahideen had infiltrated ten thousand men into Kabul in preparation for a final battle. Kandahar was close to falling by the end of the year. Just as the Soviet/PDPA advantage in helicopters had been offset by the Stinger, by late 1988 the PDPA armoured force was being counteracted by the Milan anti-tank missile then in Mujahideen hands. As 1989 opened, the Mujahideen and the PDPA each fielded about 125,000 fighters. Admittedly, there was still fragmentation within the Mujahideen, who were still orientated towards a guerrilla war. However, the PDPA faced the problem that a good

▲ Among the most effective troops in Afghanistan were the Soviet Union's élite paratroopers

number of the troops fighting for the Kabul regime were forced conscripts who would desert at the first opportunity. Even if, as appears likely, the PDPA falls, there could be a struggle to fill the power vacuum between pro-Iranian guerrillas and pro-Western guerrillas. Some feel the return of the former king might be the best compromise, particularly if he left the Mujahideen fighters alone to return to their independent way of life.

Analysis

In many ways, the Afghan guerrillas contradicted most normal patterns of successful irregular warfare. However, their long tradition of guerrilla fighting and the ruggedness of their existence and their homeland combined to overcome many seeming disadvantages. Normally, the Soviets have been successful at using divide-and-rule tactics in their satellite states, and this tactic might have been expected to work in the fragmented Afghan society. However, the common Islamic faith, a faith it should be noted which encourages militancy, provided the cohesion to keep the guerrillas fighting. Although Soviet strategy is based on the use of military power as a means to let the Communists consolidate political power, the political process proved markedly unsuccessful in Afghanistan; hence, the Soviet military commitment grew, rather than diminished.

The Soviet command structure proved particularly cumbersome during the conflict, as orders often had to pass through Moscow and Kabul before reaching field commanders, thus slowing reaction time and hindering flexibility, both grave disadvantages in a counter-insurgency war. Another serious mistake was that the Soviets tried to control the country without really occupying it. At no point did the combined Red Army/Kabul Army control more than twenty per cent of the country. Without attempting to pacify areas and then expand control, the Russian equivalent of the oil-slick strategy, the Soviets granted the Mujahideen most of the country in which to manoeuvre. Admittedly, the depopulation strategy followed by the Soviets did prove effective at removing the guerrillas' base of supply and support. However, such harsh tactics served to harden even more the will of the stubborn Afghans, and brought widespread support for the Resistance.

Soviet units operating in Afghanistan were often composites designed for thrusts along the roads. As a result, battalion-sized motor rifle/tank/combat support teams became the primary striking force. An Army equipped, organized and trained for combat in Western Europe or Manchuria had to adapt to a counter-insurgency war. The period between 1984 and 1986 saw a significant improvement in small unit tactics, particularly for airmobile and airborne troops. Even Soviet airborne troops, however, had to overcome their heavy dependence on armoured personnel carriers. Motor rifle units were still limited primarily to the roads throughout the war, and were dependent upon heavy logistical back-up. The best counter-guerrilla forces, as throughout the history of counter-guerrilla warfare, proved to be élite light infantry such as the Spetsnaz, mountain, airborne or airmobile. The Spetsnaz often operated in Mujahideen dress, using the pseudo tactics which had proved so effective in Kenya, Vietnam and Rhodesia.

Relying heavily on artillery and airpower, the Soviets developed the relatively effective use of observation posts located on mountain tops, surrounded by minefields and supplied by helicopter. The barrenness of Afghanistan allowed this tactic to work better than in most parts of the world. The Soviets did finally increase their use of infantry patrols, but to nowhere near the extent of the US in Vietnam, or UK forces in their successful counter-insurgency campaigns. Instead, Afghan militiamen were normally used for patrolling in the mountains.

Considering the length of the conflict, Soviet casualties were surprisingly light, no doubt because Kabul regime troops actually saw the bulk of the combat and because the Soviets relied so heavily on airpower, using it for aerial surveillance, depopulation through bombing and seeding mines, interdiction and ground support. The helicopter proved the most invaluable weapon, though its use in the mountains presented some problems. Deployment of a large number of helicopter pilots to Afghanistan did grant the Soviet armed forces a large pool of combat-experienced pilots, and also gave invaluable experience at making their helicopters more 'survivable', even against the Stinger, which they might encounter on the battlefields of Europe. Development of helicopter reconnaissance tactics should prove particularly valuable wherever the Soviet Army is deployed.

Other combat adjustments made by the Soviets included the deployment of ZSU-23 self-propelled AA guns, gun trucks and self-propelled howitzers in the mountains where tank guns did not have the necessary elevation to engage targets on the heights. Just as the United States found that the lighter M-16 was better suited to counter-insurgency operations, the Soviets adopted the AK-74 and its 5.45mm round for service in Afghanistan. The need to engage guerrillas at longer range also influenced the Soviets to triple the normal issue of SVD snipers' rifles, from three per company to nine.

The Soviets worried far less about world opinion than had the US in Vietnam and, hence, deployed mines almost indiscriminately around the countryside, randomly killing animals, women, children or fighting men. Around garrisons, the minefields were often used as much to keep in the Kabul regime conscripts, press-ganged off the streets in most cases, as to keep the guerrillas out. The guerrillas encouraged desertion by assisting deserters to reach refugee camps or to join the Resistance.

Another negative factor affecting the Soviet ability to wage a successful counter-guerrilla war was the ineffectiveness of the Kabul regime. Within the PDPA there was constant squabbling between the Parcham and Kalq factions, which eroded the ability of the military, political and religious establishments to function. Even the Afghan Communists retained some of their native independence as well, preventing the Soviets from ever exerting full control over the regime, though they did manage to finance the war by piping natural gas back to the Soviet Union. Perhaps the greatest control was exerted over the Kabul intelligence service, WAD, through its KGB advisers.

The religious issue remained the most critical factor throughout the campaign. Even at home the Soviets faced problems with their own Muslim population, who were not happy with the war against fellow Muslims in Afghanistan. Both Karmal and Najibullah made a show of leading an Islamic state, often attempting to bribe religious leaders to support the regime.

Within Kabul, many sympathizers provided money, food and intelligence to the Resistance, eventually forcing the Soviets to withhold information from their counterparts, thus eroding efficiency and sowing mistrust.

What finally gve the Resistance their victory was the resilience and self-sufficiency of the average Mujahideen. The movement had not been 'created', but had grown from a national unwillingness to be conquered. The decentralized nature of the guerrilla movement made it hard to control, but also hard to defeat. Although most Western countries decry individual ownership of firearms, it was the case that the rural Afghans, who were traditionally riflemen with their own weapons, were able to defend their country successfully against one of the most powerful armies in the world.

The flow of arms to the Resistance increased, AK-47 rifles coming into the country from China and elsewhere, while many other AKs were captured from the Soviets. Such weapons were the best arms for the Afghan guerrillas, since captured ammunition would be usable. Later, the flow of heavier arms, particularly the Stingers, gave the Afghans much greater ability to combat Soviet technology. By later in the war, the Resistance could even put their own captured armour into the field and had their own captured artillery. However, mortars and rockets, due to their portability, remained the primary Resistance indirect-fire weapons.

In combination, the Afghan Resistance was successful because it was based on a highly independent people with a long tradition of guerrilla warfare. They were united by a common religion in Islam, a religion which does not encourage meekness but rather fighting for one's beliefs. The Afghans were armed when invaded, and lived in a country particularly suited to guerrilla warfare. The long borders with Iran and Pakistan gave the Afghan Resistance both safe areas and sources of supply in countries linked by the same religion. Eventually, the flow of aid from Pakistan, Saudi Arabia, the US and China would have a significant effect as well.

Politically and militarily, the Afghan guerrillas proved unsophisticated; but from their childhood the Afghans had been raised on a tradition of rugged individualism and a warrior ethic. When combined with their strong Islamic faith, these factors created an implacable foe for any invader.

ANGOLA

The war against Portugal for Angolan independence was fought by three guerrilla groups. For the most part, the MPLA, UNITA and FNLA had concentrated on defeating the Portuguese, though conflicts between the Marxist MPLA and the two other groups began to appear during the final stages of Portuguese rule. After the MPLA gained power in 1974, the others continued their struggle against the new Marxist regime. Until 1976, both received CIA aid, though to nowhere near the extent that the MPLA was receiving Soviet aid.

Even after the US Congress cut off aid in 1976, the anti-Marxist guerrillas continued their fight, though with some difficulty, particularly as large numbers of Cubans – around 25,000 – had been sent to Angola to assist the MPLA. The situation for FNLA and UNITA looked even more dire under the Carter administration, which became an at least passive supporter of various Marxist governments. As a result of negotiations by the Carter government, in 1978 an agreement was made with Angola, Zaïre and Zambia. This agreement promised US aid for all three countries, and required Zambia and Zaïre to stop supporting FNLA and UNITA.

Of these two groups, FNLA had initially appeared most viable, under Holden Roberto. With support and sanctuaries from Zaïre, FNLA had been tying down a large number of Cuban troops and harassing the Marxist regime throughout northern Angola.

UNITA, on the other hand, had not initially appeared as dynamic under Jonas Savimba, though Savimba himself, with a PhD from a Swiss university, was a highly intelligent and charismatic leader. His power was primarily in southern Angola, where the Ovimbundu tribe makes up about forty per cent of the country's population. Savimba had received initial guerrilla training in China, and hence had a sound understanding of the importance of winning over the local population, a point which would prove of critical importance in later UNITA successes. UNITA would also receive substantial support from Pretoria, in return for helping inhibit SWAPO raids into Namibia, then under the control of South Africa. By 1981, it had become apparent that Savimba and UNITA were really the guerrilla force to be reckoned with in Angola. While Roberto had gone into exile and FNLA operations had been severely curtailed, UNITA held about one-third of the country, though a couple of isolated government garrisons remained in place.

By interdicting the Benguela railway line, UNITA had stopped the flow of copper from Zambia and Zaïre as well, inflicting severe economic losses upon the Marxist governments which profited from this trade. The large Cuban presence was now heavily concentrated in the cities, where UNITA-supporting urban guerrillas hit at them whenever possible. Though run by the normally efficient East Germans, Angolan intelligence was faring poorly against the guerrillas, due to their widespread support among the population. Even with fifty thousand Angolan government troops, over twenty thousand Cuban troops, three thousand East Germans and fifteen hundred Soviets, the Marxist government was losing ground monthly. The supposed 'People's' Army had virtually no support among the people.

During daylight hours, heavy Angolan/Cuban columns, supported by MiGs and helicopters, could go wherever they wished, but at night UNITA controlled the roads in up to half the

▼ Members of the Mozambique resistance trained by South African special forces personnel to operate against the Communist government of Mozambique

▲ Members of the Mozambique resistance 'on parade' with an assortment of weapons, including the ubiquitous AK-47

country. As a result, the government strategy was to try to control the population centres, the Cabinda oilfields, and the main communications lines, while trying to reopen the Benguela railway. In the bush, the MPLA troops were not very effective, particularly since many were drawn from urban backgrounds. Even the government's Long-Range Penetration Unit, whose main mission was reportedly to assassinate Savimba, proved ineffective in UNITA territory, because they received no local co-operation; in fact, the locals quickly reported their presence to UNITA troops. The Marxist government also attempted a disinformation campaign, linking Savimba with the regime in South Africa.

Savimba had sixteen thousand regulars, some of whom had been fighting for fifteen years, and about five thousand militia. Regulars, who operated south of the Benguela railway, were organized in five-hundred-man battalions, while the guerrillas, who operated north of the Benguela railway, operated in fifty-man units. Included within the regulars were about five hundred Angolan-born Portuguese who supported Savimba.

The guerrillas were particularly adept at ambushing government patrols, or trains moving along the railway line. A combination of tough discipline and high morale made UNITA an extremely efficient irregular force. Additionally, members of UNITA went through a five-month initial training course, then each year returned for a three-month refresher course, thus guaranteeing a high degree of small unit skills as well. Although the Clark Amendment had banned US support in 1976, China, Morocco, France, Saudi Arabia and some other Gulf states continued to give financial support to Savimba.

Though the war was expensive for Savimba, as is usual in counter-guerrilla wars it was far more expensive for the Angolans and the Soviets, costing $1.6 million per day. The Angolan economy was in a shambles, with diamond, coffee and iron production at only a fraction of capacity, and half the country's food being imported by 1978. As the UNITA strategy was to wage guerrilla war all over the country, tying down more and more troops and continuing to disrupt the economy, the costs to the Marxist government could only continue to rise.

▲ Member of the Mozambique resistance learning to fire a rocket launcher

In 1981–2 South Africa began carrying out cross-border operations into Angola against SWAPO, with at least tacit assistance from UNITA. In return Savimba's troops were supplied with captured weapons. While the people living in Savimba's 'Free Angola' were relatively happy with their lot, those living under the Marxist government were becoming more and more unhappy about the Cuban presence, as were many Angolan government troops, who viewed the Cubans as arrogant and unwilling to fight. The presence of helicopters on the government side was a real disadvantage for UNITA, though, since Cuban troops could be inserted so easily, but the use of heavy MGs by UNITA to some extent discouraged the use of rotor airpower. In fact, the only real danger from airpower in 1983 was from napalm, which was dropped against UNITA concentrations when attacking garrisons.

By 1983 the areas under Savimba's control were well organized politically, and provided a ready food supply. Hygiene in UNITA and, to a lesser extent, in supporting villages was quite good by African standards as well. Using numbers of captured Soviet trucks, UNITA could easily move troops or supplies, while a good radio communications net linked the thirty-five thousand regulars and guerrillas under arms by 1983. So efficient was Savimba's rule that at Jamba, the capital of 'Free Angola', there was a secretarial school to train clerks and a machine shop to make parts for captured Soviet weapons.

The government position continued to worsen as they now really controlled only about one-third of the country, with another one-third contested. Cuban envoys could only move with massive support, and still were frequently ambushed. One growing advantage for UNITA was the great distance from Angola to the Soviet Union and Cuba, making Soviet support relatively difficult. By the autumn of 1984, UNITA was harassing the Angolan capital of Luanda by constant interruptions of its power. FNLA still carried on operations in northern Angola, crossing from Zaïre to hit Luanda or other nearby targets. So threatened were the Cabinda oilfields that the oil companies hired ex-SAS and ex-Special Forces troops as guards. Putting economic exigencies ahead of ethics, Chevron-Gulf was supporting the Marxist regime. By 1985, too, the Cuban commitment was up to around thirty to thirty-five thousand men.

Often the South Africans would carry out cross-border operations which pushed the Cubans back, after which UNITA would occupy the area when the South Africans pulled back. In the autumn of 1985 the Angolan government, growing desperate, launched an offensive designed to eliminate UNITA. Although UNITA did suffer casualties, the MPLA suffered far more, up to ten thousand, in fact. UNITA kept the government on the defensive, however, by carrying out operations with the South Africans in 1986–7. To avoid a complete rout, ten thousand more Cubans had to be flown in. During December 1987–January 1988 the Cubans, with heavy air support, were committed to fighting around the besieged Cuito Cuanavale garrison. Equipped with Stingers, however, UNITA knocked down dozens of aircraft.

Now with South African artillery support, UNITA victories continued throughout 1988, in one battle seventy Soviet tanks being knocked out or captured. The Cubans, East Germans and Soviets increasingly faced growing hatred from the people, as well as an ever-growing risk of

AIDS, an endemic problem in Africa. As a result of negotiations with South Africa, by 1989 the Cubans were starting to withdraw, theoretically all to be out by 1991. Without them, the MPLA would appear to be in deep trouble, a fact seemingly acknowledged when MPLA leader Jose Eduardo Dos Santos agreed to direct negotiations with Savimba in July 1989. It is, of course, possible that these negotiations are being used to play for time, since the South Africans have withdrawn material support for UNITA in reciprocation for the withdrawal of the Cubans.

One of the greatest advantages UNITA retains is Savimba himself, who dynamically leads the guerrilla war from within the country, rather than being a figurehead leader living beyond the combat zone. Without South African support, some believe that the UNITA capital of Jamba could be taken; however, this might actually be to UNITA's advantage as it would extend MPLA supply lines well into the heart of UNITA-controlled territory, and force UNITA to engage in a full guerrilla war. As of autumn 1989, UNITA remained fully in control of at least one-third of Angola, retaining the initiative in striking at government forces when and where they pleased. If the Cubans do pull out by 1991, it is entirely likely that UNITA will take Angola.

MOZAMBIQUE

Mozambique, another former Portuguese colony, also saw a Marxist regime take power after the departure of the former colonial government. FRELIMO, the Marxist guerrilla group which took power, has been opposed since 1977 by RENAMO, another highly successful anti-Marxist movement. Resistencia Nacional de Moçambicano (RENAMO), under Alfonso Dhlakama, has won widespread popular support, due to the reign of terror instituted by FRELIMO in Mozambique. Initially, RENAMO operated out of Rhodesia with support from the Rhodesian SAS and CIO (Central Intelligence Organization), but in 1979, with about a thousand fighters, it moved its base of operations into Mozambique.

When support from Rhodesia ended in 1980, South Africa took over, using many former Rhodesians serving in the SADF special forces. Some members of the No. 5 Recce Commando, made up of former Selous Scouts, for example, worked with members of RENAMO to create a special raiding unit. SAMI, the South African intelligence agency, added support by supplying captured arms. As in Angola, South Africa found supporting the anti-Marxist guerrillas a useful counter to unfriendly regimes aiding Marxist guerrillas operating against Namibia.

Throughout the 1980s, RENAMO has operated very successfully throughout Mozambique from small bases, receiving support from local villages. Many people support RENAMO as the only opposition to what amounts to widespread Soviet colonialism in the country; by 1982 the Soviets had four to five thousand 'advisers' of various sorts in the country. RENAMO's campaign was waged primarily against the economy and communication lines, though ambushes of FRELIMO troops were also carried out successfully.

In 1984, when FRELIMO agreed to stop supporting guerrillas operating against South Africa, South Africa reciprocated and agreed to withdraw its support from RENAMO, though it should be noted that SAMI made large deliveries of arms to RENAMO before the agreement went into effect. Nevertheless, RENAMO strength continued to grow, often drawing on FRELIMO deserters disillusioned with the Marxist regime. In many provinces, RENAMO gained control of the countryside, isolating the provincial capitals and carrying out a campaign of sabotage. In areas under their control, RENAMO took the popular step of encouraging capitalism.

By 1985 RENAMO had over fifteen thousand combat troops, while FRELIMO required the presence of twenty thousand troops from Zimbabwe just to keep open its railway links with neighbouring countries. Raising the ante, in January and again in March, 1985, RENAMO hit the airport at Quelimane. FRELIMO, deprived of most freedom of movement, despite the presence of large numbers of foreign troops, was virtually isolated in garrisons and forced to resort to heavy convoys for movement between these garrisons.

One of RENAMO's real strengths has been a clear-cut policy setting forth what they are fighting for. In 1985 this was stated in their manifesto as follows:

1 The removal of the Communist dictatorship.
2 The establishment of a democratic government of national unity.
3 Free elections.
4 Respect for the people's traditions and customs.
5 Respect for human rights and liberty.

To counter RENAMO's popularity, FRELIMO used a twisted version of pseudo operations, having troops masquerade as RENAMO and carry out atrocities against villages.

Had the US, British and South African governments given RENAMO their support, they could very likely have toppled the Marxist government by late 1985 or early 1986. By 1986, so isolated were the provincial capitals controlled by FRELIMO that they could only be supplied by air in most cases.

When the FRELIMO strongman, Samora Machel, who had held power since 1975, was killed in a plane crash in October 1986, the ruling party was weakened even more, in the struggle to fill the power vacuum. With twenty-five thousand full-time fighters in action by mid-1986, RENAMO controlled up to eighty-five per cent of the country. Special 850-man shock units

▲ The Contras view their fight against the Sandinistas as a religious battle against 'Godless Communism', though in actuality many priests within Nicaragua support the Sandinista government

equipped with recoilless rifles and mortars, and coming directly under the command of President Dhlakama, were used against FRELIMO garrisons and other key targets.

As discontent grew among the population, many of the other African regimes helping to prop up the Marxist government began to tire of the long war. Although eight to twelve thousand troops from Zimbabwe remained, in 1989 Tanzania pulled out eight thousand troops, allowing RENAMO to occupy many towns. With little US aid – in fact, the US Department of State was actively working to aid the Marxist government – RENAMO appeared in 1989 to be slowly winning the war. Should the removal of additional foreign troops take place, victory would appear almost certain. As in Angola, the emphasis on building support among the people was RENAMO's greatest strength. The guerrillas had realized what all good guerrilla forces must: the people lead to victory.

NICARAGUA

After the defeat of the Somoza regime and the institution of the Marxist Sandinista regime in Nicaragua, initial resistance came from about six thousand former Nicaraguan National

▶ Members of the Contras were trained in Honduras, the Canal Zone, and elsewhere in Latin America. Here they learn small unit patrolling from US advisers *(US Army)*

Guardsmen, along the Honduran and Salvadorean borders. Many of the officers leading this group, known as the 'Jackals', were graduates of Fort Benning, Fort Bragg or the Jungle Warfare School in the Canal Zone. Under the leadership of Juan Carlos, this group had a relatively short existence, and had ceased operations by 1983. The bad reputation of the National Guard under Somoza had prevented this group from gaining any public support within Nicaragua.

Far more popular were the FDN Contra guerrillas, who began their operations about the time the Jackals ceased. Of the four to five thousand FDN guerrillas, few had been in the National Guard, a point in their favour. As CIA aid for the FDN became known, and the Hondurans, who had allowed them to operate from their territory, became worried about Nicaraguan reprisals, the FDN moved into bases within Nicaragua.

Also operating against the Sandinista regime at this point were the Misorasata, an alliance of Indians along the eastern coast, and Eden Pastora's ARDE. Pastora, known as Commandante Zero, was a former Sandinista officer who had become disillusioned and left the regime.

Giving some credibility to the Contra cause was the fact that most of their political leaders had been enemies of Samoza, and now viewed the Sandinistas as just as bad or even worse. The Contras, of course, wanted to overthrow the Sandinistas, but it appears that the US was backing them primarily to force the Sandinistas to stop exporting their revolution, particularly to El Salvador.

Contra raids within sixty miles of Managua soon jolted the Sandinista leadership, which was losing public support continually, due to human rights violations and a failure to hold popular elections. From liberators, the Sandinistas had quickly become oppressors. The Sandinista policy of relocating or even annihilating peasants near the border, to remove potential Contra support, only served to drive many peasants into the Contra fold. At the same time, many former loyal Sandinistas joined the Contras because of their dislike for the large numbers of Cubans and Russians now freely roaming Managua. Alarming the Sandinistas even more was the US assault on Grenada, which fuelled fears that the US might invade. With US Congressional approval of a $24 million aid package for FDN, plus the September

▶ As the Sandinistas tried to export their revolution, the US responded by training counter-insurgency troops, such as this Guatemalan paratrooper *(Soldier of Fortune)*

▶ ▶ US Ranger advisers (note 'Ranger eyes' on the back of the caps) train Contras in the methods of rope tying *(US Army)*

1983 bombing of Managua by ARDE Cessnas, things looked grim for the Sandinistas.

September 1983 also saw attacks on Castillo, a Sandinista fortress, using mortars and recoilless rifles. These relatively portable stand-off weapons were used on other raids as well. When prisoners were taken, the Contras normally treated them well and encouraged them to join, a process which became easier due to the opposition to the Sandinista regime of the Catholic Church.

The Sandinistas did take one highly effective counter-guerrilla step, which was the formation of the BLIs. These were specialist, highly mobile, counter-guerrilla forces, able to stay in the field for extended periods hunting the Contras. Realizing the importance of small unit patrolling, the Sandinistas also deployed four- to five-man patrols along the borders to interdict and act as early warning against Contra incursions. Increased efficiency in late 1983 and early 1984 hit ARDE the hardest, forcing a retreat into Costa Rica. Nicaragua's location, however, meant that infiltrators could enter from bordering countries as well as the many waterways, including the sea, and the Contras soon grew particularly effective at using the waterways for mobility. By early in 1984, FDN was stepping up its attacks against power lines, oil depots and other economic and communications targets.

A bomb blast almost killed Eden Pastora in 1984, but he was already losing support due to his unwillingness to work with the FDN, lack of real action against the Sandinistas and his posturing for the international press.

American civilians, some ex-Special Forces soldiers, as well as some CIA agents, worked with the Contras teaching them guerrilla techniques and also lessons from Afghanistan. Also useful was the CIA's *FM 95-1A Guerrilla War Manual* in Spanish for the leaders, while a simplified version was supplied in comic book form for the regular guerrillas. This manual stressed the importance of propaganda, as well as gaining the support of the local population. It also covered guerrilla organization and training, and the selective use of terror in a guerrilla campaign. All in all, it was a compact and efficient manual on how to carry out a war against the Sandinistas. CIA support of the Contras was condemned in the US press, however, after it became known that the US intelligence agency had assisted the Contras in mining Nicaraguan harbours.

In 1985 a loose alliance of ARDE, FDN and MISURA, known as UNIR, was attempted. Former US Special Forces demolitions experts taught the Contras techniques for making improvised mines to place along the Nicaraguan road network, and also taught them such harassment

▶ Contra bases are certainly not luxurious, but they do offer a haven between operations into Nicaragua

tactics as planting old hub caps as well, to confuse the Sandinista engineers with mine detectors. The Sandinistas continued to strike back, hitting an FDN camp on the Honduran border in spring 1985 with a rocket attack. The FDN soon bounced back, though, cutting the Managua–Rama Highway soon after. This and other such missions were carried out by Contra long-range patrols, which often gained strength while on operations by picking up Sandinista deserters.

Just before Easter 1986, the Sandinistas carried out an ambitious operation, crossing the border into Honduras to hit an FDN base. However, FDN penetration patrols returning to the base hit them from behind, inflicting heavy casualties and driving off the attackers.

In May 1986, Eden Pastora finally gave up the fight in southern Nicaragua, and sought political asylum in Costa Rica. The FDN, however, was buoyed by the approval in October of a $100 million aid package from the United States. By that point, the Sandinistas had 119,000 men under arms, by far the largest army in Central America. In an attempt to stop Contra operations, they were mining infiltration routes and sending their Irregular Warfare Battalions on long-range missions. However, like the Rhodesians before them, they were becoming involved with sealing borders and carrying out cross-border operations on the assumption that their problem was a strictly external one. They were not addressing the political problems which had given the Contras widespread support within Nicaragua.

Although the Contras were menaced by Hind-24 and Mi-17 helicopter gunships, the arrival of Redeye and Stinger missiles soon gave them suit-

◀ Many Contras received training in other Latin American countries from US personnel *(US Army)*

able protection and allowed them to knock them down. With Oliver North's co-operation, the American magazine *Soldier of Fortune* offered a one-million-dollar reward to any Nicaraguan pilot who defected with a Hind. As a result, the Sandinistas grounded most helicopters until 'reliable' Cuban crews could be brought in. Through Oliver North's network, which would later achieve notoriety in the Iran-Contra judicial hearings, an airlift was flying supplies in for the Contras, often resupplying them deep within Nicaragua.

During 1986 and 1987, a large coastal area came under the control of Miskito Indian guerrillas, who were reacting to a campaign of virtual genocide being carried out against them by the Sandinistas. Initially, the Indian guerrillas received little outside help, but after forming an alliance of various Indian groups into YATAMA in 1987, they gained some FDN aid.

By this stage, the Nicaraguan economy was in a shambles, as the Sandinistas attempted to support their large army with few real sources of hard currency. A large proportion of the population was now anti-Sandinista, in many cases actually stoning Sandinista soldiers. Hitting at the economy even more, in December 1987 the Contras launched an operation to take over three gold mining towns in north-eastern Nicaragua, which they seized and held for periods of hours or days, inflicting heavy casualties on the Sandinista defenders in the process.

In March 1988 the Sandinistas carried out another cross-border operation into Honduras to hit Contra bases just before a scheduled peace conference, but members of the US 82nd Airborne Division and other units were deployed on a 'training mission', thus discouraging the Sandinistas.

The US Congress has now cut off aid to the Contras, though it is likely that a smaller, more mobile Contra force will continue to operate against the Marxist government.

Analysis

It is noteworthy that all the Communist countries suffering from problems with guerrillas are Soviet orientated. Those regimes whose guerrilla forces trained along the classic pattern of guerrilla warfare advocated by Mao, realize the importance of winning the support of the people, while the Soviets, Angolans, Mozambicans and Nicaraguans seemingly do not. In Angola and Mozambique, particularly, the areas under counter-revolutionary guerrilla control are more effectively and more benevolently administered, setting an example for other segments of the population. Although all of these regimes came to power through guerrilla warfare, most were based on urban cadres. Tough local guerrillas, used to operating in the bush, have consistently defeated the better-armed and more numerous government forces.

Generally, the intelligence services of the Marxist governments, even with assistance from the Soviets, East Germans and Cubans, all known for competence in this field, have had little success due to the widespread popular support for the guerrillas, though torture and double agents have on occasion netted important information.

An extremely important factor in the successes of UNITA, RENAMO and the Contras has been the real belief in a cause, the belief that they are a true army of liberation. They have been willing to undergo real hardships and, in some cases, to continue fighting for many years. On the other hand, the Marxist regimes they have been fighting,

▲ Contras on a forced march to build endurance for penetrations into Nicaragua

▶ Contras received training in basic military skills from US advisers *(US Army)*

which came to power fighting against colonial or dictatorial governments, have in some cases become even worse than those they replaced, and in this way soon lost popular support. The presence nearby of countries hostile to Marxist government has also been of great assistance to the guerrilla movements, granting a haven and source of supply. Soviet airpower, particularly the Hind helicopter, has been a useful counter-guerrilla tool, but the distribution to the guerrillas of Stinger and Redeye ground-to-air missiles has evened the odds considerably.

The United States has proved itself an unreliable ally, offering intermittent aid to counter-revolutionary movements, but also offering support to the Communist governments in many cases and ignoring the true freedom fighters. Had the United States fully backed UNITA, RENAMO and the Contras, it is entirely likely that one or more of the groups would have been successful in toppling the Marxist government of their country. Even without US aid, these three guerrilla movements have helped absorb Soviet and Cuban resources to the extent – particularly with the Soviet reversal in Afghanistan – that Communism has been on the defensive during the 1980s, rather than the offensive as it was throughout the fifties, sixties and early seventies. The Mujahideen in particular have been an inspiration to other anti-Marxist guerrillas, by showing the way with tactics against Hind helicopters and other Soviet weapons.

Still other Marxist states face guerrilla wars of their own. Just to name one, the Marxist regime in Ethiopia is fighting an insurgency by the OROMO guerrillas. With the record economically, socially and politically of certain Marxist states, especially on human rights, such insurgencies are certainly not surprising. The question is, then, whether it is in the West's best interest to encourage these insurgencies, or to pull back and see whether the reforms beginning to sweep the Communist world can accomplish the same ends with less bloodshed.

15 NOTES CONCERNING A COUNTER-GUERRILLA STRATEGY

The counter-guerrilla campaigns, both successful and unsuccessful, covered in this book have brought to light certain common factors which can determine success or failure. Most important in fighting against an insurgency or guerrilla war is that the government being defended must be basically viable, or there must be a deep-seated willingness to make changes to make it so. The Dhofar Campaign in Oman is a good example of this, in that the government of the old Sultan was not viable, and it is very unlikely that the insurgency could have been defeated had he remained in power. The ascendance of his son Qaboos, however, who was willing to make immediate reforms, laid the groundwork for a highly successful counter-insurgency campaign. On the other hand, the Soviet Union in Afghanistan continued to support a non-viable puppet government, and thus had little real basis for countering popular support for the guerrillas.

Assuming the government is basically sound, steps must be taken to win the population away from the guerrillas. These steps can take the form of economic or political reforms if needed, an information or propaganda programme to convince them of the virtues of the government (it should be noted that such information must rest on a sound basis of fact), removal of the motivation to be a guerrilla, and the encouragement of economic stability. Generally, the peasant class, which often supports guerrilla movements, is motivated by simple things – fair treatment from local police or administrators, provision of education and medical facilities, and a bearable standard of living. If these are present, it is doubtful if insurgent forces will be very successful.

Obviously, before attempting to implement a counter-insurgency strategy, clear political and military goals must be established. A strong leader, who can ensure that these political and military objectives and policies are compatible, is also desirable. Such a leader can ensure co-operation between branches of the armed forces, government bureaucracies, the police and the intelligence services. And, make note, such co-operation is highly critical. If government and security send confused or contradictory messages to the guerrillas and population at large, it is much more difficult to carry out a focused campaign.

While a political solution is being worked out and a 'hearts and minds' campaign is being waged through civic action, military and police must hold the line and begin retaking any parts of the country of which the guerrillas have won control. It is of vital importance that the military personnel respect the population in carrying out these operations. Guerrillas trained in Mao's style of guerrilla warfare will have been working hard to convert the population; hence, ill-treatment from security forces will only assist them. If guerrillas have been attempting to intimidate the population, fairness on the part of the military will quickly win tacit if not active assistance, and frequently will garner substantial intelligence.

Decisive action must be taken early to counter guerrilla depredations and maintain law and order, though the temptation to put repressive measures into effect immediately can backfire. Still, to allow security forces to do their job it may be necessary to implement special legal powers.

◀ US Special Forces personnel are trained to work with either guerrillas or counter-guerrillas, as it suits US foreign policy *(US Army)*

▶ A member of the US Army Special Forces uses a Robert Parrish knife, an invaluable weapon or tool when operating in the rough conditions of guerrilla or counter-guerrilla warfare

The population will usually remain supportive if such powers are used with restraint, and selectively. In fact, the population will welcome moves which protect them from intimidation and remove guerrillas from their midst. Sound, timely intelligence can allow surgical application of special powers, as well as lead security forces to guerrilla camps or storage dumps.

It must constantly be borne in mind when dealing with the population that normally only a very small percentage of the people will be active supporters of a guerrilla movement. Probably only a relatively small percentage will be active government supporters as well. Most are just trying to get on with their lives, but may be frightened, or waiting to see what happens. This majority are the ones who must be won to defeat an insurgency successfully. In working with the people to gather intelligence, gain local military assistance, or carry out civic action, language skills are highly important where a multiplicity of languages exist.

Both food denial and population control are desirable, to make day-to-day living for the guerrillas more difficult and thus sap his ability to carry on aggressive action. However, forced population and food control can alienate the population. Hence, if a protected village system is used it should be one which offers the people a better rather than a worse lifestyle in their new home. Likewise, food denial programmes should be handled in such a way that farmers are not denied a market for their crops. Instead, the government should buy the crops, then supervise the distribution, or should supervise through a middleman who will exercise controls to prevent food reaching the guerrillas.

The maintenance of morale among the population, the security forces and the government is also very important. Along with this, perhaps as an integral part of it, is the necessity to retain the will to fight. Many guerrilla wars have been won because the guerrillas were willing to outlast their opponents. Both the Indochina and Vietnam Wars are classic examples of this type of victory, as are Afghanistan and Rhodesia.

Militarily, the security forces must wrest the initiative from the guerrillas, and as soon as possible put them on the defensive. Highly trained and mobile light infantry which can operate in small patrols and stay afield for extended periods are often the best type of force for counter-guerrilla operations. Troops such as the US Army Special Forces or British SAS can live rougher than the guerrillas, move faster and thus track them through desert or jungle or across mountains to deny them safe havens. There is a tendency in many armies to want to use all of the technologically sophisticated weapons in the arsenal against guerrillas, but the Special Forces Infantryman, Mark I, remains the most sophisticated counter-guerrilla weapon. Scout Dog, Mark II, is often the best supplementary weapon. Admittedly, air support, intrusion detection systems, artillery and the vast array of modern weapons can be used selectively to support counter-guerrilla campaigns; however, guerrillas are basically highly mobile light infantry, and it takes even more mobile light infantry to defeat them.

Such light infantry should be used for saturation patrols around infiltration routes. It should also be trained to operate well at night to deny the guerrilla what are usually his most friendly hours. Guerrillas normally make extensive use of ambushes; members of counter-insurgency infantry units should be even more adept at ambushes. They must learn, to paraphrase Spencer Chapman, that the jungle, the mountains and the desert are all neutral, favouring whichever side learns to use them most effectively.

When carrying out counter-guerrilla operations it is necessary to have good intelligence about the guerrillas' location; often aerial surveillance or small local scout parties can alert the reaction force. Good counter-intelligence is also important to prevent the guerrillas from learning about an upcoming operation. The effective use of long-range reconnaissance patrols can often allow air strikes or artillery to be called in on guerrilla bases. The guerrillas can also be decimated using raids or ambushes, particularly by stay-behind parties after a patrol leaves an area, since guerrillas will often scavenge. Infiltration routes may also be mined, or supply caches boobytrapped, though such operations must be selective so the odds of affecting the civilian population are kept to a minimum.

Getting the local population involved in the counter-insurgency is normally desirable as well. Arming and training local militiamen not only shows villagers that the government trusts them and considers them a valuable element of the population but also frees members of the police or military, who would otherwise have been tied down on static security duties, for more mobile operations. Assistance in building simple stockades or other protection for the villages, perhaps by assigning an Army engineer to work with the villagers, not only increases their security, but once again gives them a sense that the military is their friend rather than their enemy. Local militiamen, now considering themselves 'soldiers', will often prove especially able scouts for the security forces operating in an area. An important point to note in countries with traditional tribal rivalries or even blood feuds is not to deploy troops from a rival tribe to protect their hereditary enemies. Often atrocities can result or, at the best, bitterness towards the government will be engendered.

As the security forces gain successes and the civil forces work on winning the population to the government's side, it is often advisable to offer

▲ These members of the Australian SAS are highly trained for jungle operations and can function well in the counter-insurgency role *(Australian MOD)*

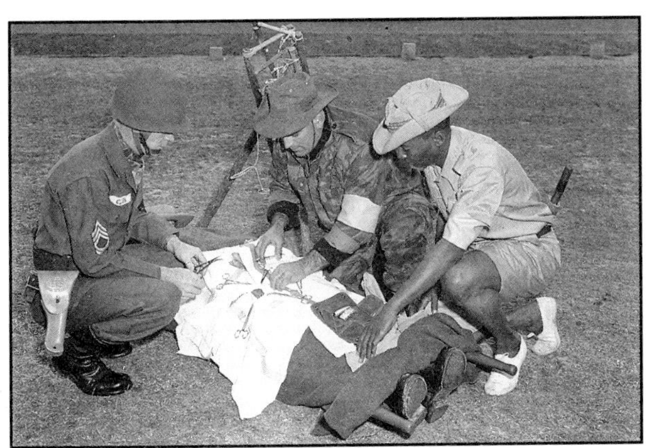

◀ Training foreign troops in medical techniques is a useful aspect of counter-insurgency warfare *(US Army)*

▼ Élite light infantry such as these US Army Rangers can be used very effectively to harry guerrillas *(US Army)*

incentives such as amnesties to lure guerrillas to come over to the government side. Turned guerrillas often bring valuable intelligence, as well as providing excellent propaganda material. In many cases, too, turned guerrillas can be used as scouts who already know where their former comrades have arms caches, camps and boobytraps. Even more effective are pseudo-guerrilla groups, often composed of a combination of turned guerrillas and members of the security forces. Such pseudo forces not only offer excellent intelligence sources and result in guerrillas being killed or captured, but are a real drain to guerrilla morale, sapping as they do the guerrilla's trust in his comrades.

Certain geopolitical factors can enhance or inhibit the chances for success in counter-guerrilla operations. If guerrillas have the support of a bordering country, this will normally make the insurgency substantially harder to defeat, since the guerrillas will have a safe haven across the border. In this case, a diplomatic offensive will have to be fought along with the internal counter-guerrilla campaign. The presence of a large, cohesive, disaffected racial or religious minority in a country offers particularly fertile ground for an insurgency. The presence in a country of extensive jungle or mountains can also make waging a counter-insurgency campaign more difficult, as these areas offer more latitude for the establishment of safe guerrilla camps.

Fighting a counter-insurgency will be costly both economically and strategically, for instance in lost agricultural or mineral revenue as a result of guerrilla operations, but guerrilla movements can be defeated if the proper combination of politico-military action is taken decisively. Guerrilla warriors are frequently highly political, but the techniques of the guerrilla warrior are apolitical. In the 1950s, he tended to be Marxist, while in the 1980s he has tended to be anti-Marxist. In either case, his techniques are relatively simple, and often effective. The techniques for countering him are somewhat less simple, but are also tried and generally effective. They do, however, take a substantial amount of will and intelligence to implement – commodities lacking in all too many governments.

INDEX